San Juan Silver

Silver

ARTHUR W. MONROE

Historical Tales of the Silvery San Juan
and Western Colorado

**WESTERN REFLECTIONS
PUBLISHING COMPANY**®

Lake City, Colorado

Cover design by Angela P. Hollingsworth
APH creative design, Lake City, CO

A Reprint Published by
Western Reflections Publishing Company
P. O. Box 1149
951 N. Highway 149
Lake City, Colorado 81235

Printed in the United States of America
Library of Congress Control Number: 2008943817
ISBN: 978-1-932738-78-0

CONTENTS

FOREWORD

For many years the author of this book has been intensely interested in the history of Western Colorado. As a U. S. Ranger, Mesa Verde National Park, from 1923 to 1926, he learned of the Cliff Dwellers, who lived in the Southwest Corner of the Great Centennial State, long before American history was written.

As the editor of a special edition of The Montrose Messenger, published on Sept. 20, 1922, he gathered a large amount of the data used in this volume. As a special writer and interviewer for the Colorado Historical Society during the winter of 1933-34, he gathered the biographies of a hundred and fifty pioneers of the Western Slope.

I am indebted to the following persons and organizations for use of material previously used by them:

The Montrose Daily Press; The Montrose Enterprise; "Early Days on The Western Slope," by Sidney Jocknick; Harry P. Tabor; Mrs. E. Z. Peterson; The Colorado Historical Society; W. M. Simmons; C. T. Rawalt, formerly editor of The Western Slope Democrat; Forest Ranger John H. Keep; L. G. Denison; Martha and Henry Ripley (deceased). I also appreciate the assistance of Lenetta Austin who helped with the typing. Thanks to Paul Adams, who drew the cover design.

Since this manuscript was written many of the people herein mentioned have passed on but their stories will live.

To all of these, as well as the hundreds of people I have interviewed, I say "Thanks Kindly."

ARTHUR W. MONROE

THE BRIDGE BUILDER

An old man going a lone highway came in the evening cold
and gray,
To a chasm vast and deep and wide;
The old man crossed in the twilight dim; the sullen stream
had no fear for him;
But he turned when safe on the other side and built a
bridge to span the tide.
"Old man," said a fellow pilgrim near. "You are wasting
your strength with building here.
Your journey will end with the ending day, you never
again will pass this way;
You've crossed the chasm deep and wide; why build your
bridge at the eventide?"
"Good friend, in the path I have come," he said, "There
cometh after me today
A Youth whose feet must pass this way;
This chasm that has been as naught to me, to that fair-
haired youth may a pitfall be;
He too must cross in the twilight dim; good friend, I am
building this bridge for him."

—Author Unknown.

THE ANSWER

The following is dedicated to the pioneers of the San Juan country, especially to W. H. Nelson of Norwood, Colorado, who blazed the trail for the first wagon road over Marshall Pass:

And so you and I, in the days that are dim,
Can look back at the bridges we built for him.
An empire we founded, our numbers were few
When the country was wild and primitively new.
The trails we have blazed that others may see
And find the way built by you and me—
The roads and bridges, o'er chasms and streams,
Were built for others with no selfish miens.
What measure of thanks, in the twilight of life,
Do the pioneers get for that early strife?
Do they ever think of the days we spent
In work and hardships unselfishly lent?
It matters not, for we confidently knew
That the foundations we laid when the country was new—
The bridges we built in the days that are dim—
Were good and strong that we built for him.

—L. G. DENISON.

CHAPTER I

SILVER—THE LODESTONE

Silver was the lodestone that attracted a great many of the West's foremost builders, brought them out of the East and transplanted them, so that they grew up with the country.

Silver was the magnet that drew thousands upon thousands of men of every type and description into the Rocky Mountain region and bade them make there a home for themselves.

It was Silver that brought national fame to the Comstock Lode in 1859—that made Sun Mountain a beehive of activity—made Virginia City a great Camp—gave Mark Twain to the World—made Eilley Orrum queen of the territory—brought Nevada into statehood, breaking the deadlock of slavery and making the Negro a free man.

It was silver that raised up the city of Leadville in the midst of a wilderness, and emblazoned the name of H. A. W. Tabor upon the international horizon. It was Silver that made Baby Doe Tabor the queen of the continent and it was the fickleness of silver that brought disaster and poverty to the House of Tabor.

It was San Juan Silver that made Ouray, Creede and Lake City great camps and it was the demonetization of Silver that changed these from booming towns to sleepy, half-deserted little villages, with grass growing in the streets and battered shacks decaying. Such was the history of the towns of the San Juan.

> I saw a silent city,
>   Houses vacant there
> Battered shacks decaying,
>   Windows all astare.

3

Where once bold people hurried,
  Seeking hidden gold,
Now just a ghostly village,
  Deserted, weathered, cold.

It was this same fickleness of silver that sent the miners down from the Silvery San Juan into the valleys below to build farms in the fertile soil, and to establish new and thriving communities, which were not dependent upon silver and its fluctuatious value.

Such is the valley of the Uncompahgre river, unsurpassingly beautiful with its green and well-watered fields. A poet has said of this vale of plenty:

"Far in Western Colorado,
  Lies a valley warm and bright,
Circled round with lofty mountains,
  With their heads all crowned in white,
There I always long to be,
  'Neath the cloudless azure skies,
There the Sun is always brightest,
  And Nature's charms I learn to prize."

But the Silvery San Juan will again come into its own. She is silently, patiently waiting for the action of Congress to put a fixed value on Silver. If this is done the San Juan will again leap into a feverish activity. Hundreds of now abandoned shafts and tunnels will be opened up and will give forth their riches to the World, and Creede, Lake City, Silverton, Ouray, Rico and Telluride will be flourishing cities.

CHAPTER II

INDIAN AND SPANISH OCCUPATION

For long ages the only inhabitants of Western Colorado were wandering bands of red men and the only record they left behind them to tell of their occupation of this beautiful land of rugged mountains and fertile valleys is an abandoned flint quarry, a goodly collection of pictographs chiseled in the sandstone cliffs, a sprinkling of arrow points, flint knives and a few pot sherds.

There are to be found and studied in the Shavano Valley, west of the town of Montrose, groups of pictographs that show three distinct ages and cultures of people, some of their picture writing superimposed, one upon the other.

The Utes for a long time have been mountain Indians, but of the people who preceded them, we know little. History tells us that one Juan de Onate came into the San Luis Valley of Colorado in 1598. He was, no doubt, the first white man to set foot upon what is now Colorado soil. Gold was discovered at Fort Garland in the same valley as early as 1600.

The first expedition of Spaniards to enter the valleys of Western Colorado was led by Father Escalante, a priest of the Conquistadores of Spain, who came up from Mexico in 1776. This expedition crossed the turbulent waters of the Gunnison River a few miles above the present town of Delta.

I have heard recently that a skeleton in armor was found in a cabin of rocks near the mouth of the Black Canyon of the Gunnison, but the story has never been verified, so I doubt its authenticity. However, it is barely possible that if such a find was made, it was the remains of one of Escalante's men who took sick and was left behind at this point on a journey through a trackless wilderness.

The following was taken from the files of Ranger John H. Keep, formerly of the Uncompahgre National Forest:

"Through the countless ages of the past, the Uncompahgre Plateau has been the habitation of men. Scenes of great fights and conquests, hunting grounds with an abundance of game, fires which devastated entire townships. And down through the countless ages the forest struggled onward.

"The earlier history of the country before the coming of the White Man is rather meagre. Whether or not the country maintained a people before the Ute Indian is still a matter of doubt. Remains of broken pottery have been picked up at various points along the Roubideau Canyon. This would indicate that a race of man, perhaps a branch of the Mesa Verde Cliff Dwellers, at one time inhabited the country. The supposition is, however, that this pottery was packed in by Cliff Dwellers on their travels from Southern Colorado, to the superb hunting grounds then found in this vicinity. There are no visible remains or indications of their having maintained a permanent abode, such as can be found in the Mesa Verde country. (Author's Note— However, during the summer of 1939 two Folsom arrow points were found near Black Canyon. These are thought to date back as much as 30,000 years.)

"Just when the Ute Indian first came into this country is also a matter of doubt. Whether they acquired it by conquest from another race, or found a virgin country awaiting them is not known. However, down through the decades that followed, the Western Slope has forever been the favorite camping and hunting grounds of the Allied Utes. In union lay their strength. Originally the Utes were called "The Snakes", and in that olden time, they occupied the territory of the Snake River in Idaho as well as a portion of Montana, Colorado and Utah. Those who now survive in southwestern Colorado and Utah, are but a small remnant of that once powerful tribe of a decade or more ago.

"When the whites first commenced their encroachment of the Western Country, the Utes controlled practically all of the mountainous sections of Colorado and small portions of the plains east of the mountains. However, they were gradually crowded back, until within a short time the Western Slope constituted their domain. The tribe then consisted of five factions, each controlled by chiefs, Ouray being the leader of the tribe dominating the Uncompahgre Valley. Winter quarters and camps were maintained along the river in the valley, while the Uncompahgre Plateau and other surrounding high country, constituted their summer camps, journeys and famous hunts. This situation prevailed for a number of years, treaties being made with the whites in respect to reservations and proprietorship, until such time as the encroachment of the whites became so great that the Utes were mercilessly removed to their present reservations in Utah and Southwestern Colorado.

"Many routes of travel were maintained by the Utes while residing in the country. Some of their main trails are still distinguishable to the present day, while others are entirely obliterated by none-use or overgrown by vegetation. There is one old trail crossing the Roubideau Canyon, about where the present site of the Roubideau-Moore Creek Trail is laid out. Remnants of another trail still exist north through East and Horseshoe Basin, crossing the numerous canyons and ramparts to 25 Mesa, thence across Sawmill Mesa to the Dry Fork of the Escalante. Another main trail was maintained by them through the forest near Dew Drop Hill on the Dave Wood Road, and thence to Horsefly Creek, and on across to the San Miguel country. Their hunts and travels were distributed over the entire plateau, as another main trail extended along the crest of the Divide the entire way. Arrowheads and other signs of their presence can be found most anywhere on the plateau.

"Interesting carvings and picture rocks can be found today, some located in Shavano Valley, west of the town of Montrose, one in Dry Creek Canyon, three miles south of the farming section, and another on the Dry Fork of the Escalante Creek west of Delta. What these rocks represent is a matter of theory. Rude drawings of deer, elk, hunters, fish and other signs are readily distinguishable. Some seem to think the drawings were made for the benefit of travelers, giving information of the resources of the coun-

try. Others are inclined to believe they were constructed
by some artistically inclined soul, giving vent to his feelings
with the crude implements which were at hand. No farming or cultivation was carried on by the Indians in the
valleys, except small patches of corn now and then. They
depended almost entirely for their living and existence,
from the game, fish and fruit contained in the country.

"The first expedition of the White Man into the country
was made in about 1774. Padre Junipero Serra, President
of the California Missions, urged the ecclesiastics of New
Mexico to undertake the exploration of a route from Santa
Fe to the Coast of Upper California. With this object in
view, Padre Francisco Silvestre Escalante, Ministro Doc-
trinero of Zuni, and Padre Antanacio Dominguez, Visitador
Comisario of New Mexico, organized an expedition in 1776,
which consisted, besides themselves, of Padre Cisneros,
alcalde Mayor of Zuni, Bernardo Miera y Pacheco, Capitan
Miliciano of Santa Fe, Don Joaquin Lain, who had accompanied another former expedition to Colorado, was official guide of the expedition, and five soldiers.

"They set out from Santa Fe July 29, taking a North-
westerly course, crossing the several affluents of the San
Juan River, which lay between them and the Rio de Nues-
tra Senora de los Dolores. Following down the river, sometimes in the canyon, at times several miles away, he left the
river at Gypsum Valley and traveled across the mesa to
the canyon of the San Miguel River, which they called the
Rio San Pedro. Encamping along the north side, he found
traces of Rivera's former passage at this point. Continuing
his travels, he struck out across the Uncompahgre Plateau
in a northeasterly direction, or probably across about what
is now Dallas Divide, or perhaps across the Ute Trail
through Horsefly Creek. He traveled through the Canada
Honda, which was doubtless the Uncompahgre River below
Ridgway. This point is spelled by him as "Ancapagari,"
and was named by him at this time Rio San Francisco. No
doubt he received the name Ancapagari from the Ute Indians, which he encountered at this place. Escalante gives
the distance traveled from the San Miguel River to the

Uncompahgre, as twenty-four and one-half leagues, which is proof conclusive, if any other descriptions were needed, of his long detours through the Uncompahgre Country. The explorations of this party while in the valley, were carried on at different points around the present site of Delta. Escalante Creek and Canyon, as well as Dominguez Creek north of Delta, were named in honor of these two explorers, who accompanied this expedition. After camping at a place which is called San Augutin (probably what is now Austin, or the mouth of the Black Canyon of the Gunnison), the expedition moved up the Muddy, down Divide Creek to the Colorado River and the present site of Grand Junction, thence to Utah, returning by a more southerly route to New Mexico.

"A period of sixty years passes by after this early expedition and the Ute is still in possession of the wonderful valleys and surrounding hills, which abound in game and from which he secures an easy living, and lives a life of comparative ease. This is interrupted by the advent of the early American and French trappers and explorers. The travels and work of these early men, were carried on over a wide territory and throughout all the Western Country. The records left by them are very meagre, as usually they worked in small numbers or alone, and were nomadic in nature, here today and some place else tomorrow.

"During the year 1837, a French trapper by the name of Joseph Roubideau came into this country, and established quarters on what is now Roubideau Creek, about seven miles west of Delta. Here he built himself a cabin, and spent considerable time in trapping the surrounding country from this point for several years. The partial remains of his abode can be found on the J. D. Dillard ranch on this creek. Evidently he did not get along well with the Utes, as his stay was short, and by 1840 we hear of him as established near Salt Lake City and working that region."

The famous scout and trapper, Kit Carson, spent a couple of winters with Roubideau on the Gunnison, trapping and exploring the breaks of Western Colorado and Eastern Utah.

CHAPTER III

SIGNS OF OTHER HABITATION

The early white men who settled Western Colorado, on coming into this vast empire found many signs of previous habitation.

A cabin was found on Cochetopa Creek that must have been built about 1840, as it was old when discovered in 1870.

The remains of a series of camp fires were found on one mesa at a depth of a foot below the ground indicated that a party of Spanish soldiers had camped there long ago.

An old fort was found on a ridge between Needle and Razor creeks, near Tomichi Creek in 1872, and some old flumes for placer mining were found in the Hot Springs Valley in the Gunnison country in 1870.

The Baker party spent a winter of extreme hardship in the Silverton country in 1859, and several members of the party perished.

In 1861 Fred Lottis discovered gold in Union Park in the Tin Cup district and washed it out with a small tin cup, hence the name of the district.

A party of prospectors were killed by Indians in Dead Man's Gulch in the Tin Cup country in 1853.

Benjamin Graham built a log fort on Rock Creek in 1870. The year 1874 saw the founding of Lake City, Ouray, Silverton and Gunnison. At that time there were signs of old placer workings in Taylor Park.

It is claimed that some of the stone used in the construction of the Cathedral of Mexico was taken from the Sawtooth Mountain on the West side of Cochetopa Pass as long as one hundred and sixty years ago.

A burned wagon and two skeletons found in No Name Gulch were thought to have been the remains of Forty

Niners who attempted to pass through.

By a treaty made in the late sixties, the Utes were given the San Luis Valley. The San Juan Treaty, whereby the Utes agreed to sell to the United States the entire San Juan Mountain district for mining was entered into in 1872 and 1873.

At this time the Utes were given the Uncompahgre Valley, which they were privileged to hold, by the Treaty, as long as "rivers shall run and grass shall grow." As the Indians subsequently broke the treaty by perpetrating the Meeker Massacre, the white man also broke it and in 1881 the Utes were moved over into the Uintah country of Utah. The Southern Utes were given a reservation in Southern Colorado and Northern New Mexico in 1888, and have since resided there.

With the coming of the year 1865 there was probably not a single habitation of white men in the entire of Western Colorado, and the land was unmolested, save for a few roving bands of Navajoes, Utes or Piutes. The fertile valleys had not yet felt the touch of the plow share or shovel and the great grey peaks of the San Juans had not felt the searing stroke of the pick. The booming of dynamite was unknown and the echoes resounded only from the crashing of an occasional avalanche, roaring down a steep mountainside.

In the year 1873, there was an Indian Agency on the Los Pinos River, near the present Flying M Ranch, and a cow camp was maintained on the Gunnison in charge of James P. Kelley and Sidney Jocknick, who in his later years wrote the book: "Early Days on the Western Slope." So far as I can ascertain the only other settlement in all this vast Western Colorado country was the homestead of Chief Ouray on the Uncompahgre River, about five miles from the present site of Montrose, where the Chipeta-Ouray Memorial Park is located.

Jocknick and Kelley were in charge of the government cattle, which were kept on the Gunnison and distributed among the Indians as they were needed. The monotony of the long winter of 1873-74 was broken by the arrival of

O. D. Loutsenhizer and a companion, who with three others were attempting the trip on foot over the mountains. But for a kindly providence and the location of the Cow Camp none of the party would have survived the trip. As it was they were weak, emaciated and nearly starved, having saved their lives by killing and devouring a lean coyote and drinking the warm life blood of a cow, which they managed to kill.

The five men remained at the cow camp for nine weeks, until they had regained their health and then headed toward the Los Pinos Agency through the deep snow drifts. Again they would have met with disaster, but for a premonition of the Indian Agent's wife, who caused a lantern to be hung on the top of Chief Ouray's cabin on a foggy night. The men were hopelessly lost, but saw the light and made the trip on to the Agency.

Loutenhizer and his companions were a part of an original group of miners and prospectors, who left Salt Lake City, and after many hardships finally arrived at the Ouray homestead. Some of these men were persuaded to remain with the famous chief all winter, but others, despite his warnings, decided to go on. The Loutsenhizer party by mere chance, made the trip to the Agency on the Cochetopa. A party of six men, headed by Alfred Packer, who had been bailed out of a Salt Lake chain gang, and hired to guide the party into the Colorado mountains, met tragedy in the region near beautiful Lake San Cristobal.

The story is well known how Packer came into the Indian Agency alone and told various stories of his experiences and the fate of his companions. The preponderance of the evidence showed that Packer had killed the men to obtain the money they carried and had existed on human flesh for some time.

He was tried in Lake City several years later and sentenced to be hanged. A gallows was erected near the site of the tragic camp, but due to certain legal technicalities, the sentence was never carried out. The state supreme court decided that a man could not be executed under state law for a crime that was committed before the state was established. However, Packer served twenty-five years in the Colorado penitentiary at Canon City, after which he was pardoned and spent the last years of his life around Denver.

His victims lie buried in the valley below Lake San Christobal, where the wind in the trees sings an endless requiem, as they sleep. These men were: Frank Miller, Israel Swan, Shannon Wilson Bell, George Noon and James Humphrey.

There are many men alive at the time this is being written, who recall Packer and his trial. Charles A. Mendenhall, of Montrose and Lake City, and Charles F. Huntsman, also of Montrose, were going to school in Lake City at the time of the trial. Mr. Mendenhall remembers especially that Packer had a great love for children.

In describing Packer, Huntsman says that he was a very peculiar man, having a large head and almost no forehead, the cranium sloping back from the eyes. The man was broad shouldered and had a wax-like complexion, a small goatee and a very peculiar voice.

William Roatcap tells of meeting Packer in a saloon on Larimer Street in Denver after he was released from the Penitentiary.

The late Judge Gerry presided at the Packer trial and John C. Bell, now deceased, was one of the prosecuting attorneys. It is stated that Judge Gerry said to Packer: "There were only six good Democrats in Hinsdale County and you've eaten five of them." However, I will not vouch for the veracity of this statement.

John A. Randolph, a reporter for Harper's Weekly, was the man who discovered the bodies of Packer's victims.

CHAPTER IV

EARLY DAYS IN LAKE CITY

The eyes of the World were focused upon the San Juan when gold was discovered on the shores of Lake San Christobal in 1874. At the time the discovery was made, Clarence Putnam Foster, who was one of the prominent pioneers of Hinsdale County, was head farmer at the Los Pinos Indian Agency. In an interview with the author on December 28, 1933, Mr. Foster told of many of his experiences in the early days of that section. Excerpts from this interview follow:

"In the Summer of 1874, Mr. Foster felt the urge to come West and seek his fortune on the frontier. He arrived in Denver in September of that year, went to Colorado Springs and then started out through Ute Pass with a wagon and mule team, headed for the Ute Indian Reservation on the Los Pinos River, west of the Continental Divide. The last night of their journey, they camped about six miles from the Agency. Shortly after they had unhitched the teams and prepared to camp for the night, a band of Utes rode up and made camp near them. The Indians had been on a raid into the Arapahoe country and were returning with three hundred stolen horses and three scalps. So that night they held a big scalp dance to celebrate the event.

"Shortly after this experience the Indian Agent on the Los Pinos, N. F. Bond, received a letter from Thompson, the Agent in charge of the Arapahoes, stating that the Utes had stolen three hundred Arapahoe horses and that they would have to return them. The matter was referred to Chief Ouray and his decision was that, when the Arapahoes had returned all the Ute horses they had stolen, theirs would be returned to them.

14

"C. P. Foster was well acquainted with Chief Ouray, who lived in the cabin next to his at the Agency. He says that, while Ouray was a great deal smarter than the average Indian, still he was no super man. He did, however, have power and his word was the law of the Utes.

"The language of the Utes was interspersed with Mexican, due to their contact with the Mexicans along the border for several hundred years. Ouray was the chief of all the Utes, which tribe consisted of several bands, namely the Wimonoches, Capotes, Tabeguache and the bands of Colorow and Shavano.

"When Mr. Foster arrived at the Agency he was given the position of head farmer, and it was his job to teach the Utes to farm. The Agency was quite a settlement at that time, there being storehouses, warehouses, blacksmith shop, Agent's House, houses for the other employees, Chief Ouray's adobe houses, etc.

"The winter of 1874-75 was just before the opening of the fabulously rich gold and silver mines at Lake City, which at this time did not exist. Rich ore had been discovered at the site of the Ute and Ulay Mine and a toll road was being built into the Lake City country by Otto Mears and Enos Hotchkiss. The intention was to build the road up through Burris Park and the site where Sherman is, to Silverton. While they were working on the road past Lake San Christobal, the two Hall Brothers found an outcropping of ore and decided to do some prospecting. That winter they loaded eighteen sacks of the ore they had found on two wagons and started to Denver with them. The snow was deep and the horses could not pull the wagons, so they put all the ore on one wagon, doubled the team and made it through. These eighteen sacks of ore brought $1000 a sack, or a total of $18,000, at the Grant Smelter in Denver.

"Enos Hotchkiss spent a night at the Foster cabin a while before he located the Hotchkiss mine, which was later changed to the Golden Fleece, and which, in a few weeks changed Lake City from a group of four or five cabins to a town of 5000 people, all feverishly trying to locate a rich lode.

"A man named Finley traded a Sharpe carbine rifle for a fourth interest in the Golden Fleece, which by the way, was on the location where the Halls had taken out their fortune. It was thought that they had only found a pocket and that it would play out. The mine broke Hotchkiss and it was sold on default of assessment work. A man named Davis secured a lease on the mine and, at this time, C. P. Foster was operating a market in Lake City and furnished him supplies. Foster was afraid that Davis would not be able to pay him, and told him so. Davis then said that if he did not strike good pay ore the next time he tried, he would quit. He went to work again, but finally gave up in disgust, and when there was one stick of powder left, he quit and started out. The man who was with him decided to use the one stick, and so shot off a pop shot in a bulge on one wall. The shot opened up a pocket and they took out a thousand dollars worth of gold. Proceeding on that vein, they took out more gold, and Davis, fearing the pockets would play out, sold out for $75,000 to Stearns, Stewart and Bartheldes of Denver.

"The new owners worked out the pockets they found and were losing money on the mine, but, figuring that they had invested too much to stop, they kept on with the work and opened up a chimney of fabulously rich gold ore.

"It was in February of 1875 that Foster and George Walton, the Agency blacksmith, felt the pull of the gold lure and, quitting their jobs, went to Lake City, where they bought some town lots at five dollars a lot, and built a cabin.

"Once when he was prospecting up the Lake Fork, Foster came upon the camp of the victims of the Packer tragedy. There were towels hanging to the branches of the trees, just where they had been left by the murdered men, and the blankets and other camp articles were lying about on the ground. He later saw Packer in jail in Gunnison.

"In 1876, when Spring had come, Foster moved into the Cebolla Valley and settled a squatter's claim. There were then three other settlers in the Valley of the Cebolla, namely, Jones, Mathias and Testerman.

"Oregon Bill, (mentioned in Sidney Jocknick's book: 'Early Days on the Western Slope', as one of the bad men of the country) whose real name was W. Speck, and who was an Englishman, was a would-be bad man. He wore long hair and boasted of how tough he was. He settled on a farm in Summit Park and started to work it, but soon had an accident in which he received a bad cut on his foot. He went to a doctor in Lake City, and was laid up there for considerable time. While he was gone Derocia, a Frenchman, jumped his claim. Oregon Bill returned to the ranch and shot the Frenchman dead, then fled to Saguache. D. J. Huntsman, the Justice of the Peace, issued a warrant for the arrest of the murderer, and Foster, being constable, was sent to Saguache to bring the man back. Oregon Bill feared he would be lynched and said he would not return to the Valley, but after Foster guaranteed his safety, he returned and was exonerated, because the settlers had no use for claim jumpers.

"A tenderfoot lad from Missouri killed a man named Davis in a cabin just a short distance from the Foster home, after Davis had teased him until the lad could stand it no longer. He was also cleared by the coroner's jury. It seems that the Missouri youth had a small thirty-two calibre revolver and the men, with whom he was batching in the cabin, teasingly told him not to pull the gun unless he intended to shoot. One day, Davis, who was prospecting for Lewis, the man who built the big LaVeta Hotel in Gunnison, and was seeking iron ore, with visions of a steel mill in that town, goaded the boy into a fight and hit him on the head with an axe handle. The boy pulled his little revolver and shot Davis through the eye, killing him instantly."

"In 1882," says Charles A. Mendenhall, "when I arrived in Lake City, there were twenty-eight saloons. It was a town of several thousand people and the Golden Fleece, the Ute and Ulay, the Hidden Treasure and other famous mines in the district were giving up their horde of riches to the world. The camp was a place of feverish activity and dance halls and sporting houses were running full sway."

The father of the Mendenhall boys trapped for fur animals the first year the family was on the Lake Fork, and later conducted the Miners Market in Lake City. Charles A., as a boy of sixteen, carried mail over Engineer Mountain from Rose's Cabin to Animas Forks. He has had almost every kind of experience with snow slides that it is possible for one man to have, without being buried by one.

Once when men of the crew of one of the mines were sick with influenza, the rest of the crew carried them down the mountain side. Two of the men, returning to the mine, found that everything had been swept away by the running of the Horseshoe Slide, while they were gone. Mr. Mendenhall says that at one time or another he has seen every slide on Hensen Creek run, and there are twenty-three of them which cross the road. These slides run every winter and are called: the Fanny Fern, Ute and Ulay, Modock, Grassy, Nellie Creek, Klondike, Twin Slides, Big Casino, Little Casino, Copper Gulch, Sunshine Mountain, Capitol, Wittemore, Galena Gulch, Lime Kiln, Wager, Independence, Shafer Basin, Horseshoe, Gravel Mountain and Boulder. All these slides run between the town of Lake City and Rose's Cabin, a distance of about fifteen miles.

Both Mr. Mendenhall and Mr. Huntsman tell of the hanging of two men, Betts and Browning, in Lake City. The two were attempting to rob a house, not knowing that the Sheriff and City Marshal were concealed inside, and when they were caught in the act, they shot their way out, killing the sheriff. They made their getaway and the marshal, whose name was Clair Smith, ran into town and organized a posse, which started after the miscreants. They were caught and jailed, but soon a mob stormed the jail and took the two out and hanged them. As they were about to be hanged, Betts said: "Come on Browning, let's perk up. Let's take a good chew before we go."

CHAPTER V

ONE MAN'S STORY OF EARLY DAYS

(Copied from the Montrose Daily Press)

By WILLIAM M. SIMMONS

You have frequently requested me to write something for The Montrose Daily Press pertaining to my 58 years of residence within the boundaries of Colorado. This I shall now try to do.

I came to Colorado with my parents late in the fall of 1866 and became one of her children. Now I am quite a well matured old fellow, having commenced upon the 14th day of February, 1936, to manipulate the wheel of my mobile of life over the 79th mile of the journey toward that "country from whence no traveler ever returns."

To condense the happenings of a lifetime in one short article is quite a difficult task, especially when that life has been spent in any of the younger states and territories. Colorado was a territory for ten years after it became the home of the Simmons family.

I was born on St. Valentine's day, 1857, in the town of Neubergh, now Cleveland, Ohio. My very young days and years were spent in and around this place with my mother and a brother and sister. Then my mother was notified to meet our father in Chicago to which place he had returned—having gone to Colorado in the fall of 1859 —for the purpose of bringing his family to the then very young and sparsely settled Territory of Colorado.

My father, as you shall see, was one who always wanted to be on the frontier. It was not strange that he should go when the Pikes Peak excitement was on, with all of its promises of the riches of gold and silver that could be gotten by merely going and gathering it up. He prevailed upon his brother-in-law, Dim McElroy, to accompany him on the trip, which he supposed could be accomplished in a

couple of months. Having acquired an old ox, an old harness, a set of wheels and axle, they rigged up a box, made
a set of thills, or shafts for the cart, between which to back
the ox, piled in their earthly belongings, and started for
Colorado. His brother-in-law, however, never arrived, on
account of "cold feet." When they got to the Missouri
river, he gave his interest to father and returned to Ohio,
satisfied to be back there with "his wife's people."

At this point he was joined by A. H. Miles, whose wife
was my father's sister, and who was ready, with his three
children, two girls and a boy, to cross the plains. He had a
team of three yoke of oxen and it did not take long for
my father to transfer his valuables from the cart, dispose
of the outfit, and continue the journey with the Miles. That
family in later years became quite a factor in the life and
affairs of the state and of the city of Denver. The history
of the state of Colorado cannot be well written without
mention of the name of A. H. Miles.

During these few years that my father, P. A. Simmons,
was in the Territory, he built the third frame house in
Denver, in 1860. It was built for A. H. Miles and was
located on Arapahoe near F—now 15th—street. In Central
City and Black Hawk he located several leads which in
later years became some of the best mines in the district.
He built the first water wheel in the camp, which was
used in the first mill in the Territory. Just at this time
came the excitement from the reports of great riches to
be had in the southern part of the Territory where a prospector from the south, by the name of Baker, had made
a discovery. It was for this prospector that the valley and
Baker's Park of the San Juan were named.

This was just the place for a man of the disposition of
my father, so he got ready and started in the fall of 1861,
trying to go in by way of the southern or Tierra Amarilla
route. But he never got there, because winter came on. He
wintered in the town of Taos, New Mexico, returning in
the spring, completely broke, to the hills of Black Hawk
and Central. By fall he had accumulated enough money
to enable him to go back to "The states." It was at this

time that my mother and her three little children were to meet him in Chicago for the purpose of going to Colorado.

However, the Civil War intervened, and father enlisted. After the War, we started across the plains for Denver. It took us just four weeks to negotiate the trip, because to guard against Indian attacks, the government would not let any teams pass Fort Carney until there was a train of no less than 25 teams. We arrived in Denver in the late fall of 1866, having seen but one band of Indians and they not on the warpath. After a stay of but a few days in Denver we moved to a ranch four miles below Golden, on Clear creek, then the capital of the territory. We remained there until the following spring when we moved back to Denver, Glenarm and F—now 15th—street.

In those early days of Denver many times men had to go to other places for employment or business. Some of you older ones may recollect that the Union Pacific had started to build their road from Omaha across the plains in the early part of 1866. As I now look back I can see the work trains hauling things needed for the new road, later to be one of the great roads of the globe. As the road came nearer Denver, giving this small city of the plains hope, dark clouds commenced to hover over, and she awoke one morning to the realization of the fact that this great railroad was going to leave her as far south of its line as it is between Cheyenne and Denver. The result was hard times in Denver, and, as above stated, the heads of families had to leave for other parts. Many of them went up to the railroad for work or for business of some kind.

My father was one who left Denver. Now that we were well and comfortably settled, he went to Bear River, Utah, the end of the road at that time, where he engaged in the store and auction business. In the course of but a few weeks, he was appointed city marshal of this railroad town of the far west, and this, in those days, was some little job for an officer to handle. The jail was usually well filled with some sort of offenders of the law. From what I understand of the location of the town it was divided by a stream, over which there was a bridge connecting the two parts of the city. The jail was in one part, the city offices and business houses in the other.

One morning one of his night men came running up to his office, and informed him that the vigilantes had hanged three of his prisoners, which report proved to be a fact. Father had them cut down and buried. No more was thought of the incident until one morning not long after, another officer came running up and told him there was a mob of a couple of hundred men down at the jail clamoring for vengeance because of the three men having been hanged. They blamed the city authorities for the act. My father immediately went down to where these 200 or more men were. The mob was composed of railroad construction men, gamblers, and hangers on about town, and were led by one of the most popular and desperate gamblers of the west, D. Tom Smith. He knew no fear, was honorable in all things in spite of being a gambler. His word was as good as gold, and if he had any difference with a man which he thought gave sufficient reason for his shooting him, he would send him word that he would shoot him on sight.

Upon arriving at the jail, with his guns and knife strapped about him, my father began to talk with the men as an officer in the interest of the law; but this only made them all the more determined to "finish" him and the town. In their anger, they were not particularly choice in the language they used to convey this information. He immediately backed into the jail, took off his guns and knife, and tried to reason with them as an unarmed citizen, not as an officer, but this reasoning seemed to make them even more emphatic in their expressions of "affections" for him and the whole city management.

He finally turned away, never, as he said, expecting to get as much as ten steps from them without losing his life, but they let him go his way while they battered in the jail, turned all the prisoners out and set fire to the building. Then they went over and burned down the newspaper office, set fire to other houses, and started across the bridge to the other part of town, with the intention of putting an end to the city officials. This was their mistake and meant the undoing of their plans and the death of some 30 or more of their number who might have later made good citizens, a credit to the nation.

As they came on, crazed now with victory, having had no resistance, they were met by one of the men whom my father had pressed into the service. He was backed by several others and some volunteers, making about 30 in number. They were fortified in a big log building with plenty of ammunition and firearms which had been confiscated from the gun store of the town. The leader of this defense ran out and told the mob that if they did not stop they would be fired upon, whereupon he was chased back to the building and shot dead in the doorway. This started the battle. When it was over and the smoke had cleared away it was found that the mob had left ten of their men there on the ground. Several more died from the wounds they had received. D. Tom Smith, as soon as he was able to attend to matters—he having walked away with a lot of buck shot and two bullets in his otherwise sound body—sent my father his usual "honorable notification," but he never had an opportunity to carry it into execution, or try to, until two years later in the railroad town of Kit Carson, on the Kansas Pacific.

The golden spike, connecting the Union Pacific and the Southern Pacific was driven at Ogden, Utah, soon after this battle, or at least within a few months and my father was a witness to this connection of the east and the west. The Kansas Pacific had now gotten as far as Sheridan, Kansas, close to the eastern border of that state and it was to this town that my father went and established a blacksmith business in the year of 1869. In the spring of 1870 the road had advanced as far west as Kit Carson, a short distance west of the eastern boundary of Colorado. This was one of the wildest towns ever known to the frontier—open saloons, gambling in full swing, and four dance halls running all night every night. At that time all the freight from the southern territories of New Mexico, Arizona, and a part of Texas was brought to Kit Carson by long trains of ox teams, to be unloaded and sent east on this new railroad.

My father moved his shops to this town and sent to Denver for his family. We made the trip with a team and wagon and it took us one week to make the journey. We spent the summer there.

As you know, this road was completed into Denver some time in May or June, just a few weeks after the Denver Pacific from Cheyenne was finished. Both of these roads are part of the great Union Pacific of the present day. The line from Kit Carson to Denver was called the Denver Extension of the Kansas Pacific, so the newsboys could go on farther than Carson. My brother and Mr. Williams got the concession on this line, he going in on the first train and I on the second. We enjoyed this privilege for some three or four weeks, until the road had been turned over to the Kansas Pacific.

Wonderful town, Kit Carson, as I look back and think of life as it was then. For some reason there was a company of soldiers camping there for a short time. One of these soldiers—a sergeant—became jealous of a gambler named Stewart, over some woman. Meeting in Tom Kemp's dance hall one morning, they began to shoot. When the fight was over Stewart had a bullet in his shoulder and the soldier and an old three-card Monte dealer, who happened to be standing on the outside of the building with his back to the window, were dead.

Stewart had a fine sorrel horse in a stable, which he now brought into use, as the company of soldiers, who had by this time heard of the shooting, were fast on his trail. I can still see Stewart, on that sorrel, almost flying over that prairie, with the soldiers right after him. They never got him, however, and later he came back. I saw that bullet taken out of his shoulder. The wound was but slight, but the whole adventure made a deep impression on me. I thought the men were wonderful.

It was here also that I saw the first prize fight of my life. It was fought under what I think they called London prize ring rules—every knock-down a round, with the usual rest of one minute between. The match took place out in the hot sun on the hot sands of Sand creek, between a little Irishman out of the company of soldiers and a big one from off the grade. The big fellow finally was victorious, but only after taking a fearful punishment. Later we boys of the town had an opportunity to talk to the soldier about that fight and I can assure you we thought it was an honor and a privilege.

It was here, too, that father met that D. Tom Smith, for whom he had been carrying a gun in his pocket for two years. Tom was tending bar in Tom Kemp's dance hall. Father went in and their eyes met, for the first time since the battle of the Bear river. A cigar was called for and was handed out. A match was called for and was handed out. It was also taken with a left hand and the cigar was lighted with a left hand. Puff, puff, puff. Smith lowered his eyes. Father lowered his. Smith went to the other end of the bar. His "hand had been called, and he manfully lost." Father sauntered about the gambling place for awhile, then went home and threw down the gun he had been carrying for two years, prepared for the most fearless man of those days, and withal, the most honorable. He was so fearless that later he was chosen marshal of a town in Kansas and met his death trailing two men that he wanted for some crime. As the story goes, they fled into an abandoned house, taking with them an axe that they found in the yard. Smith followed them in alone and they killed him with that axe, thus ending the life of a good officer, a good friend, and an honest man, one of those strong, fearless men that took part in the building and settling of this now great and peaceful west.

Another exciting incident occurred soon after we had gotten settled in our home in Carson. Early one morning we heard quite a number of shots about a mile back of us on the prairie where the hundred head of work cattle were being herded by five Mexican men and one boy of about ten years. These shots proved to be an attack by the Indians, who had started on the warpath and commenced their attack with the raid on these poor night herders. All five men were killed, but the boy escaped by hiding among the cattle and working his way into a dog hole. After the attack was over he came in and gave the alarm. Men went out and got the bodies, which were buried in a grave 30 feet long near our shop. The Indians continued their murderous attacks all along the line of the railroad where there were any camps or men out on night duty. Many lives were lost and some were saved by fleeing into the town of Kit Carson. This, I believe, was the last Indian raid in Colorado until the Meeker massacre in 1879, although there had been one in 1869 on the Divide near Colorado City, now Colorado Springs.

Charley Jennison was city marshal in Carson the summer of '70, having just been married to Miss Irene Leonard, a very young girl. Charley was well known as an officer who generally got his man. One day I heard a gambler, who was expecting to be arrested, say that he would go with Charley if he had a warrant. Otherwise, he would not be taken. A few minutes later, Charley himself appeared and attempted to place the gambler under arrest. When the gambler refused to go with him, he produced a gun, but the gambler, unperturbed, stood a few feet away and dared Charley to shoot, which he did not do. He put up his gun and went after a warrant, returning shortly with the document. This time the gambler went quietly along with him. This little story shows that the men, though gamblers of those rough times, could be manly when properly approached.

It was said of Jennison that he "would die some day with his boots on." Apparently to disprove this statement, when he was shot, it was thought fatally, his wife hurried to him and pulled off his boots. But he recovered, only to be shot again in Del Norte—this time to die—with his boots on, before his wife could reach him. No one could deny that Charley was a bold and fearless officer of those wild times, and one can hardly say more than that of any man.

During the years we lived in Denver, my brother and I carried the Denver Tribune, an evening paper, and the Rocky Mountain News, a morning paper. In those days, all the papers had to be folded by hand for the routes, and we carriers became quite proficient in the work. We had to be at the office of he News at 4:00 a. m., fold our route, and be delivering before daylight. My brother was on the West Denver route. One morning Sandy Steele, the brother of Wilbur, formerly of the Post, went along with him, just for fun. They had a pistol along for the purpose of shooting some dogs that were giving some trouble, but I think the only thing they shot was Sandy. The gun went off accidentally in my brother's pocket, passing through the upper part of Sandy's leg. He recovered from this injury, but was killed by accident some time later in the Paradox country. A load of wood tipped over on him.

In '72 we moved to Colorado Springs. My father built a two-story house on Huerfano street, known as the Lafont house, which was used as a billiard hall and hotel. Failing in this enterprise he sold some land he owned in Harmon, now a part of Denver, and built the Eagle hotel, just around the corner from Lafont house, on Te John street. In this hotel my mother, sister and friends made the first flag that ever floated on the summit of Pikes Peak.

On July 3, 1873, Dr. Allen, with three of us young fellows, started for the top of the peak, with the aim of signaling Colorado Springs by means of a flag code he knew. We arrived at timberline that first day, camping there for the night, with plans to start early on the fourth for the top. From timberline to the summit in those days was a hard climb over open country, mostly rocks, and when we finally reached the top, we were disappointed to find that we could not see Colorado Springs and could not be seen from there on account of the clouds that hung over the peak all that day.

However, during the summer of '73 a good trail was built to the top of the peak, via Skink's cabin, Jones' ranch, the Lakes, and on to the top. Over this trail, I made 23 trips as foreman of a pack train of 25 burros, my father having the contract for packing all the timber, lime, furniture, and everything else needed for the installation of a government signal station on top of the peak. Some one else had the contract for the wood that they would need for the long winters that were to follow. Getting to the top with these loads was a continual, day and night struggle. Forty years later I made the trip in that cog railroad coach with Mrs. Simmons, who had but a couple of days previously become my wife. She had promised that she "would go to the ends of the earth" with me, and she made good that promise, at least in that one direction. Forty years, a lifetime in itself, had passed between the time that I had made the climb as best I could and the trip in the comfortable cog-railroad coach. When I shall have driven an automobile to the top and finally shall have flown over it, I shall be satisfied that "the world does move."

During the winter of 1874 and 1875 a prospector, who was a very fine singer, came to town from the San Juan, and by spring he had sung his way into the hearts of nearly everyone in the town. Colorado Springs had gone crazy—as Colorado Springs did, and I think always will—over the reports from a foot racer to a gold mine. Many men got ready to go, among them Alva Adams, who has become one of the bright stars of this great state; O. P. Posey, who later became a millionaire; John Wingate, now of Durango, and my father and his family. We had saved enough from the second failure to buy a half dozen burros, 25 cows, two yoke of oven, and a good wagon. With these we started toward the San Juan, expecting to go by way of Del Norte, where Adams, Posey and Wingate had gone and established a hardware store. My brother drove the herd of cows, while I drove those two yoke of oxen all the way—up Ute pass, on and into South Park, down Trout creek, down the Arkansas to where Salida is now, up Poncha creek and over the Poncha pass, on down and into the great San Luis Valley to Saguache, where we lived for another year. The trip had taken two weeks. The bridge over the Rio Grande river at Del Norte had been washed away, so travel in that direction was impossible for awhile. Saguache was still in its infancy. Father was appointed street supervisor and gave us two boys a job plowing and scraping the street with our work cattle. There, in a home of adobe, which we built ourselves, we remained until the following spring, when we broke up camp and started for Lake City.

While we were in Saguache, we learned that Otto Mears, among others, was trying to get a road through into the San Juan in opposition to the one that went through Del Norte. They got in touch with Enos Hotchkiss, whose brother, Pres., was operating a sawmill. (I can see Uri and Willie, little shavers then, running about the place.) A toll road company was organized. Enos Hotchkiss got the contract, and work was begun that spring. Most of it had to be done from the Ute Indian agency, at that time located on Los Pinos creek, some few miles south of the place where Gunnison now stands. A short time after the work was started a man by the name of Richardson came along with, I think, two teams of work cattle, three yoke to the team. He wanted the company to go with him into the valley of the Gunnison and the Tomichi. My father and brother went, leaving me to look after mother and sister in camp and to take care of the stock. I think Mr. Richardson remained there for several years, establishing the town of Gunnison. My father also took up a location just east of the town as it is now, but he never went back to take care of it.

It was just before we reached Saguache that Alfred Packer, the man who killed five men near the spot where Lake City is now, escaped the authorities. He was not captured for several years. It was also during the winter of '73 and '74 that a party of prospectors from Salt Lake City, Utah, were in this valley with Chief Ouray.

During the summer of the year 1874 the road got as far as San Christobal Lake, where my father had gone to see how they were making out and incidentally, to see what data he could get that would enable him to present his case logically when he should go to Denver for the purpose of raising funds to continue the work. While at the lake he said to Enos Hotchkiss, "Enos, there is a mine up there. Some day go up and locate it; and if you don't mind, locate me in." The mine, which afterward became the Golden Fleece, was located all right, but there were so many of the boys that wanted in that father's name was forgotten.

When father returned from his trip to Denver he provided us boys with three yoke of oxen, and a good four-inch wagon filled with supplies, and started us on the way to the road camp, a distance of 120 miles with only the Indian agency between. My brother was then 18 years old and I was 17. When we arrived at the camp we found that the men had advanced as far as Burris Park. We followed them, but we found almost insurmountable difficulties in our way. The road was new, much of it had been washed out by recent rains, the hills were steep, and we were too heavily loaded. One hill in particular caused trouble. It was called the "Fourth of July hill" and was long, steep, and crooked. Another difficult place was where the timber had been cut down right in a narrow gulch with the dirt scraped in on top of the stumps and logs. This piece of road has gone by three different names in its history— "Hell's Canyon," "Hell's Delight," and "Hell and Repeat."

We were not allowed to go back home because Enos needed the cattle for plowing on the grades as well as our own assistance. This we did, staying with him until the last thing was loaded into the wagons one Sunday morning. We had left our wagons up on the hill, carrying the supplies down to the forks of the Animas. In order to get our wagons down, we had to pass them down over some benches of rocks which were blasted out while we loaded the wagons. These shots completed the most wonderful road of its day, a road connecting the forks of the Animas, in the heart of the San Juan mountains, with the outside world. It was storming fearfully when we started out and by the time we had reached the top of the range many of the stock had been down in the snow. We camped in the timber at the head of Burris Park, to roll out the next morning from under a foot of snow that had fallen during the night. Having little to cook, we were soon on our way. The storm had cleared away and as we came lower we found less and less snow. In Lake City there was no snow at all and the sun was shining, making it look to us like an oasis in the desert, by contrast. There seemed to be nothing under heaven but sunshine, warmth, clear water and high willows.

CHAPTER VI

CHIEF OURAY AND CHIPETA

Chief Ouray, the famous leader of the Utes, was born a Navajo, according to John Lucero, now of Montrose, who formerly lived in the San Luis Valley country and near Taos, New Mexico, where it has been supposed that the Chief was born. He states that, contrary to this belief, Ouray was not born in Taos, but was taken captive in a battle between the Spaniards and Navajoes and was raised at that Indian pueblo. He learned to speak Spanish and the Ute language, and became an interpreter. Later, he joined the Utes and became their most famous chief. His Spanish name was Burule', his Indian name was Lule' and the English became Ouray. Chipeta, his equally famous squaw, was probably born in the San Luis Valley about 1850. Her Spanish name was Guadalupita, which in English was shortened to Chipeta. The Indians used a pronunciation very similar to the English. She was supposed to be the daughter of the chief that preceded Ouray in command of the Utes. As the Utes were not good historians, the exact time and place of her birth cannot be determined.

Some authorities state that the two had one son, who was stolen by the Arapahoes. Others state that they had no children. They were united in marriage some time before 1878. They lived at the Los Pinos Indian Agency for four or five years, and were known to many white people who are still alive. E. C. Dunlap, of Montrose, tells of seeing Chief Ouray in the South Park country of Colorado in the seventies, and later, he states, he was at the post at Fort Crawford, in the Uncompahgre Valley, when the Meeker women, taken captive at the time of the Meeker Massacre, and held for some time by the Utes, were returned to their own people.

William and Enoch J. Shepherd, who came into Colorado in 1863, told the writer that the famous Chief often came to their home in Canon City in the year 1876. It is not known whether he was married to Chipeta at that time or not.

When Mrs. Chauncey Mills came first to Ouray, Chipeta, Chief Ouray and two other Indians rode behind her stage from the Post to Ouray and stayed at the same hotel in that town.

Chipeta and her friends always stopped at the Orvis Hot Springs, near Ridgway, while on her way between the Reservation in Utah and the Southern Ute country. Mrs. Orvis, who still lives on the place, knew her well.

Ouray and Chipeta were frequent visitors at the home in the Cebolla valley, where Mrs. R. B. Lines, now Mrs. Hyde, formerly of Montrose, spent her childhood, and the squaw often took the children to school, driving her own team of mules.

In her latter years, Chipeta became totally blind and lived on the reservation of the Uintah Utes in Utah. She was operated upon once for cataracts, but removed the bandages too soon and never regained her sight.

Chipeta was a friend to the white people who were coming into the country to settle Western Colorado, and it was largely due to her efforts that the Meeker women were returned home by the Utes.

She died in 1924 and was first buried on the reservation. Later the body was removed to the Uncompahgre Valley, and placed in the tomb in the Ouray-Chipeta Memorial Park, about three miles south of Montrose, which is a memorial to the two famous Utes. In this park is also a concrete tepee covering the spring, where Ouray and Chipeta often drank, and also a monument erected by the State of Colorado to the memory of Ouray, as well as the grave of Chipeta's brother, Chief McCook.

> Chipeta walks at midnight,
>   When stars are gleaming bright,
> With the spirits of her people
>   Beneath the pale moon's light.

She treads dim, long-unused trails,
    That know no time or tide,
Chipeta walks at midnight,
    With her chieftain by her side.

When the ghosts of Indians walk,
    And spirit voices sing,
Chipeta comes at midnight,
    And stoops beside a spring.

She sings a deathly silent chant,
    That naught but spirits hear,
Chipeta walks at midnight,
    In places she loved dear.

The late Mrs. Martha Ripley, pioneer of Ouray, wrote the following, which was published in the Montrose Daily Press on Saturday, June 4, 1927:

"OURAY THREW ONE SHELTERING ARM AROUND HIS BELOVED TRIBE AND THE OTHER AROUND WHITE MAN'S INTERESTS AND WENT WITH A CRUSHED SPIRIT TO THE SEAT OF JUSTICE.

"Memorial Day, May 30, 1927, while pondering over the events of the past, concerning the history of the early days on the Western Slope of Colorado my thoughts filled with gratitude as never before, for the many kindnesses shown to us, the pioneers of the western slope, by Chief Ouray, and his wife, Chipeta. My children came with beautiful flowers to be laid on the graves of our loved ones, and then I asked them if they would not take me to the tomb of Chipeta, too. And so, while the people all over the Uncompahgre Valley were placing flowers of tenderness on the graves of their loved ones, it was my pleasure to enter the gate and place with tearful reverence, flowers at the tomb of Chipeta, to whom so much is due. When doing this I recounted to my children how, many years ago, at the time of the Meeker Massacre, I packed a flour sack of condensed milk, and different things for my babies, ready at a moment's notice to fly to a certain cave near our home in the town of Ouray and perhaps escape the war-tossed Indians from the war scene at Meeker.

"The men of Ouray, who, by the request of Governor

Pitkin 'to keep close watch on the Indians' were busy making walls of defense north of town to the best of their
ability, for since no word had as yet come from Chief
Ouray, we did not know what his attitude might be to-
wards the whites at such a time.

"But the white men had not yet sounded the depths of
the character of one of earth's greatest noblemen. Like
Jesus, he was not understood, but he proved equal to the
demands of the hour, and when he spoke, it was in terms
of peace for us, and stern reproof and command, to his
tribe. So no wonder half of my flowers were laid with
loving reverence, at the foot of the monument erected in
honor of Chief Ouray—yes with a little clearer sense of
how the women felt who came to the tomb of Jesus with
spices.

To me, the shaft erected, is a sublime thought. We do
not need Ouray's body. Better without it, perhaps. For as
it is, we see more clearly what the rough-hewed weighty
shaft stands for—"in memory" of a noble life of service.
And also in memory of the preservation of the life of
many an old pioneer. Proving an Indian's heart or soul is
as white as God saw it when He said, 'It was very good.'
And Chipeta—a fit help-meet to this chief—a queen among
the queens of womanhood.

"As Jesus said of the woman who poured 'the precious
ointment' upon his head—'she has done what she could.'
This can surely be said of Chipeta, who was always the
friend of the whites.

"About eleven years ago, soon after the publishing of
the book my husband, Henry Ripley, and myself wrote on
pioneer life—'Handclasp of the East and West', I sent
Chipeta a copy with words of gratitude from us as the
whites she befriended, written on the fly leaf. I asked the
superintendent if an interpreter could read both that and
the other expressions of gratitude to them written in my
story. This was done and the Superintendent wrote me
that the tears rolled down her face as she listened. She
meekly said that she was glad if she had ever been of help
to the whites.

"It is a satisfaction to us today to know she learned we were grateful and remembered her.

"Chief Ouray did not have to bear the pangs of leaving this wonderful valley—so adapted to the wild nature of the Indian.

"We have been told by those who seem to know, that he died of a broken heart, brought about in a measure by the Meeker Massacre. It is possible if the white man could have awakened to Ouray's worth as a man and a friend, he might have been with us today, but as it was, he went to another reservation, which cannot be taken from him.

"I recall, Ouray, for reasons thought by him to be good, would not allow the ones who participated in the Meeker Massacre to be tried by the impetuous spirit of the enraged people of the Western Slope, for as he said in the presence of a representative of my husband's newspaper: 'You are my enemies—I cannot expect justice from you, '. . . . the 'Great Father' (we irreverently call Uncle Sam) 'shall see we have justice'.

"The writer may never know why the Indians all came back free, but this she does feel now, that great wisdom and love for the whites as well as the Indians, was shown by the 'great Father' at Washington. . . . .

"When the testing time came, Ouray threw one sheltering arm around his loved tribe, and the other around the white man's interests, and went with spirit crushed to the seat of justice, ruled by the Great Father, who failed him not.

"There is one in all the world who understood him—his wife, Chipeta. Perhaps her last days were not as dark as we thought them—for she had memories—some of which we are only wakening to enjoy.

"In the light of this widened vision of what we owe to Chief Ouray and Chipeta, shall we not include them in our floral offerings on Decoration Day? a privilege for our children and our children's children?"

Ouray was the ablest Ute chief known to history. His record is an exceedingly creditable one. He ruled his people with a rod of iron but he had their interests at heart. They relied upon his superior judgment and made him "head chief of the Ute nation." He became the representative of all the Utes in their transactions with the United States government.

As the stream of miners and prospectors poured into the San Juan and the mountains were found to hold rich minerals, the Utes were pushed farther and farther back.

From time to time they were induced to relinquish huge slices of their best hunting grounds to the government. By the Kit Carson treaty of 1872 they relinquished all of their land excepting a strip covering about three-fourths of the western slope. A year later by the Brunot treaty they were forced to give up another slice from the southern half of this strip. By the terms of this treaty the government was to pay them an annual sum of $25,000. Years passed and not a dollar was appropriated by congress. Naturally the Utes believed they were being cheated.

Then squatters were continually trespassing upon their reservation in defiance of Ouray's protests. In spite of these grievances Chief Ouray urged his people to be patient. He realized the folly of measuring arms with the United States troops and did all in his power to keep peace. For this service the government paid him a salary of $1,000 a year for a considerable period.

Nevertheless a storm was brewing. The Indians resented the intrusion of the white man, and the white man was equally impatient with the Indians' interference with the march of civilization. "The Utes must go," became the cry throughout Colorado and by an unexpected trend of events, this came to pass.

In the spring of 1878 Nathan C. Meeker was appointed agent of the White river Utes in northwestern Colorado. "Father Meeker" as he was called, was a benevolent soul with the best intentions, but he knew nothing about Indians. He wanted to make them self-supporting and set about teaching them to farm. He intended also to educate and Christianize them. But the Utes did not take kindly to Father Meeker's program. They had their own ideas as to how they should spend their time and much preferred hunting or horse racing to work or study.

There was no serious trouble, however, until a strip of their racing ground was ordered plowed. Then a bullet whizzed by the plowman's ears.

The Utes became more and more disagreeable until the agent in alarm complained to the commision on Indian affairs and finally was forced to put in an appeal for soldiers to protect him.

A band of soldiers was sent from Fort Steele, Wyoming, under Major Thornburgh with five men accompanying them to the agency to investigate matters before the soldiers were brought inside the reservaion. Thornburgh was afraid to trust himself with them and refused.

After halting two days they marched on toward the agency. In a narrow ravine where the trail crosses Milk Creek they were surrounded and attacked from ambush. Thornburgh and a number of his soldiers were killed. The remaining soldiers built a breastwork of wagons and boxes and held the ground for six days before relief came.

Joe Rankin, a scout, who had slipped away under cover of darkness, rode for help, making the distance of one hundred and sixty miles to Rawlings in twenty-eight hours.

The soldiers were in a pitiable plight when Colonel Wesley Merritt with his force of six hundred men arrived and lifted the siege.

Soon afterward the Utes, after first stealing all the rifles from the agency, fell upon Father Meeker and his associates, killing all but one, a messenger who had left immediately before the attack.

Mrs. Meeker, her daughter Josephine, and a Mrs. Price were taken captives and although unharmed suffered many hardships before they were finally rescued by General Adams.

This tragedy occurred while Chief Ouray was away on a hunting expedition. When word reached him of the uprising, he immediately sent a command to the White River Chiefs to stop fighting.

But the damage had already been done and the result

was the removal of the White River Utes to the Uintah reservation in Utah.

Chief Ouray died in 1880 and his death opened the way for the removal of the southern Utes to the Green River.

To the time of his death Chief Ouray and Chipeta lived in their little home on the Uncompahgre where they rendered many a service to the white man.

In 1882 after the removal of the Utes the land in the Uncompahgre and Grand valleys was opened for entry and farms began to flourish where the Indians had roamed.

In June, 1883, the first railroad train whistled into Montrose and the Uncompahgre valley. Four years later this road was completed to Ouray.

CHAPTER VII

OURAY, THE QUEEN CITY

Beautiful Ouray, the Gem City of the Rockies, came into being about the year 1874. The San Juan country was very isolated and it was a long, hard trip to the mines it contained. Many made the trip through Del Norte and on through Antelope Park to Silverton, which was established about the same time. Others came around through Saguache, over Cochetopa Pass and through the Ute country.

Among the first white men to arrive were William Shepherd, J. C. Frees and James Marston. There were no roads, and there were many mud holes and steep hills galore.

There were not many white people in Colorado in the year 1863, the year William Shepherd and his brother Enoch came into this state, their father having preceded them in 1860. The journey across the plains in those Indian days was a dangerous one, and the wagon trains were burned ahead and behind them. However they arrived safely in Denver, and soon moved on to the little settlement at Mountain City, half way between Central City and Black Hawk.

The father was a blacksmith and his two sons have followed that profession nearly all their lives.

One of their first recollections of Colorado was seeing a man named Van Horn hung on Bates Hill in 1864 for shooting another man.

The elder Shepherd, in addition to his blacksmith trade, was a Methodist preacher and walked from Central City to Denver, a distance of forty-five miles to preach. He was a personal friend of Col. Chivington, who was in command of the troops at the Battle of Sand Creek, in which an entire camp of Indians was killed, with the exception of two little girls.

39

The Shepherd family moved to Canon City in 1868, where they operated a blacksmith shop. Later the father and two elder sons took up homesteads of 160 acres each. They had the first ranches in the Lincoln Park district.

The year 1876 saw the family moving to Fairplay, where they also operated a blacksmith shop. A short time later they were running a sawmill on Oak Creek, between Canon City and Rosita, in the Greenhorn Range country.

In 1877, William Shepherd, with Frees and Marston, came into the Uncompahgre Valley, following a company of Negro soldiers, who had been compelled to build their own road. Going up the far-famed Son of a B----- Hill, they lost everything out of the wagon, except the camp equipment, and had to go back after all the blacksmith tools and supplies. Mr. Frees wept as he looked back over the hill with paraphernalia strewn all along its steep slope.

In 1878 William Shepherd and Gus Seibert operated a pack outfit and carried supplies in the San Juan country. Since 1905 he operated a blacksmith shop in Ridgway until his death.

Mrs. Sarah Randall Jarvis Orvis claimed to be the first white woman in Ouray, having come to that town in 1876. The next year she settled on the ranch, where she still lives at the time this is being written.

As a child on the frontier, Mrs. Orvis saw many thrilling things on the overland trip from Illinois to Salt Lake City and back to Julesburg, Colorado. In 1875 she was married to A. H. (Billy) Jarvis and they came to Gunnison, where they lived on a ranch for a time. There was not much of a town in the Gunnison Valley and they soon decided to move farther westward, so they came on to Ouray, which at that time was known as Uncompahgre City, and was in San Juan County.

A son of Mrs. Orvis was the first person buried in the Ouray cemetery, which property was deeded to the town by a Mr. Paquin.

The Jarvis party was the first to come over Log Hill Mesa on the way into the Ouray district. They had to let their wagons down over the south rim of Log Hill with ropes. They came into the country to stay and it seemed like a Paradise to them. They lived on the Stough place for a time and also on the Stanton place, then moved to Ouray for a while, before squatting on the ranch in 1877, which the Orvis family still owns. This is a very valuable ranch, for it contains the far-famed Uncompahgre Hot Springs, for which the valley was named.

In 1878, Mr. Jarvis became ill and started out to Pueblo for medical care, Mrs. Jarvis staying behind to hold the ranch against claim jumpers. Jarvis died before reaching Pueblo. When there was an Indian scare, Mrs. Jarvis took the children to Ouray and then returned to the ranch to hold it against all comers. Her brother had built her a fort which was connected with her kitchen by a tunnel, and here she stayed until the scare was over. She states that at the time of the Meeker Massacre, the Indians around her were as scared as the white settlers.

President Grant ceded the land of which her land was a parts back to the Indians, but still she stayed on the place, and she is there yet. At one time, when there was an Indian scare, she and her children, together with the Moody and Noland families, loped a team of oxen all the way to Ouray.

In those days they did not have many conveniences in the home. They put the endgate of a wagon on hinges in place of a window on one cabin and at one time the family had the only glass window in Ouray. For doors they used bed blankets, and they slept on pine bough beds.

Mrs. Orvis says that the Indians did not prowl at night but if they went on the warpath at night it was time to watch out. There came a rumor of Indian trouble to Ouray once and the minister of the Episcopal Church was on guard. Some one was joshing him, saying that they thought he was saving souls. He replied: "I am saving lives now."

A boy named Johnny Long was working for the family at one time. He was staying in the camp house and went out to go to bed one night. He heard a noise inside the house and ran back after help, declaring there was a bear in his quarters. Investigation showed that a cow had entered the premises and chewed up all his clothing and every article she could eat.

In 1882, Mrs. Jarvis was married to Lewis F. Orvis, who came to Central City, Colorado, in 1860. He came into the Uncompahgre Valley with Ben Parliaman and Johnny Neville, by wagon. One winter, 1878, he went out after a herd of cattle and spent the whole winter driving them back into the valley. Some days he would only go a mile or so. It took men of iron to stand experiences like that.

The Orvis' had a contract to furnish hay for the stock at Fort Crawford one winter and received $48 a ton for it. They sold a ton of hay one winter to a man named Corbut in Ouray, for $100.00, and hated to part with it even at that price. One sack of oats cost them nine dollars.

The family had many thrilling experiences with claim jumpers and more than once came near losing the place and their lives as well.

The Orvis ranch was always popular with the Indians because of the hot springs. The redskins always stopped there to bathe and dance when they were in the valley. The Indians all over the state knew of the springs.

Mrs. Orvis says that the squaws and papooses would come into her house and sit on the floor. They would pick bugs out of their hair and crack them between their teeth. All the Indians called her "Sis" and would say to her: "This is Ute Country. When you go away?" She would reply: "When the ponies get fat."

Her mother kept her little sister picketed with a rope so she would not run away. The Indians got a kick out of this and would say: "Papoose no get fat. No grass."

In her last years Chipeta was bitter toward the white men. She told Mrs. Orvis that she owned all the land between the Hot Springs and Ignacio and she did not like the encroachment of the Whites.

CHAPTER VIII

OLD TIMERS

George Rhodes Hurlburt, who was recently killed in a fall from a cliff, at the age of 88, while actively engaged in his work as County Surveyor of Ouray County, had a long and thrilling life in the San Juan country. Coming into Colorado in 1873, he helped survey some coal land around Cocheros and Walsenburg. He came to Silverton in the summer of 1875 and to Ouray in 1877. As Assistant County Surveyor, he helped survey timber lands near Silverton. During the winter of 1877 and 1878 he traded with the Indians of the Uncompahgre Valley, and also acted as interpreter. In addition to this work he did some placer mining in the San Miguel River in 1878.

In 1879, Hurlburt helped lay out the town of Telluride, and built the first cabin in Naturita Canyon, remnants of which still remain. This cabin was used as a hunting lodge.

He carried mail between Ames and Rico during the winter of 1879 and 1880, and in 1883 joined C. A. Wheeler in the surveying business. He discovered the Bachellor Mine in 1893, and for a time was a third owner of it. This is now the east half of the Banner-American and has produced more than $2,000,000.

In the winter of 1884, Mr. Hurlburt was carried two thousand feet down a mountainside near Silverton by an avalanche, but was able to dig himself out. He took part in many rescues of snow slide victims. He surveyed thirty miles of the highway between Creede and Lake City, and was City Engineer of Ouray when the waterworks and sewer system were installed. He was County Surveyor of Ouray County for many years.

Charles Leighton McKinley came in to Ouray as a boy in 1882. At this time the camp was booming and everything was wide open. The trip to the gold camp was made on a buckboard from Gunnison, seven people in the vehicle, which was driven by Pete Buskirk. The first night the party stayed with S. H. Schildt at Barnum, where the Half Way House now stands, and the following day came over the old Cutler Cutoff to Fort Crawford on the Uncompahgre, near the present location of Colona, where were stationed some five hundred soldiers.

During this summer, McKinley's grandfather was on a jury which convicted Andy Bigger of murder, after the latter had carved seven notches in the handle of his gun, each for a man he had killed. This same Grandfather operated the Wheel of Fortune Mine in Imogene Basin one winter.

At this time Dave Day was publishing the "Solid Muldoon," Charley Armstrong was cook in a mine, and Johnny Donald, George Hurlburt and William Rathmell were there. Down by the river, old "220" and the Gold Belt Theatre were in full swing. Bob Brookfield operated a faro game at the White House Saloon, Louie Hohl was the oldest baker, Shorty Davis ran a meat market, "Baby Jim" Knous, uncle of Senator Lee Knous, was town marshal, Jesse Benton was sheriff. Captain Jackson, who built the brick house below town, now used as a County Home, owned the Saratoga Mine. The Captain had been one of Quantrell's Raiders in Kansas, and told McKinley that he once secretly met his friend, Jesse James, on the Log Hill Mesa road, when the latter was being hunted and could not show himself.

The town of Old Dallas, located where Dallas Creek joins the Uncompahgre, was thriving, with about twenty stores and saloons, well patronized by the freighters and cattlemen.

Many of the old timers of Ouray remember the Cudigan hanging. Mr. and Mrs. Cudigan had adopted a little girl, and it seems, were very cruel to her. They made her sleep in a straw pile in the winter time, according to some reports, until her feet froze and she died of exposure. The Cudigan ranch was on Dallas Creek, but the couple were at the Del Monica Hotel in Ouray. The hotel was stormed by a mob, who took them to a place below town and hung them. It was a cold night and Mrs. Cudigan was barefooted.

Mr. and Mrs. Chauncey E. Mills are among the early pioneers of Ouray, who still live there. Mrs. Mills, who was first married to Richard Cogar, came to Ouray in 1880, and Mr. Cogar was connected with the Allied Mining Company at Camp Bird and the Agnes Mining Company. When they started to keep house in Ouray they had eleven pounds of flour and some rice and dried peaches. All provisions had to be hauled in by ox team, and, though they had money, they could not buy food. Flour was $11 a hundred, eggs $1.50 a dozen and lemons $1.25.

They were in Ouray when a Negro, who had killed a chambermaid at the Beaumont Hotel, was cremated in the cage at the jail. A mob took the jail keys away from Jesse Benton, the sheriff, and set fire to the jail. After the man was burned, a small boy came up the street, shouting, "Roast coon for breakfast."

Mrs. Cogar once saw Sheriff Benton shoot a man off a mule for putting his boy on the stove. On her trips over the ranges, Mrs. Cogar always went armed and was held up several times. She says she is not afraid of any man, but is only afraid of a mouse. She is a dead shot and has had occasion to use her skill as a marksman.

When she came in by stage from Alamosa, Mrs. Cogar had to tie her two boys in the stage to keep them from being bounced out.

Mrs. Mills built the Cogar Sanitarium in Ouray and operated it for many years. Mr. Cogar died in 1920 and his widow was married to Chauncey E. Mills, whom she had known for a long time. Mr. Mills, at an early age, went on an emigrant train to Manti, Utah, where his father worked as a carpenter on the Mormon Temple. From there they went to Price, where, at the age of twelve years, Chauncey drove a freight team to Fort Duchesne, in the Ute Reservation. In 1889, he came to Ouray and engaged in freighting, driving stages and teams, also packing for the John Ashenfelter firm.

He left Ouray with others one morning in 1893, headed for the Revenue Mine. Arriving at Windy Point, a horse went off the road and they were trying to get him back into the tracks. A snow slide came crashing down upon them and swept the outfit down the mountainside. Two men behind Mills were killed. A man who was standing three feet from him was killed. Another standing fifty feet from him was killed, but Mills happened to catch hold of a telephone pole and saved himself. The men killed in this slide were: Hank Metcalf, John Swain, Charley Winn and Neighbor White.

Eighteen six-horse teams were on the road once when the big Water Hole Slide ran and killed twenty-three horses and five men. They went over the tops of the slides with their pack outfits, not taking the time to shovel through them, for they never knew when a new slide would run.

Wildie Roy Andrew was born in Lake City, March 21, 1878. At the age of four years he was taken to Ouray, where he attended school. He states that he helped dig the horses out of the Water Hole Slide near the Camp Bird Mine. He also remembers the Cudigan hanging and the cremation of the Negro in jail.

There were many killings in Ouray in those early days. Jesse Benton killed a man named Lucas in front of the Dixon House, and a Chinaman was killed for an attack on a white girl. The Sanderson Hotel burned in 1886 and the Dixon House was destroyed by fire in 1893. The Ashenfelter mule barn burned in 1909 and fifteen mules and one horse were killed. A runaway team ran into another team standing by the sidewalk, and the wagon tongue was thrust clear through one horse and part way through another. One Ed Leggett was shot in a dance hall fight. Once the cage at the Virginius Mine dropped and killed five men.

James A. Beatty, better known to the citizens of Montrose as "Doc" Beatty, came to Leadville, Colorado, in 1879, and the same summer was on Bear Creek, about five miles from Ouray, mining with Harry Youman and two other men. On the Fourth of July, he walked into Ouray and had dinner. This was the year in which the Meeker Massacre took place, and a runner came through the mountains to warn the miners of a suspected general uprising of the Indians. Youman, Beatty and Minor Minor fled to Lake City and joined the Pitkin Guards. The uprising failed to materialize and the men worked in a saw mill for a time, as it was too late in the fall to go back to the mine.

A short time later the firm of Gilbert and Howell hired Beatty and Gene McGregor to move a saw mill from the Dallas to Gunnison and on the way there, they met the soldiers escorting the Meeker women back to civilization, after their harrowing captivity among the Utes.

For the next few years Beatty worked at various places throughout Western Colorado, and then settled on a place near Roubideau Station, below Delta, where he had bought a ranch from a horsethief named William Pitney. The last time Pitney was seen alive by Beatty, he saw the man riding a fine horse on the Horsethief Trail, near Ouray. Soon after passing him, two other men came along, following Pitney. Later the two men returned with Pitney's horse and he was seen no more.

In 1892 the Beatty family moved to Telluride, then Durango and the next year, they came to Montrose, where they have lived since that time. For many years "Doc" was a leading veterinary in Montrose.

E. C. Dunlap came to Colorado from Iowa in the year 1870. With his father's family, he settled on a ranch twenty-five miles east of Fairplay. While the family was living there the country was full of Indians and there were many scares. When the Meeker Massacre occurred, the whole country around South Park was in an uproar. Dunlap's father-in-law was killed by Indians and the body lay for three days before the troops came and buried it.

The spring of 1881 saw the family moving to the Western Slope, making the trip by wagon through Salida, over Poncha and Cochetopa Passes to the Indian Agency on the Los Pinos river, where they camped for a while. Then they traveled over the Blue Mesa and came into the Un-

compahgre Valley where they spent a time at Fort Crawford.

The Dunlaps went from Fort Crawford to a point on
the Plateau River, where the Meeker women had been held
in captivity by the Utes, and there settled down for a few
months. They spent a winter snowed in, and as they were
going out to Grand Junction in the spring were accosted by
Sheriff Bowman and his deputy, Rowe Allison, who thought
they might be members of the Howard gang of cattle thieves.
They were taken to Grand Junction, where they were identified by the Russell brothers who had known them at Fort
Crawford. Later the sheriff and his deputy met up with
Howard on Kannah Creek and a battle ensued, in which
the leader of the rustlers was killed.

Most of the years following this until 1905, Dunlap was
engaged in operating sawmills in various parts of Western
Colorado, and working the present Veo ranch on the Big
Cimarron River. In 1905 he went to work assisting with
the construction of the Gunnison Tunnel, and while thus
engaged suffered the loss of his right leg in an accident.
Since that time he has resided on a farm near Montrose.

The history of Western Colorado is closely entwined
about the lives of Mr. and Mrs. Louis Fournier, who now
live in Pleasant Valley, several miles west of Ridgway. Mr.
Fournier was born and raised in Ponrouge, Canada, and is
a Frenchman. At the age of twenty years, with three other
Frenchmen, he set out for Colorado, coming as far as St.
Elmo, in the Gunnison region, by train. They had planned
to secure work at the Mary Murphy Mine there, but the
mine closed the day they arrived. They walked on to Glenwood Springs, and suffered many severe hardships, Mr.
Fournier's younger brother, a lad of seventeen, dying on
the way. None of the party could speak English, which
made their experiences doubly hard to bear.

Mr. Fournier has been identified with the development
and progress of the San Juan region ever since that time.
He has worked in many of the mines in the Telluride
district. The men who came with him from Canada are all
dead now, but Fournier still carries on at this writing.

He was in Telluride when a snow slide killed sixteen men at the Liberty Bell Mine, and also swept away all of the mine buildings. A rescue party sent to the aid of the sixteen men was killed by another slide.

Mrs. Fournier, who was born Josephine Noel, is the daughter of Sim Noel, who came to Antonito, Colorado, in 1879. The family followed a year later. Mr. Noel operated a section house on the new railroad to Antonito and also ran a saloon in a tent.

When Mrs. Fournier was five years old a bunch of bandits came into the town, rounded up all the citizens and proceeded to take all the valuables they found. Mrs. Noel took the children to the mountains for safety. One of the robbers was killed and the others got away, passing, in their flight, the very tree beneath which Mrs. Noel and her children were hiding.

In 1881 the family moved to Durango, where Mr. Noel operated a hotel and saloon. In 1883 they went to Silverton and on up to the Ironton district, packing in with mules. Mr. Noel and Louis Blanchard located the Saratoga Mine. The winter of 1883-84 was so severe that the party moved into Ironton to escape dangerous snow slides. Food was scarce as the snow was too deep for pack trains, and the men had to go on foot to Ouray and carry back flour and other supplies to keep their families from starving.

The Spring of 1885 saw the family moving to Ouray, where the father operated the Sanderson Hotel, until it burned in 1886, after which Mr. Noel took up a ranch at Noel, on the headwaters of Leopard Creek.

CHAPTER IX

TIME TURNED BACK

The late Henry C. Fink came to Lake City in 1887, after graduating from the Cincinnati Law School. His aunt's husband, Judge McKenna, was superintendent of the Ute and Ulay Mills at that place.

Of the trip from Gunnison to Lake City, which was made in a buckboard, Mr. Fink said that way out in the wilderness all four tires came off the buckboard and the passengers had to rustle all sorts of wire to fasten them on with. They were served the evening meal at Gateway by Mrs. Mendenhall.

After a short visit with the McKenna's, Mr. Fink decided to seek other fields, so the Judge suggested that he go on to Ouray. Fink inquired as to the price of the trip and was told that it would cost him twenty-five dollars to go by buckboard to Sapinero, by train to Montrose and buckboard to Ouray. By far the shortest and cheapest way was up across the American Flats, a distance of only about fifteen miles. So he decided on this. He and the Judge made the trip to the Frank Hough Mine, well above timberline on the Flats and walked down the famous Bear Creek trail into Ouray. Of course, in the early days, many people made this trip on foot, but in the later years it has been made by few. The American Flats is the largest above-timberline area in the United States, and at the present time is a desolate and lonely place.

Arriving in Ouray the two men asked the price of a bed at the Beaumont Hotel and were told that it would cost them $8.00 a day to sleep there. The Dixon House however, was a little cheaper, about $4.50. Meals for the two were $3.75.

At this time, Mr. Fink was somewhat of a tenderfoot,

and, when a cold summer rain and hail storm hit them on
the American Flats, he sincerely wished he had stayed in
Cincinnati.

The trail on American Flats was hard to follow and
the two got lost several times. It was midnight before they
finally arrived in Ouray.

Mr. Fink engaged in the practice of law in Ouray until July of 1888, when he received an appointment from
President Cleveland as receiver for the United States Land
Office at Lake City. In this capacity he had to carry large
sums of money from Lake City to Gunnison, where it was
expressed to the United States Treasury.

In September of 1888, Fink was ordered to move the
Land Office to Montrose, which he did. Large amounts of
money were brought into the office at that time, and one
night he slept on his revolver with $25,000 in cash hid in
rolls of paper under the safe. Altogether he spent ten
years as receiver for the U. S. Land Office. The remainder
of his life was spent in the active practice of law at Montrose.

Samuel S. Boucher was a placer miner on the San
Miguel River as early as 1881, having come into Colorado
in the year 1879 and spent some time in Denver. After
spending three months in Durango in 1881, he moved to
the San Miguel River, where he worked for wages on a
placer mining outfit operated by parties living in Keokuk,
Iowa. The flume they put in cost about a half a million
dollars. He assisted in several cleanups and found that the
place was rich in gold. He says he never did know why
the company stopped the work, unless the superintendent
held out the profits. Mr. Boucher saw strips of amalgam
two feet long almost pure gold. The hydraulic process was
used in the placer mining, the nozzles being six and eight
inches in diameter.

Boucher asserts that the Dave Wood place on the Dallas
is the scene of the earliest placer operations in the Uncompahgre Valley. His cousin, Elmer Bernard, worked
this place as early as 1877.

After leaving the San Miguel country, Mr. Boucher became a member of a survey party that surveyed from the top of Dallas Divide down to the town of Ridgway. Then they went to Delta and ran the survey for the Denver & Rio Grande Railroad up the river about twenty-five miles, after which the party went down to the Utah state line and ran a survey back to Grand Junction. They tried to go through the Black Canyon of the Gunnison, but were unable to get very far up the formidable canyon that was before them. At that time Grand Junction was a very small town, only one log house and a bunch of tents.

Returning to the Ridgway country, Mr. Boucher spent six years as assessor of Ouray county, and since retiring from this position he has operated a drug store in Ridgway. This town, when at its best, had a population of six hundred people, and the big Mentone Hotel, built in 1890, was crowded most of the time. The town had five saloons and the round house for the Rio Grande Southern had forty-eight men at work, with a payroll of $6000 a month. There was also a creamery with a $5000 payroll, and a flour mill that distributed $6000 a month. Now the town has about three hundred people, the round house employs seven men, and there is no creamery and no flour mill.

At one time the Camp Bird Mine was paying three-fifths of the county taxes, giving into the county treasurer $76,000 out of $100,000 taxes each year. At the time Mr. Boucher was assessor, the Camp Bird had produced $25,-000,000 in gold and has been producing ever since.

The American Nettie, an old producer of the Ouray district, has about fifty-two miles of underground works, of which nine-tenths are natural caverns, in which pure gold was found in the dust of the floors.

CHAPTER X

A GOOD INDIAN

Addison Josiah Baxter came to Olathe, Colorado, in 1890, where he worked for four years. At the time he came to Olathe, there was not much to be called a town. The little old log building that was a store, post office and saloon still stands across the road from the section house.

He worked for several years for the "Hip, Side & Shoulder" Cattle Company, owned by Carlisle of Pueblo, in the Blue Mountains of Utah. One time while he was on this job, he and his pal, Charlie Snell, were riding down toward the Colorado River, when they suddenly came upon the hideout of the McCarty gang of outlaws who had a short time before this robbed a bank in Delta. In this robbery, two of the bandits were killed and bills of various denominations were spread all over the streets.

Another time, when they were riding, Charlie Snell sent Ad down through a dry wash, while he rode on the ridge above. Mr. Baxter soon encountered a flock of small owls. He was curious to know what they were doing, and investigated. He found that they were picking the meat off the bones of a dead Indian, who had been hung to a tree.

He also spent some time herding cattle for the Smith outfit on Black Mesa near Crystal Creek. There were three or four cowboys, whose duty it was to round up and brand the calves. Their supplies were carried on pack horses, and the remuda consisted of about twenty-five head of horses.

William Davis Jay, the son of Samuel and Elizabeth Harper Jay, was born in Winfield, Cowley County, Kansas, on the twenty-first of April, 1872. At the age of four years, in 1876, he was brought by his parents into Colorado, the family crossing the plains in a wagon. The father and

53

mother had been in Colorado, at Denver, in 1861, and '62, Mr. Jay being stable man for the Government troops stationed at that place and hauling supplies for the Government.

The two returned to Iowa in 1863 and then went to Kansas, where Samuel Jay hauled supplies for the Caw Indians, making trips from Kansas down into the Indian Territory.

In 1876 the family came to Pueblo, where they stayed a short time, after which they moved to Canon City, from which place Mr. Jay freighted to Ouray. The family started to Leadville and spent a winter in the town of Nathrop, near Salida. At Leadville, he worked in a smelter and engaged in teaming. He was there at the time the first train was run into that town.

From Leadville, they went to Maysville, also near Salida, and followed the D. & R. G. Railroad as it slowly crept over the Continental Divide and down into Sargents. There Mr. Jay operated an eating house for the Railroad Company, established a hostelry of his own in 1883 and then moved to the town of Old Dallas in 1884, where he became the owner of a hotel, which he operated until it burned with the rest of the town a few years later.

In 1890, when the Ridgway-Telluride section of the Rio Grande Southern was built, William D. Jay became clerk and baggage master at Ridgway, which position he held in 1891 and in 1892 he entered the train service. From that year until 1923, he was on the various runs of the Rio Grande Southern, between Ridgway and Durango.

George Heavrin was born in Burlington, Iowa, in 1870. He was taken to Joplin, Missouri, at the age of two years, and when he was four years of age, his parents brought him to Colorado, stopping at Denver, Pueblo and Canon City. Then the family went to Rosita, where they stayed for three years, the father freighting from there to Canon City.

The winter of 1876 was spent in Del Norte, and the following spring, 1877, the Heavrin family went to Alpine, where they spent a year, going from there to St. Elmo, where Mr. Heavrin helped lay out the town. Alpine and St. Elmo are in the Gunnison district.

Moving to the Gunnison Valley above Delta in 1883, the family stayed there until the spring of 1885, when they returned to St. Elmo, to remain until the fall of 1887. James Heavrin, the father of George, was a miner and worked in the various mines in and around the towns in which they lived.

In 1887, they again returned to the North Fork of the Gunnison and lived on a farm. George left home and worked as a freighter in Pitkin, hauling ore for Charley Neale, and the next winter made railroad ties. In the winter of 1888 he hauled ore from Gold Hill to St. Elmo, working for Jim Boyd.

The family moved from Hotchkiss to a farm near Olathe, and George worked for the farmers and punched cows in various parts of Western Colorado. After spending three years near Olathe, George moved the family to Hastings mesa, where they lived for two years, after which they moved to Delta again. While on Hastings Mesa, Mr. Heavrin worked at the Larry Finch sawmill.

George Heavrin then took up a ranch on Hastings Mesa, where he worked in the summer time and worked in the mines around Telluride. This he did for sixteen years, and then sold the Hastings Mesa ranch to Boyd Collins and moved down into the Paradox Valley, where he spent ten years. He hauled ore for the Carnotite mines and for two years operated a feed stable in Naturita. He drove teams for Mel Turner, W. R. Rader, and the Hartman Brothers, also for Harry Watt.

He lived for six years on the Leopard Creek side of Dallas Divide, where he and W. R. Jones operated a store and post office and a ranch and bunch of cattle.

Jones and Heavrin went to Florida in 1924, and stayed for a year or so, when Heavrin returned to Montrose for a time and then went to Southwest Missouri, where he owned a farm. He stayed there about eight months and then returned to Ouray, where he worked for the Banner-American Mining Company until 1933.

Virdie Lewis Hotchkiss was born in Vermillion, Nebraska, January 29, 1867, and died March 4, 1934. When he was two weeks old, his family moved over into South Dakota, where the father, Roswell Hotchkiss, operated a grist mill until Virdie was nine years old, then the family came across the plains to Saguache, Colorado, later moving on to Ouray County, where with his brother, Preston, Roswell Hotchkiss established a store in the town of Portland.

After the Indians were taken out of the Uncompahgre Valley in 1881, Virdie Hotchkiss' father homesteaded the place, across the river from Colona, where the Virdie Hotchkiss family still reside. Virdie made one trip to Kansas with a hundred head of horses, which he and his brother, Charlie, sold in that state. Charlie returned to Colorado, but Virdie bought some race horses and went down into Texas, where he spent a time in the racing game.

Selling the race horses, he went up into Oklahoma and took part in the land race into the Cherokee strip, taking up a 100 acre ranch, living there a year and then selling out and returning to the Uncompahgre Valley.

He worked for fifteen years for a man named Gere, but in 1898 quit his job and went up to the Klondike region in Alaska and the Yukon Territory, where he leased placer mines and worked for wages for a year and a half, making about $5000 in his ventures there.

He returned in 1900 to Montrose, and when Gere died, Virdie L. Hotchkiss was made administration of the estate. He was married to Cora Lamb and settled on the Gere ranch.

After moving back onto the old home place, Virdie L. Hotchkiss became firmly established in the cattle business. He homesteaded and bought land until he owned 4000 acres on Beaton Creek, which he used for summer range for his stock. This acreage he sold in 1927, and thereafter took his stock into the Forest Reserve in the Sanborn Park region.

When he worked for Gere, he helped drive beef to

Ouray every week for the markets of that city. In those days the cowboys worked throughout the year. The cattle were driven to different ranges for each of the seasons. They did not winter feed the cattle in pastures, as the country was not fenced and there was plenty of open land for everyone. It costs more to winter the stock than it did in the old days so there is less profit in the business. In those days all the cow outfits were big ones, with from two to five thousand head of cattle. Today the big outfits have given way for the smaller companies, the individual stockmen.

During his lifetime, Virdie Hotchkiss operated livery stables in Montrose, Ouray and Lake City, at various times.

Fayette Herman Posey is descended from General Thomas Posey, who was a close friend of George Washington, and took an active part in the American Revolution. The Posey and Washington families were closely related through intermarriage, and Fayette Herman Posey has some very interesting documents which bear out these statements.

He was born in Henderson, Kentucky, on February 18, 1865, and lived there until he was twenty years old. His father was a planter, and his grandfather had been a big slave holder. Therefore the father and grandfather were Southern sympathizers in the Civil War. F. H. Posey was educated in the public and private schools of Henderson.

When he was twenty years old, in 1885, Posey came to Denver with Robert Walker, also of Henderson. At this time the cattle business was the rage and the two youths had a desire to get into that game. In Denver they stopped at the old Del Monica of the West Hotel, which was cattlemen's headquarters. Lee Seehoun, the clerk of the hotel, was married to a cousin of Mr. Walker. They stayed there for a month or six weeks, and then met Charles E. Taylor, who had gone from Henderson to New York a few years before. He was a man of untiring energy and ambition, and at this time had an office at Sixteenth and Larimer Streets, near the Tabor Block. Mr. Taylor told the two young men that he was going to drive a bunch of cattle

over Tennessee Pass in May and he offered them a job
assisting in the drive. The cattle belonged to Taylor and
Chase.

They helped to drive the stock over the Divide and
located a ranch on the Grand River, now the Colorado. The
cattle were taken to summer on the Castle Range. The
foreman of the outfit was John Mortimer Baxter, a min-
eralogist. Taylor was also interested in the mining game,
being connected with the Groundhog Mine on Battle
Mountain. He established the Mining Exchange in Denver
and at one time could have sold his interest in the May
Mazeppa Mine at Doyle, east of Gunnison, for a million
dollars.

The cattle drive occupied six weeks of time and they
came out on the Colorado River about 15 miles east of the
County Seat of Eagle County, which is the town of Eagle.
At that time, however, the County Seat was Red Cliff.
They built corrals and pastures, and made cabins to live in.
The country was alive with deer and elk. They were near
the mouth of what is now called Posey Creek, which flows
into the Colorado opposite Red Dirt. At the present time
Posey Creek is diverted over a divide for farm use. The
new Dotsero Cutoff of the D. & R. G. W. R. R. runs
through the old Posey homestead.

Before the year 1885 had come to a close, Chase purchased the interest of Taylor in the cattle outfit and F. H.
Posey became his partner. In the spring of 1892 they traded
this ranch for a place in the Brush Creek Valley, below
Eagle, securing the new ranch from Art Hockett. They did
not keep this ranch long, but in the fall of the same year,
sold out and bought an interest in the Brunswick Hotel for
"gentlemen only," on Sixteenth street between Larimer
and Lawrence, in Denver. They bought the interest of
General Taylor of Lake City, who was later lieutenant governor of Colorado.

Then came the panic of 1893, and Posey lost everything
he owned. So with a bunch of Colorado pioneers, he
made the run into the Cherokee Strip of Oklahoma. On
the same train they went into the strip on, was Judge

George W. Bruce, who today is Judge of the Seventh Judicial District of Colorado. Posey secured a lot in the town of Perry, Oklahoma, built a house on it and lived there all winter. One day this land was an open plain. The next day there were 30,000 people on it. A man from Texas tried to jump Posey's claim, but the Colorado boys came to his rescue and the lot was saved.

In the spring of 1895, Mr. Posey returned to Denver and then started to Alaska. He got as far as Port Townsend and then returned to Portland, where he met a man he had known in Pocatello, Idaho. This man was interested in the Bingham Springs in the latter city, and offered Posey a proposition to sell the spring water in case lots in Portland. Posey accepted the position, and also established a commission business, which he operated for a few months, after which he returned to Denver, where he became connected with the N. B. McCrary Wholesale Grocery Co., as the Western Slope representative.

Montrose was the most central point so Posey made his headquarters here. He liked the town and became established in a room over the J. E. McClure Bank, which is now the Montrose National Bank. The four grocery stores of the town were operated by E. J. Mathews, J. C. Frees, C. J. Diehl and Olen Spencer. After Posey had been with the firm for five years, the business was sold and Posey accepted a position with the Bragdon Firm of Pueblo, and handled the same line of goods in the same territory. After five years with them, he became connected with the Morey Mercantile Company of Denver, a position he held until 1911, when he retired and engaged in the life insurance and real estate business. He had acquired considerable property in Montrose and finally retired from his other business to put in his whole time taking care of his own interests.

He was married in 1898 to Mrs. Virginia Marshal Brown, whose first husband had been the son of a Governor of Kentucky, and also Secretary to the Governor. Mrs. Posey has one daughter, Mrs. George Anderson of Pawling, New York.

General Thomas Posey, F. H. Posey's distinguished ancestor, besides being a close friend of General Washington was the second Governor of Indiana, was Lieutenant Governor of Kentucky for four years, and was State Senator from Louisiana.

There is a county in the state of Indiana named after General Posey and the county seat is Mount Vernon.

Una Belle Alderson Thompson was born in Exeter, Scott County, Illinois, February 9, 1861. It was during the early days of the Civil War. Her father was one of the first men to volunteer in that war and he served clear through the war, and spent three months in the Confederate Prison on Belle Isle.

John Alderson, the father, was a deputy sheriff, the family living over the jail in Winchester. One night, when he had a young man named Fred Haller, who was accused of cutting up a couple of old ladies, in jail a mob stormed the bastile and threatening the sheriff's family, took the boy out into the street and shot him.

After coming to Colorado, the elder Alderson one day took his younger daughter, the sister of Mrs. Thompson, on a trip to Red Rock Canyon, a tributary to the Black Canyon of the Gunnison. The girl met a tragic death, when a gun carried by the father, was discharged into her body. The heart-broken father sent his young son after help and stayed in the canyon all day with the body of his daughter.

Mrs. Thompson recalls another interesting episode in the early family history, while her father was in the sheriff's office in Illinois. Two convicts had escaped from the Indiana State Penitentiary and made their way into Illinois. Sheriff Alderson learned that one of the men was in his county and, taking his sixteen year old son with him, went after the desperado. He found him out in the timber on a certain ranch. He captured the fellow and asked him where his partner was. He was told that the other convict was at the farmhouse. So, leaving the sixteen year old boy to guard his prisoner, the sheriff went down to the house and made the second capture.

Mrs. Thompson came into Western Colorado by train

in 1886. The first winters were spent at Eureka, near Silverton. They had to lay in supplies to last throughout the winter, for they were snowed in for several months at a time.

James Ivey Lick was born in Mountain Home, Baxter County, Arkansas, October 3, 1890, and was brought by his parents to the Uncompahgre Valley at the age of two months. He went through school in the town of Montrose, and since that time has followed various pursuits, engaging mostly in mining and milling.

His father, Francis August Lick, had made a previous trip into the valley and had helped General MacKenzie take the Indians out in 1881.

Mr. Lick helped the Williams boys haul the lumber to erect the first uranium mill in the United States. The work was superintended by a Frenchman named Appollo, who was the representative of Mme. Curie, the famous French scientist, who discovered radium.

Among other experiences, Mr. Lick recalls the time when a bunch of Utes from the McElmo Canyon country surrounded their wagon train, and one of the Williams boys traded whiskey to the redskins for the safety of the cavalcade.

In the days when he was a boy, Lick says, it was a common occurance for the cowboys to ride into town and shoot all the lights out. He says, also, that the cowboys in Western Montrose County often wrote their names on the cliffs with uranium ore, not knowing what it was.

At the time his father was in the valley, before the Indians were removed, there was a trading post almost on the spot where James I. Lick lived a long time.

John Foster Wilson was born in Harleton, Union County, Pennsylvania, and lived there until 1881, when he went to Poughkeepsie, New York to attend a business college. In 1882, he went to Nebraska where he spent a couple of years, and came to Montrose, Colorado, in 1884.

He arrived in Montrose with the sum of eleven dollars and it took five of that for meals and lodging for the first day and night. He secured a job with the Buddecke and

Diehl General Merchandise store on the Busy Corner site and worked for them for several years, sleeping on the floor in the store and spending spare time at study.

He worked for a time for the Heil Clothing Company after severing his connection with the Buddecke & Diehl firm, and in 1891 he bought out the Bessaue Company, which was in the building where the Western Colorado Power Company is now located, and in 1897 moved to the Busy Corner site.

He was married in 1890 to Cora Alice Smith, and to them were born two children, Sylvia Eyre, who died in 1918 during the influenza epidemic, and John Foster, Jr., who passed away recently.

The first Mrs. Wilson died on June 8, 1900, and in 1905, Mr. Wilson was married to Amy Miller, who survives him, and resides in Montrose.

During the early days in Montrose, John Foster Wilson saw many things of interest. At one time he saw $50,000 in gold on a poker table. Jim Kyle ran the Loutsenhizer Hotel when Wilson came to Montrose. Wilson was instrumental in setting out most of the fruit trees in the valley. He had the third automobile in Montrose, an old Maxwell, with carbide lights and all the other early day equipment of the well-built automobile. Bill Torrance had the first car and Dr. Schermerhorn the second.

John Foster Wilson, Jr., was born in 1894 and lived in Montrose practically all his life, with the exception of a term spent in the Polytechnic Business College in Oakland, California. Since 1913, when F. E. Cotton bought out his father's business, the younger Mr. Wilson worked in nearly all the men's clothing stores in Montrose. He worked in the Cotton Store, for Mabry's and for Tom Alvord, sold clothes on the road for a while and operated the Sugar Bowl Candy Store with Robert L. Spalding, and the Busy Bee Drug Store, with Horace S. Price.

Jacob Alexander Lawson was born in Wytheville, Virginia, on August 9, 1859. He lived there for six or eight years and then moved to Haywood, Grayson County, where he lived until he was twenty-six years of age, when he came to Delta, Colorado. This was in 1886.

He arrived in Delta with K. C. Collins and Martin Collins on the ninth of March, during a spell of snowy, wet weather. There was mud everywhere, there being no gravelled roads at this time. The three men walked out across Rogers Mesa and had to take the old Ute Trail to Crawford. The first night of the trip they stayed at a ranch house on the Mesa and slept on the floor. They waded the North Fork of the Gunnison when it was full of slush ice. At this time there were only about a dozen cabins on Rogers Mesa.

Mr. Lawson had a job awaiting him as a sawyer in the H. C. DeLong sawmill near Crawford. There they turned out the lumber for the first house erected in the town of Paonia. This lumber was purchased by Tom Wand, old timer of that town.

Later Mr. Lawson went to Telluride, where he worked for wages, returning to Crawford to spend the winter. The following spring he bought a team, drove to Telluride and spent the summer hauling ore and mine timbers for the Gold King Mine and the San Juan Consolidated Mining Company.

Returning to Crawford the following fall, he took a 160 acre claim, by squatter's right, lived on it a year and sold his right to it to Riley Stoner, of Kansas, for $1000. Then Lawson went to Telluride and took a 160 acre place on Boomerang Hill. This was May 5, 1891. He sold his ranch to a mining outfit for $6000 and bought more land farther west on Turkey Creek Mesa, from Andrew Kellock. He bought land until he owned fourteen houndred acres. He later sold six hundred acres to John McKnight on an $18,000 contract, but had to take the land back. At the time of his death he owned some 1440 acres on Turkey Creek Mesa.

CHAPTER XI

TWO MEN WHO NEVER GREW OLD

Many people grow old at sixty years, some grow old at eighty, but few of us live to see the ripe age of ninety-eight, and, if we do, we seldom retain our faculties the way Judge Gray did. He saw several generations come and go.

John Gray was born March 13, 1841, in White Creek, New York. In the Judge's own words he "was born in the light of the moon and a tallow candle at White Creek, N. Y., famous for its street shade of sugar maples." Says Judge Gray: "My first recollection is of wormfuge and castor oil—a noisy open air political meeting, during the presidential election of 1844 is a distinct memory; also news of Taylor's victory at Buena Vista, borne by carrier pigeons, and published in the New York Herald. When five years of age, with my father and mother, I remember seeing Henry Clay, P. T. Barnum and Tom Thumb on the New York and Erie Canal; Clay's imperial brow, and striking face of intellectual brilliance, yet generous and kind, was indelibly traced upon my memory as I sat upon his knee.

"After a course in the common District School, where the important curriculum was a daily cordial with a stick in it, popular in that period as a discipline to mental activity and manly endurance, and three years in an academy, I entered law school at Poughkeepsie, N. Y., graduating in 1859.

"Attracted to Kansas by the great debate between Lincoln and Douglas and the rosy reports of undulating plains, waiting to be turned into fields of golden stores, and the thought of starting in life upon the ground floor, unhampered by the deference required to slow promotion in the

64

old settled communities, I bade adieu to the ties of home for experiences new and yet to learn. St. Joseph, Missouri, was the terminus of railroad communication with Kansas. Arriving over the Illinois Central at the Mississippi River, where passengers were conveyed by ferry to connect with the Hannibal and St. Joe railroad, the ferry boat could not cross because of the floating ice; but joining two young dare-devils, we got sticks and jumped from one cake to another, making the trip about two hours before the boat crossed. The wealth of Croesus would not tempt me to another such fool exploit.

"At St. Joe, I was told that Troy, county seat of Doniphan County, was a good place for a young sprig. It was 15 miles, over a dusty road, on a melting hot day, that on foot, I made the trip. About half way a man in a buggy, driving a fine roadster passed, looking neither to right or left. I said then that I would never pass a traveler in a conveyance and not take him in, and I never have.

"There were twenty lawyers in Troy. The land office was located there—about as many saloons, the court and bar being the principal patrons. Not pleased with the outlook, I started another fifteen miles on foot to Atchison.

"About half way, stopping at a house for a drink, I fortunately met a man to whom I afterwards became a strong friend—Col. A. G. Ege. He had two horses saddled and his son conducted me to Atchison, where I sought the office of Otis and Glick—the latter now known as one of the governors of Kansas, and whose statue is in the art gallery of the U. S. Capitol building. They were the leading firm in Northern Kansas."

This firm gave Judge Gray the privilege of reading in their office and batching quarters upstairs, in return for the janitor work. After about a month in the office, the attorneys decided that Gray might be worth something to them and they gave him their Justice of the Peace work to handle.

In March, 1861, when just twenty years of age, John Gray was admitted to practice in the U. S. District Court in Kansas. The Civil War broke out the same year and Gray tried to enlist, but was refused admission into the army because of a peculiar pulse in his left arm. He was, however, accepted for the militia and was made a first lieutenant and aide de camp on the staff of General Drake. The militia was mustered into U. S. service to assist in repelling the Confederate army under General Price.

Although he was prosperous in Kansas, Judge Gray suffered from nervous headaches there, and, seeking a change in altitude, he came to Silverton in the spring of 1883. Forming a partnership with C. M. Fraiser, he enjoyed a good practice, and sank his money in mining speculations.

In 1887 the Judge came to Montrose, where he established an office in a little building donated by James McClure. At this time he possessed $260 in cash and four horses and wagons. The second day after the establishment of the office, he received a fee for defending a horse-thief, and after that he did well. He served three years, from 1891 to 1894, as district attorney for the Seventh Judicial District. He was also county attorney at the same time and was town attorney of Montrose, and also served the town as mayor.

One time Judge Gray met on the street a small and raggedly dressed girl. He asked her name and was told that it was Elsie Vandegrift, and the little girl said: "I always go to court when I know you are going to talk." The Judge became interested in the young lady and gave her a chance to study in his office. Today the lady is Elsie Lincoln Benedict, World famous psycho-analyst and lecturer. The Judge receives letters from her regularly now.

Judge Gray was for many years the outstanding attorney and speaker in Western Colorado. He had an extensive vocabulary and his speeches were eloquent.

John Gray is descended from distinguished ancestors. His grandfather was Dr. Joseph Gray, surgeon of the Rhode Island Regiment, in the American Revolution. His father was Dr. Henry Gray, prominent Eastern surgeon. Lucy Bancroft was the wife of Dr. Joseph Gray and the sister of George Bancroft, the famous historian. John

Gray's father, Dr. Henry Gray, married Mary Niles in 1840. Mary Niles was the daughter of Sarah Huntington, whose father, Samuel Huntington, was a signer of the Declaration of Independence.

John Gray was married to Mary Elizabeth O'Driscoll, and the two had seven children, four of whom are still living. They are Annie Ruth, of Hollywood, California; Joseph, who is the father of eleven children; John, unmarried; and Mary Olive, who is at home. She is a very accomplished musician and entertainer. Another daughter, Theodosia, died in 1917, during the influenza epidemic.

Autobiography of John B. Morgan, member of the House of Representatives of the Twenty-Fourth General Assembly:

The subject of this sketch breathed his first breath on October 17, 1858, by the side of the old stage road half way between Vandalia and Salem, Illinois, in Marion County.

The house in which he was born was of the old double log house variety with a large entry between and a wide, high porch across the entire front. His first memory dates back to the time when he was about sixteen months old. An old aunt who was rather feeble, while walking too near the edge of the porch fell off and broke one of her legs. Her screams, the hurry of people to her assistance and the general stir incident to the occasion made such a lasting impression upon his mind that it remains to this day.

Soon after this my parents moved to a homestead taken from the Government on the payment of $1.25 per acre. The great strides in this part of Illinois have all been taken during the lifetime of the subject of this sketch. My recollections are somewhat cloudy for a few years after this until the beginning of the Civil War. I recall the death of my grandfather, Hardy Foster, who was the first man to settle in the township that still bears his name. The drilling of the soldiers, preparatory to going to the front, the drilling of the small boys left at home and their charges upon the hidden enemy, the return of the boys in blue and the happy families that hurried to meet them, the wounding of Uncle John Foster, Captain of the 11th Illinois at Fort McCalister, the killing of an Aunt by the Bushwhackers in Missouri, the coming of Uncle Wes Morgan from Rock Island where he was held as a prisoner of war by the North, made such impressions on my childish mind that the lapse of time has not and can not erase them.

In my boyhood, the three events of the year were hog-killing time, the time of making pumpkin butter and running off maple sugar, of these hog-killing day was most important as all the neighbors would come in to assist in the killing and take part in the feast that always followed. The corn bread cooked in the "big skillet" in front of the fire with bright coals under it and bright coals piled on the lid; the spare ribs hung up in front of the fire with the grease dripping into the pan below; the sweet potatoes baked in the ashes; and the extras, which were not many, were viands fit for a king and they were eaten with a relish by a homely, kingly people.

When only a small boy I was sent out into the field with a yoke of oxen to do some dragging with a small tree to which the oxen were hitched. All went well until they began to get hot and thirsty, when they walked off without saying, "With your permission" and did not stop until they were out in the middle of a pond. It took sticks and clods and many of them before I could persuade them to come out and then they made up their minds it was time to quit and started for home. They came to the bars, passed through and did not even stop until the barn was reached. Today I am helping to pass laws to keep boys older than I was then from working at all, notwithstanding the fact that we all know that the habits of industry are learned early in life.

For hours, days it seemed to me then, I sat in the old loom and held the threads for my mother while she hooked them through the sley and the harness preparatory to weaving the cloth out of which she made our clothes, sometimes colored with walnut bark, sometimes colored blue and sometimes woven of black sheep's wool. The first "boughten" suit came to me when I was sixteen years old. Up to that time I had worn nothing but what my mother had spun and woven by hand. We were just as proud of our new suits then as boys are today of theirs and we were at least as happy and more contented.

Our new home was a frame, one-story house with one large room, a lean-to and smoke-house attached. Again I pass through a haze until I started to school in the little old school house a quarter of a mile away. Homemade seats of a very unassuming kind, a small blackboard in one corner, with the long birches over the top, the hobby horse that the boys must ride occasionally, the old recitation benches made of puncheons, the marks of jack knives everywhere, the long rows of boys and girls standing in the spelling classes, the debating societies, the spelling bees, the fighting of the boys, the hard punishments inflicted by the teacher, the games of three-cornered cat and stink base, the cries and the laughs, the joys and the sorrows, all these are memories dear to all who have put away childish things.

My home was a very simple but in many ways a very happy one, made up of father, mother, three girls and six boys, all living in this small, poorly constructed house. The result of this simple, almost out-door life is shown in the fact that the nine children are still living, the youngest past fifty years of age. Pleasures at that time were very different to the pleasures of today. Up to my 12th year, I doubt if I had ever had as much as twenty-five cents in my possession at one time. Christmas came and went without a present but my mother always tried to have something extra on the table on Christmas Day. Our neighborhood store was a quarter of a mile away. On that day we always "got the Christmas gift" of Mr. Jones, the merchant, which consisted of one ball of candy, half dough, and about the size of a large marble. It was not much but our wants were few and we were happier than boys of today with scores and scores of presents.

My memory calls me back to the time when all the light we had at night was from the old grease lamp with

its wick and the home made candles, which I often helped
to make. I distinctly remember when the first "coal oil"
lamp came into our house and the first cook stove came
when I was almost a young man. Many a night I have
lain down on the floor with my head to the fire to study
my lessons because there was no candle or no oil in the
lamp.

Opportunities for an education when I was a boy were
not so plentiful as they are today. Then a boy went to
school and worked because he was ambitious, today many
boys study because a teacher demands it. Then, we had
few pleasures compared with today, but we enjoyed what
we did have better. The first book I ever owned, as my
very own and that I had earned myself was a Ray's Third
Part Arithmetic. I had just begun to get interested in addition and subtraction, my older brother had the arithe-
metic and I wanted it badly, but could not for a long time
figure out how I could earn it. At that time we lived chief-
ly on corn bread, which we took to a mill and had ground.
This we did each Saturday. I told my brother I would
take the grist to the mill all summer, if he would give me
the arithmetic, and he did so. All summer long, while the
other boys were playing, I must get up on old Dan with the
sack of corn in front of me and ride off to the mill a half
a mile away, wait sometimes two or three hours and then
come back home with the sack of meal in front of me.

Many times when over-balanced, the sack would fall to
the ground and I would have to wait for some casual pass-
er-by to help me get it on the horse again.

My early education was in a country school in Marion
County, Illinois, later I attended High School in Kinmun-
day, Illinois, but did not graduate. Still later I attended
the Valparaiso Normal University, Indiana, from which I
graduated in 1884, from the Scientific Course, with the
degree B. S. Sometime later, I earned the degree of Master
of Arts from this same University. It was a hard pull and
a long siege, as I had to earn my way by working during
the summer at $15 a month and "keep," until I was far
enough along to teach. Then by staying out and teaching at

$35 per month, I was able to earn enough to finish all the education I ever got except in the schools of hard knocks, the best school that anyone ever attended.

My early home was near a very large forest and in this I used to wander days at a time, picking flowers, digging up rare roots and studying the bird and animal life. My corner of the yard at home had more variety of flowers than any in the country. It was to this early habit I suppose that I owe my habit of wandering about. Four years as teacher in country schools in Illinois and I graduated and became principal of Patoka, Illinois, High School, a fine position for a young man at fifty dollars per month and with three teachers under me. My wanderlust started me westward where I became principal of H. S. at Trenton, Nebraska, and remained for six years. It was here I met and afterwards married Mary Hall. In 1893 my ambition, I thought was satisfied when I came to Colorado as teacher at Garrison, now Hooper, Colorado. In Colorado I have held many positions. Organized Saguache County H. S., the first County H. S. in the state, where I remained as superintendent eight years; organized the Montrose County High School, stayed one year and resigned to accept a position in Iolani College, Honolulu.

The Paradise of the Pacific held me for two years. The first year as teacher and the second year as principal. No land in all the World has such a charm for me as that one. It is a Paradise indeed, a half way place between Colorado and Heaven.

I have often thought it would be an ideal place to die in, as the transition would not be such a shock as from other places upon this mundane sphere. The lure of my childhood days again crept into my veins, the opportunity was offered, and I accepted the chair of English in the North Eastern Imperial University of Japan. Eight of the happiest years of my life were spent in this institution. An institution of very high rank, up-to-date in every particular and doing work the equal of the leading universities in this country. With a strong corps of teachers, many of them Christians, who are wide-awake in every way, highly educated at home and abroad and doing the work equally as well as the professors in this country, it was my pleasure to work.

In these eight years friendships have been made with the student and professor classes that are prized beyond words to express.

I have found them unusually honest in business, cautious of friendships especially with the foreigner, devoted to the Hudaist faith and ancestor worship, and loyal to their country even until death. The highest ambition of the Japanese boy and man is to give his life for his country.

My work in the school room was satisfactory in most ways, the students were always respectful, and did their work as well or better than the same grade of students in this country.

The Japanese student is superior to the American student in science, equal to him in mathematics, and inferior in literature and general world knowledge.

As a reward for my labors over there (I suppose well done labors) His Majesty, the late Emperor Mutsuhito, conferred upon me the decoration, The Fifth Order of the Rising Sun, an order of merit, which has been conferred upon few in this country.

In May, 1921, I arrived again in this country, having resigned my position in the University the year before. After spending a year in travel, during which time my wife and I visited in Siberia, Manchuria, Korea, China, Hong Kong, Philippine Islands, Singapore, Penang, Ceylon, Arabia, Egypt, Palestine, Italy, Switzerland, Germany, Belgium, France, England, we returned to Colorado and are now settled on a farm one mile out of Montrose.

For some reason, the Democratic Party of Montrose County settled upon me as the candidate of that party for Representative in the Twenty-Fourth General Assembly and somewhat to my surprise and disappointment, I was elected. And so here I am in this great and wonderful old pile of stone trying to help make laws for the grand old state of Colorado, although my life's work has not developed my abilities along that line. What a man may be called upon to do in this World "You niver kin tell."

Done under my hand this 21 day of March, 1926,

(Signed)   JOHN B. MORGAN.

The above autobiography was written by John B. Morgan for filing in the records of the Twenty-Fourth General Assembly of Colorado, of which he was a member.

Mr. Morgan, since retiring from the legislature, was superintendent of schools in the City of Montrose. Until recently he was always very active in educational matters and was a much-beloved citizen of the community in which he resided, until his death in 1938.

CHAPTER XII

CAME IN '78—BEEN HERE EVER SINCE

Aylmer F. Reeves of Montrose, Colorado, has been a resident of the state continuously since the spring of 1878. He has been actively connected with the life and growth of this state for many years.

He was born September 26th, 1858, in Dublin, Ireland, previous to his birth his parents had been in America and were American citizens.

His father, Thomas Wigglesworth Reeves, was an attorney at law and practiced in the courts of Ireland and England until his death in 1864.

His mother, Jane Saline Reeves, was a resident of New York and died and was buried in that city.

Shortly after his father's death the family came to New York, where he attended public schools and later the Irving Institute at Tarrytown, New York.

In 1870 his family moved to Leavenworth, Kansas, and from there by wagon to Manhattan, Kansas, and thence to Clay Center. The country west of Leavenworth was sparsely settled and Clay Center was in the process of becoming a town, there were but two main stores, being Aaron Dexter's store and corral and Higgenbottom's general store. Custer's Cavalry was stationed at Clay Center and scouted the plains from that point. He assisted in laying out the town of Clay Center, being axe and stake man for the surveyor.

Later the family moved back to New York and A. F. Reeves became a petty cashier for Alfred Marion and Company, then doing an extensive foreign exchange business at 54 Exchange Place, New York City.

He attended the Centennial Exposition in Philadelphia in 1876 and shortly afterwards went to Texas by way of

Dallas to Denton, where he was engaged by Benjamin to ride the train from the Brazos to Caldwell, Kansas, through what is now Oklahoma.

In the year 1878 he drove through with a bunch of wild horses and after disposing of them in Wichita followed the trail by Great Bend and Dodge City to Colorado, arriving in Denver the latter part of August of that year. There he engaged in farming with Mr. Lincoln a few miles from the city of Longmont, later moving to Central City, where he was employed by the McFarland Brothers, millwrights erecting a mill at Dumont, Colorado, and later a stamp mill at Lump Gulch.

From there he returned to Denver and was employed for a short time as shipping clerk for the George Tritch Hardware Company and later in the same capacity for the Richmond Brothers and Farnsworth, who assigned their business to C. D. Gurley, who closed it out to the George Tritch Hardware Company.

Then he became employed by the Denver and Rio Grande Railway Company in their fight for right of way through the Royal Gorge with the Santa Fe. Later he was stationed at Cimarron for a time for the same company.

In 1879 he made a trip horseback from Denver to the scene of the Meeker Massacre on the White River, coming through where now Grand Junction is located and up the Gunnison and Uncompahgre Rivers to Ouray and then from there to Del Norte, back again over the Sante Fe Trail to Pueblo and Denver. The Uncompahgre Valley was then occupied by the Ute Indians, Chief Ouray's camp was located about three miles south of Montrose.

In 1886 he was employed by the Great Western Stage, Mail and Express Company, successors to Barlow and Sanderson, who were staging between Gunnison and Lake City, Montrose, Telluride and Ouray with headquarters at Montrose.

In the same year he became associated with the Reeves and McFann Furniture business in Montrose. This was merged into what was known as the Montrose Furniture Company with five members, A. F. Reeves, George Stough,

Harry Holcomb, Len Mathers and Samuel R. Sutcliffe.

He joined the State Militia in 1888 and held positions as sergeant, lieutenant, captain, major and lieutenant-colonel in Company I of the Second Regiment and Company E of the First Regiment.

In 1890 he sold out his interest in the Montrose Furniture Company and entered the real estate business, purchasing the interest of F. H. Reinhold, who was the successor of Selig and Eckerly, the founders of the City of Montrose. He has been engaged in the real estate and insurance business ever since.

Mr. Reeves was married in 1884 to Pauline M. Ott, of New Orleans, Louisiana, the ceremony taking place in Denver, and they had five children. They are: Mrs. Leo Foster of Denver, Herbert Demetrius, who was associated with his father in the real estate business until his recent death; Aylmer F. Reeves Jr. of Greeley, Thomas J. Reeves of Montrose, and Alfred E. Reeves of Denver.

During his residence in Montrose Mr. Reeves was elected to the City Council and served about seven years; he was also a charter member of the city fire department. He was superintendent of irrigation for the nineteen counties on the Western Slope to which position he was appointed by Governor Thomas; he also held the position of fruit inspector for a number of years. He was appointed postmaster at Montrose by President Wilson through Congressman Edward T. Taylor in the year 1914 and held this position for nine years; during that period of time his son H. D. Reeves conducted his real estate and insurance business. Surrendering the office of postmaster he returned again to real estate and insurance in which he has been engaged ever since.

Flavious Josephus Hartman was born on a ranch about twelve miles below the town of Saguache, Colorado, on the thirteenth day of April, 1880. Edward Randolph Hartman was born on the same ranch on the sixth day of September, 1878, and Sidney Carlton Hartman on the fourth of October, 1883. Their early boyhood was spent on this place, the two older boys going to school there.

Very early in life they witnessed the hanging of a man named Clements, who had killed his brother and sister-in-law, and buried them in shallow graves near Saguache, and they recall seeing the posse searching for the bodies. A high board fence was built around the scaffold and only a few were permitted within the enclosure. However, the boys climbed a tree and watched the event.

In June, 1893, the family moved to Maher, Colorado, where they spent some time with an uncle, E. R. Hartman, and then, in the fall of the same year, they came into the Uncompahgre Valley and the father purchased the place which is still known as the Sanitarium Place about four or five miles south of Montrose. After living on the place for a time, the elder Hartman sold it and then repurchased it. Altogether they lived there from 1893 to 1916.

Joe and Ed Hartman attended the Union College in Lincoln, Nebraska, and Sidney attended high school in Montrose. After finishing their schooling, Joe and Sid bought a small bicycle shop, located at the rear of the building now occupied by the Pinkstaff Grocery. After operating their shop in this location for about three years, they moved into one-half the building east of the Daily Press office, where they stayed for two years.

They soon found that they had outgrown this location so they built the building now occupied by the City Steam Laundry. Many of their fellow citizens thought this was a foolish move as the place was too large for their little shop. However, the Hartman Brothers were men of vision and ambition and so they moved into larger quarters. After occupying this new building for a few years, they needed more space to carry on their business, so they purchased property near the middle of the same block, and built a larger building. This was in 1912. Three years later the firm of Hartman Brothers had outgrown this place of business and purchased the corner lots to the east and extended the building to Uncompahgre Avenue, and in the year 1919 the annex on North First Street was built.

The firm of Hartman Brothers Inc., has grown up with the automobile business. Started in the year 1904, the institution has been built up into one of the most complete automobile concerns in the State of Colorado. On their nearly 26,000 square feet of floor space they have every department for automobile repairs and service.

The first automobiles handled by Hartman Brothers were the first two automobiles in the town of Montrose. One was a two cylinder Oldsmobile owned by Dr. Fred Schermerhorn and the other was an Autocar owned by W. O. Redding. Joe Hartman tells us that in 1905 Bill Torrance built an automobile in the building now occupied by the Gilchrist Feed Store, and when he had finished the car he could not get it out of the door, so had to tear it down again, move the machine out and rebuild it. He had no differential and broke axles as fast as he could put them in.

The first time the Hartman boys were out of Colorado was in 1903, when their father took them to the World's Fair in Chicago.

Ed was married to Miss Molly Mock on September 27, 1899, and to this union two children were born, a son, Alonzo and a daughter, Clara Mae.

Joe was married on Christmas Day 1907 to Ruby L. Barnett and has two sons and a daughter.

Sid was married on May 12, 1912, to Mable Kennedy and he, also had two sons and a daughter.

Since about 1902, Walter Marion Wittmeyer has moved practically all the houses and buildings moved in the town of Montrose, and has moved many others throughout Western Colorado.

Born in 1876, on the eighth day of June at Portsmouth, Ohio, he lived in that town until he was four years old; then, with his family, he moved to St. Joseph, Missouri, where he lived for four more years, after which the family went to Oberlin, Kansas, where they lived until the year 1890.

It was while in Kansas that Wittmeyer learned the house moving business, working there with a man who did that kind of work. His parents went to Arkansas and he spent a part of the next few years in that state.

In 1901, at Carthage, Missouri, he was married to Eva
A. Viers and the couple came out to Norwood, Colorado,
where they spent about a year, Mr. Wittmeyer working on
a new irrigation project. In 1902 they came to Montrose
and here they have raised their family. They have three
daughters, Mrs. William Mills, Misses Ruby and Marian
and a son, Floyd.

All the years he has spent in Montrose, Mr. Wittmeyer
has engaged in house moving and concrete work. Altogether he has moved several hundred buildings and has
undertaken some very difficult jobs. One time, after another man had attempted to move a fourteen room house
from Coventry to Redvale, and failed, Wittmeyer was called to the job and put it in the desired location.

He once brought a house down the steep, narrow road
off of North Mesa at Menoken. To do this he had to split
the house in two endwise and take half of it down the
hill at a time. He has moved houses from a few feet to
twenty miles.

One time he helped move a Diesel engine weighing 23
tons a mile up the mountain side near Ouray. Another
time he took two houses across a large irrigation canal.
Still another time, Wittmeyer moved a slaughter house
across a swamp on a pontoon bridge.

It has become an established fact that if a building can
be moved, Wittmeyer can move it and, whenever that sort
of a job comes up in and around Montrose, he is consulted.

Wilbur Toothaker was born in the little town of Dick-
mont Corner, seventeen miles north of Bangor, Maine, on
July 10, 1847. At the age of seven years he moved to Rock-
ford, Pike County, Illinois, where his grandfather owned
a ranch on the Mississippi River, later moving to a farm,
which his father secured at Summer Hill, in the same
state. There he went to school, and he says he suffered
much hardship, because in those days the children had not
overshoes, but only hard leather boots.

He spent many of his days guiding an old blind horse
hitched to his father's cultivator, in the cornfields.

At the age of seventeen years, on February 17, 1865,

Toothaker was inducted into the Union service in the Civil War, and served until the ninth of July of that year, when he was mustered out. He saw no active service in battles, although his outfit was following the Confederate General Johnston. Once when the men expected to be in a battle, and thinking that they would be condemned if they were killed with a deck of playing cards in their pockets, many of them threw their cards away. Mr. Toothaker's war service was in North Carolina, but he was mustered out of service in Louisville, Kentucky.

Coming into Colorado in 1888, he spent a year in the Maher region in Northeastern Montrose County, and then came down to Montrose, where he spent six years hauling lumber for the Hiebler and Hamblin mills, which were located in various mountain regions around Montrose. He was working in the saw pit of a mill when the boiler blew up once. He said it was a very funny sensation to be standing in the roar of the mill, when the explosion came suddenly and then a deathlike silence. Some of the men were jumping around on the sawdust pile, all trying to run. Only one man was hurt. After the explosion they came down to Montrose and secured the boiler that had been used in the drilling of the Artesian well, on South First and Uncompahgre, and took it up to the mill.

Mr. Toothaker has spent many years on the farm later owned by Sam Kettle, above Colona. He says that at the time he came to Montrose there were many saloons and it was a rough town.

In the old days the singing schools offered a popular source of amusement and he attended many of these.

Mary Mabry lived to be 101 years old. Half of this time was spent quietly in Montrose. She was born in Millidgeville, Georgia, one hundred and five years ago, on the second day of May, 1834. She came with her grandfather to Texas and there was married to Joel Mabry in 1855. Her husband preceded her in death fifty years, and is buried in Hawkins, Texas.

Her son, William Mariott Mabry, was born in Hawkins, Texas, on January 10, 1856. When about 18 years of age he went to Phoenix, Arizona, where he met up with John B. Killian, J. W. Goldsmith and Joe Kistler, and they bought a bunch of cattle and drove them through from Springer, New Mexico, to Montrose, which was then a very small town. This was in 1887. Shortly after arriving in the Uncompahgre Valley, Mr. Mabry purchased property from the Willerup Estate and built the house where he still lives on West Main Street. At the present time he owns other property in Montrose.

For five years he worked in the Buddecke & Diehl store on the site of the Busy Corner Drug Store, and made several trips to Chicago and New York to buy the latest goods. After this he engaged in the mercantile business for himself for many years, being associated with J. F. Krebs in the firm of Krebs & Mabry, with O. L. Jessey and with P. C. Cook. He sold the store to Gordon & Buskirk in 1917 and was out of the business until 1920 when he took it back and operated it with T. W. Schutz. He recently retired from the business entirely.

He was married in 1897 to Marie G. Green and they have no children. However, they took Mrs. Green's cousin, Agnes Berry, at the age of three years and raised her. She is now married to D. G. Hayes, who is chief clerk in the commissary department at the Colorado State Penitentiary at Canon City.

When the Mabrys came into Montrose, it was a small village, with horses, buggies, wagons, muddy streets and the neighborhood where he built his house was a wilderness of trees and willows.

Joel Mabry, the husband of Mary Mabry and father of William M., served in the Indian wars in the Seminole Country of Florida but was soon discharged and sent home to operate his grist mill to feed the widows and orphans of the soldiers. At this time the women did all the work in the fields, carded and spun the cotton and wool and generally took the places of their husbands who were fighting Indians or in the Civil War. Mr. Mabry owned a stopping place where both Union and Confederates were welcome, the place being operated on a neutral basis.

Mary Mabry came to Montrose with her son and resided near him most of the time for fifty years, occupying her own house near the Mabry home.

Dr. Barnett Birch Slick was born in Washington, D. C., on September 6, 1867. He attended kindergarten and had a private instructor until he was seven years old. His father was one of the youngest captains in the Union Army of the Civil War, being around twenty years old when he held that commission. When the army was mustered out, the elder Slick was acting quartermaster in Washington, and was a close personal friend of Dr. Egnew, President Garfield's physician. Captain Slick, after the war, became a clerk in a government office, and the family lived part of the time in the city and part of the time on a big plantation on Arlington Heights, now the national cemetery. They had their own Negroes, and a Negro mammy took care of Dr. Slick in his younger days.

The Slick family did much entertaining in their home and many celebrities of the time came to their house. Included in this list was one Shepherd, who, Dr. Slick said, was the World's first racketeer.

The family moved to Gibbon, Nebraska, when the doctor was seven years old. He went to high school there and later moved to Como, Colorado. This was in 1887, when the Peabody Placer Project was at its height. The Peabody interests employed no one but Chinamen. It was at this place that Dr. Slick got his first experience with placer mining and he indulged in that work much of the time since then. He worked as a machinist and watchmen in the South Park Railroad Round House, making money in the summer to allow him to attend the Gross Medical College in the winter months.

He completed the course in 1891, having won first prize with his laboratory slides, which were exhibited at five prominent medical colleges. While in school he served as resident physician for the Colorado State Woman's Hospital. After getting out of the medical school he served his interneship in various hospitals. He won his place at the

Colorado Woman's Hospital in a competitive examination with thirty-five doctors.

He went to Minturn in the spring of 1891 to take a job as a railroad fireman. A former roommate's wife suffered an accident and Slick treated her and thereafter was called upon to do the medical and surgical work.

Coming to Ridgway in 1892, Dr. Slick conducted an office here and engaged in the practice of his profession until his death. He also gave much of his time to mining, being connected with the Sutton group of claims, with a mill near the Bear Creek Falls. His company spent $482,000 on this property in two years.

Dr. Slick spent much money and many years of his time in investigating the placer projects along the San Miguel river. He said that at one time there was a big settlement at Pinion, on the San Miguel. All that remains of this town now is the cemetery, a silent city of the dead to tell of glories past.

The San Miguel River is very rich in placer gold, and Dr. Slick said that the fact that so many companies have gone broke there is due to crooked superintendents, who reaped all the profits at the expense of the syndicate or company furnishing the money.

The Doctor said that the San Miguel Valley has one of the biggest gravel beds on earth. It is six miles long, two miles wide and a hundred feet deep, and all rich in gold deposits. He saw thousands of placer machines at work in the years he was in Western Colorado and knew as much about placer mining as almost anybody.

Placer operations were carried on in the Amalgamator Flats near Naturita fifty years ago. A great deal of money has been spent on the San Miguel and many cleanups have been made. Some have made mistakes, however. Some of the ditches and flumes constructed for miles are not even on a water grade and have been abandoned because of their inefficiency.

Robert Lee Smith knows more about the Montrose water pipe line than any other man alive. For many years he was connected with the water department of this city. He was born in Allegheny County, North Carolina, on November 1, 1867, and moved to Virginia at the age of six years, where he attended school until he was about twenty years old.

In 1888 he went to St. Joseph, Missouri, where he spent a few months before coming on to Colorado in March of 1889. In Gunnison, he worked for the La Veta Hotel for a few months and came on to Montrose in the fall of 1890. Then he went to Telluride, where he worked for about two years, after which he returned to Montrose again, and has resided here since that time. He worked for Halley & Dawson at their warehouse two and a half years, and for the Hiebler and Hammond Saw Mill at Government Spring, south of Montrose, and a saw mill for old man DeLong in the Muddy country near Crawford.

On May 1, 1900, Robert L. Smith took charge of the city water pumping plant on West South Fourth Street, where water was pumped from wells in the gravel of the river bottom. This pumping plant was built in 1888 and operated until 1905. In that year the City of Montrose acquired the rights to the Cimarron water, brought down from the Big Cimarron River by the Cimarron Canal, which was completed in 1905. The reservoir on Cerro Summit was partially filled that winter. The first pipe line installed between Cerro Summit and Montrose was of wooden pipe and it was only recently replaced.

In the summer of 1915 the City of Montrose abandoned a part of the wooden pipe line and connected on to the Gunnison Tunnel, and have since secured a part of their water from the tunnel.

Married in November of 1895, to Miss Dora Dennison, Mr. Smith has six girls and one boy by this union. The girls are: Stella M. Christie, Virginia Wilkins, Roberta Dillon, Cornelia Humphrey, Muriel Lambert, and Mary Mills. The boy is Orion Smith.

The first Mrs. Smith died in December, 1913, and in the fall of 1921, Mr. Smith married Mrs. Stella Lambert, and has one boy by this wife, who passed away in August of 1931.

For ten years, he was a member of the Montrose Volunteer Fire Department, and recalls many of the larger fires that have occurred in Montrose. He helped fight the fire which destroyed the Arlington Hotel on the corner of North First and Cascade, and assisted in removing the body of a Mr. Nerivs, representative of the Deering Farm Machinery Company, who was burned to death. He remembers that another man was burned to death when the Pomeroy Hotel, situated where the Nye Building is now, was burned. At the time of the Arlington fire, George Harlan was the fire chief, Mrs. Ed Smith operated the hotel and Joe Calloway was the clerk.

The old Belvedere Hotel burned on New Year's Eve, 1893. The Fireman's Ball was in progress, when the fire broke out. The firemen had on their new uniforms, and had to run to the fire station, which at that time was on the corner where the Rose Arctic Ice Cream Co. is now located, and pull the old hand hose cart to the scene of the conflagration.

Nearly all of the livery stables that Montrose has had have burned at one time or another.

Mr. Smith says that the artesian well, better known as "Iron Mike," was drilled on the corner near the Belvedere Hotel, within three feet of the fire plug.

Mr. Smith was for a long time a member of the K. P. Lodge and during this time filled all of the chairs of the lodge.

When the Gunnison Tunnel was opened in September, 1909, President Taft was the guest of honor and officially opened the tunnel and brought forth the water. All the sheriffs of Western Colorado acted as a special body guard in Western uniforms, ten gallon hats, bandanas, blue flannel shirts and corduroy pants, each with a Colts .45 in his holster.

Taft was a guest in the judges stand at the Western Slope Fair, with his personal bodyguard, Captain Butts, who later went down with the Titanic. Robert L. Smith, as deputy sheriff, was also in the stands and was personally introduced to the President and his aide. He recalls that

Taft himself congratulated Miss Bertha Hull, now Mrs. Ed Campbell of Montrose, for winning the Cowgirl's Relay Race.

Eugene Louis McGregor was born near Powderhorn in the Cebolla Valley, Colorado, on August 3, 1889. When he was six months old the family moved to the town of Olathe, where Eugene went to school until he was seventeen years of age. During this time he also did considerable work on the farm where the family resided.

When he was seventeen years old he went to work in the mill of the Liberty Bell Mine near Telluride, where he worked for ten years. His most exciting experience was when eight hundred pounds of ore was dumped onto him from a bucket while he was at work in an ore bin. He saw the shadow of the bucket coming and hugged a large timber so that he was not crushed to death. However, he received several bad cuts on the head in the experience.

Gene McGregor spent four years in the sheep business, but for the past twenty-five years has been engaged in blacksmithing and machine shop work, operating his own shop in Montrose at the present time.

He was married to Miss Blossom Tarkoff in 1911 and has two children, a son and a daughter. Mr. McGregor's father freighted supplies into Western Colorado before the coming of the railroad.

J. W. Topliss was born in Council Hill Station, Joe Davis County, Illinois, November 9, 1859. His father was a small town blacksmith and moved from place to place. He received most of his schooling in Galena, Illinois, and Diamond Grove, Wisconsin, and in Grant and Lafayette Counties in Wisconsin.

Mr. Topliss first came to Colorado in 1880, at which time he settled in Granada. In 1881, he moved to Canon City and moved over the Divide into Western Colorado in 1890, bringing in a bunch of cattle and horses. In 1891, he freighted in the Ouray district, hauling ore and supplies to Red Mountain, Sneffles and other points in the San Juan.

Returning to Kansas in 1892, he lived there a few years and then returned again to Western Colorado. In 1909, he moved into the little Cimarron Valley and has lived there since that time, farming in the summer and often prospecting in the winter. For a year in or about 1923, Topliss helped guard a bunch of convicts, who were engaged in highway work.

His has been the life of a farmer and laborer and he has had his ups and downs. He has had no outstanding experiences, although he has helped in the development of Western Colorado.

John William Roatcap was born in Cooper County, Missouri, on October 24, 1864. He lived there for eight years and then removed to Fredonia, Kansas, where his father, D. S. Roatcap, operated a grist mill. In January 1882, he and his brothers left Kansas and came into the Lake City country. It was winter and they worked in snow waist deep all winter, cutting out 200,000 feet of logs, which they sawed into lumber the following summer.

The Roatcap brothers sawed the lumber that was used in building the scaffold upon which Alfred Packer was to be hung. However, the scaffold was never used, the sentence never carried out, and the twenty-two hundred feet of lumber was used for other purposes.

In later years, after Packer had served twenty-five years in the state penitentiary, at Canon City, and was paroled, Roatcap saw him frequently at the Humberg Bar, on Fifth Street in Denver, and stated that he often bought the man a glass of beer.

In September of the year 1883, the Roatcaps came down into the Uncompahgre Valley and settled on a ranch on California Mesa, which at that time was known as Cushman Mesa. To William Roatcap and his wife belongs the distinction of changing the name of the mesa. Once the two were riding on horseback and talking about it. They decided that a land so large and beautiful should be named after a large and beautiful state, so decided on California.

Water was secured from the Cushman Ditch to irrigate their fields. On this ranch William married Miss Nettie Park and raised nine children, seven of whom are still living. They are: Walter and Robert of Montrose, Mrs.

Arthur Rose of Delta, Mrs. Wilbur Rusho, of Montrose, Mrs. Goebel Ficklin of Grand Junction, and Louis of California. George, another son, died a few years ago. The ninth, a son, was run over and killed by a train in 1927.

During his many years in Western Colorado, William Roatcap lived much in the out-of-doors. He operated sawmills on Horsefly and in the Paonia district. He prospected for a time almost every year for more than twenty-nine years, six of which were spent in the Carnotite fields of Western Montrose County.

At the time he first came into the Uncompahgre Valley, there were sixteen saloons in Montrose, and exciting events were not unusual. Once, stated Roatcap, a man was hung to a telegraph pole near the depot for stabbing a "friend," after a quarrel. Another time, two men met in the alley behind the Busy Corner Pharmacy. One of the men had come here from Colorado Springs to kill the other, and took two shots at him when they met. The second shot went through the man's chest and made a hole so large that a silk handkerchief was pulled through it twice. But he recovered his health and was later a partner to Mr. Roatcap in a sawmill.

One Jack Watson rode up to the well on the main corner in Montrose, which was owned by the city, to water his horse. Roatcap, with other men, was standing by the well. The stranger spoke not a word, but turned when the horse had finished drinking and walked across the street. There he met the city marshal, and started shooting at that individual, who lost no time going under the high board sidewalk, getting a shot in the heel as he went. Watson mounted his pony, rode around the block, came to the watering place again and asked:

"Boys, what town is this?"

Among other things Roatcap told of a battle between the Lambert gang and the Blackwells down by the River Bridge on Main Street. There were about twenty-five shots fired and Jim Blackwell was wounded in the arm.

Many of the buildings in Montrose were constructed of lumber sawed by William Roatcap at his mill near Iron

Springs. In his last years he owned the tax deeds on the famous old Conkling Mine on the Big Cimarron River. He also owned several other claims in this vicinity.

He was a great hunter and killed many bear and captured a number of cubs, which were exhibited in other parts of the state.

Peter Nelson Dahl was born in Frederickshaven, Denmark, on the 20th of June, 1857. When he was fourteen years old he came to America, coming first to Utah, where he worked in the mines. He was employed at the Frisco Mine, Northwest of Beaver for two years. Then he went to Eureka, about seventy miles south of Salt Lake City. Most of his work was in silver and lead mines.

In 1883 he came to Western Colorado in a wagon. There was no road and they had to follow the Indian trails. The party stopped a short time in Grand Junction, and over night in Delta, which was, at that time, a very small town. Coming on across California Mesa, they arrived at the place where Cushman was putting in his ditch, which was to bring water from Dry Creek. Cushman and Tom Rowan had settled on ranches on the south end of California Mesa. The Dahl party were looking for work and, finding none there, they came through Coal Creek Valley, which was only sage brush, the ranches of the future not having been taken up yet.

From Coal Creek they came down through Poverty Basin, now called Dead Man's Gulch, which received its name from a Mexican sheep herder, who accidentally shot himself while camping in the gulch.

On Spring Creek Mesa there were two ranches, one owned by the father of the late W. A. Neugart of Montrose and the other by William Upton, whose son, Walter, still lives on his father's place. Jim and Jesse O'Neill had a ranch near Happy Canyon, and there were a few ranches in the neighborhood of Uncompahgre, where work was starting on the construction of the Montrose and Delta Canal. Mr. Dahl received a contract to construct the second mile of the ditch and then continued to work on it until its completion. The canal was built with teams and scrapers.

Joe T. Faussone was born at Montalenghe, Italy, May 17, 1879. He came to the United States in 1900 and located in Ouray, where he worked as a rock miner at the Virginius Mine. Later, with the financial aid of his brothers he attended school, living with the J. W. Haney family.

He managed to learn enough English to qualify as a grocery clerk for his brother, who was at that time operating a store in Ouray. Later Mr. Faussone rented a small ore mill, and worked the tailings that came from the Bachelor Mine, and made fairly good money.

He joined his brothers in Rock Springs, Wyoming, in 1904 and worked as a grocery clerk in that town, later returning to Ouray.

In 1909, he visited in Italy and was married to Anna Trivero, whom he brought back to Ouray with him. He then became a partner of his brother, Dominic, in the grocery business and there remained until 1921, when he moved his family to Montrose and built a home. He engaged in light farming and other activities there until his death in 1927.

CHAPTER XIII

THE BOYS OF 1890

Burell Emerson Hitchcock was born in Onawa, Iowa, on the tenth of November, 1878, and shortly after his birth his father brought him into Colorado, taking part in the gold rush to Black Hawk, where the elder Hitchcock engaged in the carpenter and millwright professions.

In 1884 the family moved to Montrose and Burell started to school, when the present Central School building consisted of four rooms. At that time Montrose was not much of a town, although rather lively at times. In those days there were several Chinamen in this little town, a situation that has not existed for many years now. The youngsters of the village made it so tough on the yellow men that they finally moved out, not, however, until they were asked to do so by a committee of citizens.

Mr. Hitchcock remembers one time when he and Don Detweiler dealt considerable misery to one of these "chinks." One evening they went to his laundry, which was in a building where the telephone office now stands. Don took a tick-tack and made a terrible noise against the window pane and his companion dropped a box of broken glass. The old Chinaman thought the heavens were falling in on him.

Another time they laid out a Chinaman called "Grinny." First the boys put a pail over his stovepipe. Then they wired the front door shut and put a railroad tie against the back door. When "Grinny" ran out the back door, the tie fell on his head with disastrous results.

For thirty-three years Mr. Hitchcock has been connected with the grocery business in Montrose. For some years being in business with the Benson-Hitchcock Grocery and for several years as the efficient manager of the Montrose Piggly-Wiggly store. He now owns an interest in a small grocery store near the high school.

This is the story of Samuel Cramer, one of the last survivors of the great War of the Rebellion, which has receded into the past of seventy-five years ago. Samuel Cramer was hale and healthy until his death in 1937 in Montrose.

He was born on the 28th of April, 1847, in what was then the Iowa Territory. He lived there on a farm for the first thirty-four years of his life, with the exception of the time spent as a soldier in the Union Army. His father died when he was 15 years old.

He enlisted in the Union Army and served with Company F., 16th Iowa Infantry, Third Brigade, Fourth Division, Seventeenth Army Corps, and his active service started in Chattanooga, Tennessee. He was with Sherman on the march through Tennessee, at the Battle of Atlanta, the March to the Sea, and was present when Johnston surrendered to Sherman at Raleigh, North Carolina. Then Sherman's army marched the four hundred miles to Washington and took part in the Grand Review, when Grant's Army was reviewed one day and Sherman and Sheridan's command the following day.

One of the most bitter experiences he suffered was when, in February, 1865, they were marching north through South Carolina. The only pike or roadway in the immediate vicinity was held by Confederate forces. Sherman fooled the Rebels into thinking that he was going to march on Charlestown but instead made a forced march through the cypress swamps and across the Saltkahechi River. It had been raining, the water was extremely cold and shoulder deep. The four thousand men of the command waded the river, even the officers going on foot. Many of them fell and were drowned, and those who got through suffered severe hardships. Even William Belknap, the brigade commander, who was later Secretary of War, and a very large man, was forced to wade the river. And, because of one man's ambition, the trip was without avail.

The bedraggled forces who had braved the river's

waters were to attempt a flanking movement and come in
on the Rebels' rear, but, because the commanding officer
of the force which remained to attack from the front
wanted all the glory of capturing the Confederate forces,
the entire movement was lost. This officer attacked too
quick and the rebels fled before Belknap's men reached the
rear.

After the war, Cramer returned to Iowa and farmed for
ten years. Then he was married to Ammi Ammerman. A
son and daughter were born to them. The daughter died at
the age of thirty years and the son is a prominent business
man of San Diego, California.

In March of the year 1880, Samuel Cramer came West
to Colorado, stopping at Buena Vista, where he spent the
summer, in the fall of that year going on to Leadville,
which was booming. Silver sold for a good price and the
camp was going strong. While he was there the miners
struck for a $4.50 wage per day. Mr. Cramer was pros-
pecting during the time he spent in Buena Vista and Leadville, and in the latter place was a teamster for a while.

In the winter of 1881, Cramer went to Aspen where he
lived for many years, assisting in the organization of Pitkin County and acting as a County Commissioner for three
years, from 1884 to 1888. He owned and operated a farm
for many years on the Roaring Fork River near Basalt.

His first wife had died and he was remarried in 1893,
and has one daughter by this union, Mrs. Earle Bryant, of
Montrose.

Selling his ranch on the Roaring Fork in 1915, Mr.
Cramer went to Florida, where he secured a farm and
feed mill in the Everglades. In seventeen years he made 18
trips between Colorado and Florida. His mill was the first
feed mill in the Everglades of Florida.

He sold his property in the South and returned to
Montrose, where he bought a home and lived here until his
death. During his last few years he gave much of his
time to the affairs of the rapidly depleting ranks of the
Grand Army of the Republic. When he came to Montrose
there were about twenty-five members of this respected

order, but today there are but two left. When Cramer went to Aspen there were 125 members of the G. A. R. in that town, while today there are none.

Mr. Cramer lived a clean and moral life and was highly respected in the community in which he resided. He helped materially in the development of the Empire that is Western Colorado.

One of the true pioneers of Western Colorado was Asbury Armlin, who first entered Colorado in the year 1877. He was born in Schoharie County, New York, on a farm on December 27, 1855, and attended the country schools of that state. At the age of twenty-one years he went to DeKalb County, Illinois, where he spent a year, after which he came to Colorado Springs in about 1877.

He worked for a few days on the railroad construction work in the Royal Gorge, then returned to Colorado Springs and with three others hired a team for transportation to Leadville, arriving there when H. A. W. Tabor was in his glory. For a time in this mining camp Armlin was engaged with a group of men, burning charcoal for sale. He spent a year as a miner in the employ of the Small Hope Mining Company.

Together with Emory Coons, who was later his brother-in-law, James Cleaver and John Caswell, Armlin went to Aspen, where they built a cabin on Castle Creek. There they prospected and hunted for a while. Armlin and Cleaver killed and carried their game into Aspen, where it was sold. There were no game laws at that time and no bag limits. The two later bought a freight outfit and freighted in the Aspen region until 1882, when they started overland to New Mexico. Arriving at the Highland Mary Mine, near Silverton, to visit Coons, who had preceded them and was operating a pack string with Fred Monroe, packing cordwood to the mines, Mr. Armlin was persuaded to remain there and took a job packing for Merrill Doud, recent sheriff of San Juan County, and father of Henry Doud, of Montrose.

Armlin later bought out Fred Monroe and, with Coons, continued in the packing business, packing supplies to the

Robert Emmett Mine, owned by Geiger, a Ouray brewer, and packing over Engineer Mountain between Silverton and the Frank Hough Mine.

Coons and Armlin sold their forty-five burros and pack outfit to John Ashenfelter and went down on Cow Creek, where they purchased the two farms they now own from Paff and Caw, later riding over the mountains to the headwaters of the Huerfano to purchase a bunch of cattle. The Armlin property consists of four hundred acres of land on Cow Creek and eight hundred acres of deeded pasture lands.

Mrs. Armlin came into the Uncompahgre Valley as Mary E. Lee, in 1880, from the Wet Mountain Valley, to which place they had come from Utah. They settled in the Park below Ouray. Mrs. Armlin says that the Indians were careful not to allow the cattle belonging to the white settlers to get across Cow Creek into the Reservation. She was married to Mr. Armlin more than fifty years ago and they have five daughters, all of whom live in the Uncompahgre Valley. They are: Mrs. Andrew Rasmussen, Mrs. Pat Stealy, Mrs. Ray Porter, Mrs. Jay Kettle and Mrs. Leonard Kinnick.

The Armlins have one of the finest ranches in Western Colorado, and were successful in the cattle business. Mr. Armlin stated that he often rounded up deer with his cattle. The ranch is in the natural habitat of the deer and bear and these animals are numerous, as well as all other kinds of wild life that is found in Colorado.

David Poplin Long was born in Wayne County, Iowa, at the town of Corydon, on April 27, 1860. At an early age he went to Indiana and then back to Iowa, thence into Nebraska by wagon. When he was eleven years old he went to Kansas and moved on into Colorado, in 1879, where he herded cows in the Julesburg district. At that time the Indians were not hostile. The settlers ate buffalo meat because it was the cheapest.

In the days that he spent punching cows, he states, there were many stampedes. The chuck wagon was always a popular place. At the age of 21 years he was riding every day. Rattlesnakes were a daily feature of the riding and had to be dealt with. However, the "Hydrophobia Cats," diseased skunks, were the animals most feared by the cowboys, as they would come right into the camp and their bite was deadly. Mr. Long knew of several men that died from being bit by these animals.

In 1889, Long came over into Western Colorado and worked at different jobs around Montrose, Delta, Ridgway and Ouray. He worked for Lewis Orvis, Sr., on the ranch now occupied by Button Porter. He worked for a time on some prospects at Monarch, but did not spend much time in the mining game, spending most of his time hauling timbers. In Ouray he worked for John Ashenfelter in his livery stable, and hauled ore from the mines. His main work for Ashenfelter was taking care of the "knock outs," the extras and sick horses.

He says that the brakeman on the Ouray train, on passing the Dark Lake station would yell out: "Next stop Ouray, the toughest city in the mountains, where they hang men, women and kids and roast coons."

CHAPTER XIV

MISSED SEVEN FIRES IN 45 YEARS

In forty-five years, James David Donnelly missed just seven of the sixteen hundred fires that called out the fire department in the town of Montrose. He was in the fire department of that city since the year 1888, and was on the job almost every day of that time.

Jim Donnelly was born in Malone, Franklin County, New York, on the eighteenth day of February, 1862. He went to school in that town and in Trout River Lines in the same state. He grew to manhood there and engaged in farming and assisted his father, who was a stock buyer.

He came West in 1879 and landed in Leadville, Colorado, on the seventh of March. Leadville was going strong then and Donnelly worked in the Crystalite Mine, operating the cage. This mine at the time, employed about six hundred men. Other prominent mines of the period were the Little Johnny and the Morning and Evening Star. All the work was done by hand, the timbers being cut and trimmed with axe, broad axe and foot adze.

Leaving Leadville, Donnelly went to Pitkin, and in February of 1882 made a trip with twelve other men through Buena Vista, over Tennessee Pass, and into the Uncompahgre Valley, going back to Leadville and returning to this valley in 1882. He worked in Gunnison for a short time for the Hammond Livery Stable, and when Hammond decided to start a stable in the new town of Montrose, he brought Jim down here to work for him. They kept around forty-five head of horses in the stable and Donnelly drove stages to various surrounding settlements, making trips to Ouray, Old Dallas, Ophir and Ames and to Telluride and Silverton, before the Ouray branch of the D. & R. G. was built.

One night he drove a little roan team to Ouray in a blizzard in just three hours and five minutes. Dr. Rowan of Ouray had been in a serious runaway and was not expected to survive his injuries, and at Fort Crawford Donnelly picked up the post doctor and took him to the bedside of the Ouray physician. Many times Jim hauled soldiers from Montrose to the fort up the valley. There were about two companies of soldiers at the post.

In 1888 the Montrose Volunteer Fire Department was organized with Doc Owens as the first fire chief and Jim Donnelly the first fire captain. Other members of the squad were (Billy) W. A. Cassell, Joseph L. Atkinson, A. F. Reeves, Frank Parliman, Frank Wyatt. A hand hose cart was used and the first fire plug was made by Billy Cassell and Jim Donnelly at the corner where the City Steam Laundry stands today.

Mr. Donnelly was in the Montrose fire department continuously from 1888 until his death and missed responding to just seven calls. There have been on an average of 33 to 35 alarms every year, making a total of nearly sixteen hundred fires. He had little outside amusement and indulged in card games at the fire house as a pastime.

Grove Rippey was the first fire chief after the city purchased a fire wagon and team. A truck is now used, and for several years preceding his death Jim Donnelly was the fire chief. The biggest fire he ever fought was the one that destroyed the Gibson Lumber Company. Other large ones were two flour mills, the Mears Hotel, the Buddecke & Diehl Store, the Lathrop Hardware Company and the Montrose Box Factory. All the fire department records of the early days were destroyed when the Mears Hotel burned in the nineties.

The Montrose department had four life members: James Donnelly, Chas. A. Gage, Fred Day and Fred Duckett. The officers at the time of Donnelly's death were: Chief, Jim Donnelly; captain, Robt. Bryant; first foreman, Fred Day; second foreman, George Freeman; secretary, B. E. Hitchcock; treasurer, J. J. Gatschet; fire marshal, Cleve Brown; driver, J. M. Gage. The other members were: F. H. Hill,

F. C. Hill, James Full, Clark Gage, Earl Day and M. Gatschet.

It is doubtful if there is another fireman in the State of Colorado with a record as good as Jim Donnelly's for long and faithful service.

The family of James Wiley Callaway have been prominently associated with the life and development of Western Colorado for many years. Mr. Callaway came into Colorado with his family in 1880, settling at fi,rst in Pueblo, where he spent about three months before moving on over to Silver Cliff. He came first to Montrose in 1882, when the town was situated near what is now South Seventh Street. He brought his family over in 1883, shortly after the business section was moved to its present site.

Mr. and Mrs. Callaway, who before her marriage was Emma Bozeman, had one daughter and five sons. The daughter, Laura, died in 1911, after serving for some time as city clerk for Montrose. The boys were William Stonewall, of Pueblo; James W., of Salida, Colorado; Charlie C., of Montrose; Joseph Albert, of Montrose, and Michael A., who was a former sheriff of the county of Montrose.

Joseph A Callaway was born in Batesville Mississippi, on November 11, 1869, lived there until he was six years old, and then went with his parents to Arkadelphia, Arkansas, where they lived until coming to Colorado in 1880. They lived at Silver Cliff for three years and then came over to Montrose. Here the Callaway brothers attended school, being students at the first school ever established in the town. It was held in a little building behind the old Post Office. Reverend Wright was the teacher.

The first four rooms of the Central School were built in 1884 and the Callaways attended school there, with John Tobin as teacher. After finishing his schooling, Joseph A. worked at various jobs around Montrose, being clerk at both the Arlington and Belvedere Hotels.

He worked for L. N. Heil in his clothing store and later, when John F. Wilson bought out Heil, Callaway worked for Wilson.

During the construction of the Gunnison Tunnel, he

operated a store at Lujane, the town at the West Portal of the tunnel. With his brother James W., he ran a grocery store where the Pinkstaff Grocery is now. Then he worked for a time for Charlie Gage in his grocery store, after which he went to Pueblo to work for White and Davis. In 1918, he returned to this side of the Divide and bought the Cimarron Mercantile Company, which he owned until 1928, when he sold out and moved to Montrose, where he died recently.

Joseph Albert Callaway was married Nov. 1, 1900, to Miss Sara Lamont and the couple have no children. W. S. Callaway is now connected with the D. & R. G. W. Railroad at Pueblo. Several years ago, he operated a pool hall in Montrose and later was connected with a railroad company at Dragon, Utah, before going to Pueblo. Charlie was for years a traveling representative of the Grand Junction Fruit Growers Association, and is now in the commission business in Montrose. James W. operates a grocery store in Salida. Michael A. is dead.

Montrose was a tough town in her earlier days and there were many fights and killing scrapes. Jack Watson shot Marshal Murphy and Judge Edwards. It seems that Watson, who was a cowboy, had come into Montrose, left his guns with Buddecke & Diehl and proceeded to get drunk. He was arrested and placed in jail. He dug his way out of the building, but later came back and stood trial. There was a dispute about some money he had had, and Watson spat tobacco juice in the judge's face and later shot the judge and marshal. He then proceeded to make whoopee by shooting up the town.

Mr. Callaway remembered when Billy Wilson killed Dick Netherly and Frank Mason killed Cal Irvin on the streets of Montrose.

Herman LeRoy Darling was born in Kalamazoo, Michigan, on February 15, 1864. In 1879, at the age of 14, he moved to Canon City, Colorado. Previous to that time he had already started in the lumbering work, which he has followed all of his life since that time. While at Canon City, he sawed timbers for the railroad to Leadville. He worked in a sawmill below the town of Salida and in one at Buena Vista. In the year 1884, he came into the Uncompahgre Valley and settled in the Horsefly district, and has lived in this valley since that time, having operated sawmills throughout this region.

One of his outstanding experiences was a trip through the Black Canyon of the Gunnison on a horse, before the railroad was built through the canyon. It was in March and he had to travel on the ice on the river, often being compelled to unpack his packhorse and carry the equipment around large boulders to keep the animal from being pushed into the icy waters of the river. At this time there was a grade camp in the Cimarron Canyon, where men were building the railroad. He stayed one night at the camp and another at the home of A. E. Buddecke in the Old Town of Montrose.

In 1893 Mr. Darling walked from Montrose to Rawlings, Wyoming, where he ran a stage for a year at $25.00 a month. He says that the present generation does not know what hard times are, even with the great depression of 1930-36.

He was in Delta when three men were killed in a bank robbery, and says that Russell and Eldon Hauser, now of Montrose, and Charlie Hauser, a brother, now deceased, who were boys then, found two of the guns which were lost by the robbers.

Mr. Darling remembers that in 1884 Dick Netherly said that people were living much too fast, and should go back to burning candles and weaving clothes from the backs of the sheep.

During the years that he has engaged in the lumber business, Herman Darling has carried on his own operations, employing from 40 to 60 men in the woods every summer, and doing wholesale lumbering, that is combined logging and sawing and running his own boarding houses with women cooks.

His favorite sport is horse racing, and Mr. Darling has seen lots of good races.

At the time he came into the Uncompahgre Valley, Mr.

Darling says, Dave Wood was the whole cheese here, although other prominent men were Dick Netherley, and Jim and Jesse O'Neil.

Charles H. Thompson was born in Bethel, Illinois, January 2, 1856. He went to school in Morgan County in the same state and spent twenty-seven years on farms around Jacksonville.

In the year 1886 he came to Montrose, Colorado, and filed on a homestead on North Mesa, a few miles north of Montrose. After spending two weeks in the valley, he went to Silverton, where his brothers were engaged in mining. He spent four years in the vicinity of Silverton, doing mining, freighting, and driving the mail stage between Mineral Point and Silverton. At that time Mineral Point had the highest post office in the United States.

Once while driving a six horse team up a mountain road in the Silverton area, he heard a commotion above him, and looking up, saw a rock slide headed straight for him. Leaping from the wagon, Thompson sought shelter under a cliff. The slide passed over him but killed two of his horses.

He was married in April 29, 1880, to Miss Una Belle Alderson, in Exeter, Scott County, Illinois, and to them were born eight children, five of whom are living. These are: Mrs. Lena Brickson, of Prescott, Arizona; Mrs. Harry Fairfax, of Helper, Utah; Ray and Mrs. Arthur W. Monroe of Montrose, and L. A. of Denver.

At one time Mr. Thompson had a string of 100 pack burros, which he used in his packing and freighting operations in the mining area. He hired packers to take care of the animals and packs. At one time, he and his brothers, Lou, Frank, Ed and Hal, owned the Sunnyside Mine at Eureka, which was later sold for $3,000,000 to a group of Englishmen. For years this mine was the largest zinc and lead mine in the State of Colorado.

Returning to the Uncompahgre Valley in about 1890, Mr. Thompson farmed on North Mesa for a number of years and then sold his farm and hauled freight for the Cashin Mine, in the Lasal Mountains in Western Montrose

County. He had to haul his freight a hundred miles through an isolated and desolate country. Following this he spent three years as Road Overseer in the Montrose district. He also served as night marshal of Montrose, chief of police and for twelve years was a constable in that town, also holding the post of special city officer.

He recalled to mind such old timers as O. D. Loutsenhizer, A. E. Buddecke, P. D. Moore; J. B. Johnson, sheriff; Billy Crane; Charley Diehl; and Frees, Osborn and Davis, merchants. Also the Ross Brothers, J. J. and Lew, Gus Frost, William Zillmer, the Nutt brothers, Sam and Tom, and I. N. Loper.

Archer Royce Dodge was born in Newport, Sullivan County, New Hampshire, January 1, 1867, and spent the first nine years of his life in that town. Then the family moved to Vineland, New Jersey, where A. R. Dodge attended school, finishing his high school course.

At the age of eighteen years, he came to Kansas, where he worked on a cattle ranch in Wakeeney County, near the headquarters of the Smoky Hill Cattle Company, which ran about nine thousand head of stock on the open prairie. In the summer of 1885, considerable friction developed between the homesteaders and the cattlemen, and the latter often tried to intimidate the homesteaders, and drive them off their newly settled land. Those who would not scare, were often found dead on the prairie. The affair became so serious that it was brought to the attention of President Cleveland, who issued an ultimatum to the stock men, ordering them to leave the State of Kansas. So the herds of the Smoky Hill Cattle Company were divided into three sections, one of which was driven into Arizona, another into the Meeker country in northwestern Colorado, and the third herd was taken into Montana. It is said that some of the old brands of this company still exist in the Meeker section.

Dodge quit his job with the Smoky Hill Company and went to Ellsworth, Kansas, where he helped in the building of the town of Kanopolis. In 1886, together with five other men, who had the desire to go farther west, he bought a prairie schooner, filled it with supplies and came into Colorado, arriving in Denver on the 1st of April.

Denver was a beautiful sight to look upon after the weeks on the desolate plains, and they were stopped many times by farmers who wanted them to go to work on their ranches.

They made camp near the hogbacks out by Golden, and had their first experience at climbing in the Rocky Mountains. After a few days rest, they returned to Denver after supplies, and Dodge took a job on a ranch for E. M. Holman. He liked the country and decided to stay. He also worked for Valentine DeVinny, who had been a school teacher in Kansas and had for one of his pupils, William Cody, better known as Buffalo Bill. Whenever Buffalo Bill came to Denver he always came out to see DeVinny, so Dodge became well acquainted with the famous frontiersman.

Dodge worked in the neighborhood of Denver for five years and then went back to New Jersey to finish his education, attending Dickinson College, at Carlisle, Pennsylvania.

Before going back to New Jersey, Dodge had worked on the D. & R. G. Railroad, when that road was racing the Colorado Midland for the best right of way into the town of Aspen.

After taking a four year college course and graduating with an A. B. degree, he returned to Colorado, working for E. M. Holman again for a season and returned again to New Jersey, where he worked at various trades, principle of which was a sixteen year term as foreman in a lumber yard. He spent two years working for the U. S. Government at the May's Landing Ordnance Department, at May's Landing, New Jersey, during the World War.

Edmond Andrew Lee came into Western Colorado when a very young baby, lying on his mother's lap, while she drove a six-horse team. He was born in Curlsville, Pennsylvania, his mother having gone back there from Colorado, where she had spent several years. His parents, Andrew Stewart Lee and Netta Edmonds Lee, had spent sev-

eral years in the freighting business in the Leadville and
Lake City countries, the venture being a successful one
financially.

When E. A. Lee was a month old his mother brought
him into Colorado and she and her husband each drove a
six-horse team, the mother holding her infant son on her
lap as she drove.

Andrew S. Lee, the father, hauled the equipment for
the first smelter into Ouray. When the Indians were taken
out of the Uncompahgre Valley, he, with about thirty
others, made a race for the newly opened land. Lee settled
on a piece of land a mile and a half below Olathe on the
river.

E. A. Lee went to school in the first school in Olathe,
which, however, was not in the town but on the mesa west
of town. The church was also on the mesa overlooking
the valley. There were eight or ten children in the little
school and they went as far as the eighth grade and stayed
in it three years. The first school house in Olathe was purchased by Lee's mother and converted into a dwelling.
E. A. Lee recently sold the house.

He was married in 1908 to Maude Corey and the two
have three children, Stewart, Miss Yvonne and Milton, all
of Montrose. Mrs. Lee died a few years ago.

As a boy, E. A. Lee worked as a cowboy and rode race
horses for Roberts Brothers, who had a race track on the
present site of Olathe. He rode the stallions Little John
and Potter, famous horses of the day, whose names are
perpetuated in the names of mesas and canyons in the
Roubideau country west of Olathe.

Those were balmy days for the cattlemen. They had
everything their own way, and the larger cattlemen were
kings of the range where they ran their stock. Some of the
more prominent cattleman Ed Lee was connected with
were Henry Paine, Old Man White, Alex Calhoun, Dave
Dillard and Preston Hotchkiss.

In those days the cowboys rode all summer and there
were about sixty of them riding the Uncompahgre Plateau,
usually making their headquarters at the Hotchkiss Camp.

Mr. Lee's parents were acquainted with Chief Ouray, in their early freighting days in the Uncompahgre Valley.

In 1900, Andrew S. Lee quit the valley of the Uncompahgre and joined the Alaskan gold rush, where he was a pioneer of the Dawson City area. His son, E. A. Lee, joined him there and spent two years in placer mining on the Klondike.

In 1909 E. A. Lee became connected with a garage in Montrose and thereafter, until 1929 followed that business. In the latter year he sold his garage and, having secured a ranch in the canyon country west of Olathe, moved there, where he now resides.

Samuel Vickus Topliss is the only man who settled on a ranch in the Old Fort Crawford Reservation to still live on the same place. He was born. in New Diggings, Wisconsin, September 5, 1865, and lived there until he reached his fourteenth year, when he moved to a farm in Lincoln County, Kansas.

In 1880 the family moved to Canon City. Samuel V. worked in sawmills west of the Greenhorn Mountains near Galena, and also worked in the Telluride Mine, which, at the time, was turning out twenty tons of concentrates every day. His father was a wagon maker and ran a blacksmith shop in Galena.

In the year 1887 young Samuel helped Enoch Shepherd drive a bunch of horses from Canon City into the Uncompahgre Valley. He stayed in the valley and took a job with the Hiebler and Hammond Sawmill on Sawtooth, after which he worked in the Terrible Mine near the Revenue in the Ouray district.

In the year 1890, when Fort Crawford was abandoned and the Soldiers' Reservation was thrown open to settlement, Mr. Topliss settled on the ranch where he lives today, having been on the place continuously since that year. He has farmed the eighty acre place and ran cattle on the Sawtooth Mountain. He has done much hunting and has killed many deer.

He remembers many things that happened at Fort Crawford when it was a lively post. The settlers were in-

vited to attend the post dances and shooting matches. One
of the soldiers, Charley Arndt, was discharged and took
up the place adjoining the Topliss place. Arndt, whose son
now lives in the Uncompahgre Valley, sold his place to
Shepherd and went to Oklahoma, where he was accidentally killed.

At this time as Topliss remembers Fort Crawford, Ed
Hayes was hauling water, Ed Ryan was corral boss and
Alex Owens was working at the Post. He states that the
two companies at Fort Crawford were the youngest soldiers in the U. S. and were certainly full of pep. They
would often steal their mules out at night and ride to
Montrose, returning in time for duty in the morning. At
the post dances there was no trouble for the sergeant-at-
arms was on hand with a big gun strapped to his belt.

Mr. Topliss was married in 1900 to Mossie O'Bannon,
and they have one son, Charles, who is a cameraman for
the motion pictures in Hollywood.

Frank Lee Wilson was born near Atchinson, Kansas,
August 8, 1872, and at the age of two years was taken to
St. Joseph, Missouri, by his parents. When he was seven
the family came to Colorado, and settled in the old mining
town of Silver Cliff. He went to school in that town two
winters, and then the family moved westward, coming to
Delta where they lived for four years on a ranch six miles
below the town near the mouth of Roubideau Creek, on
what is now called the Bloomburg Place.

In 1886, they moved to the town of Parachute, on the
Colorado River. The name of the town was later changed
to Grand Valley. There the Wilson family lived until 1889,
when Frank moved to Lake City, which at that time was
a prosperous mining camp. Mr. Wilson worked in the
Hidden Treasure Mine, the Lille, the Champion and prospected on Hensen Creek. He did some contract work for
miners in Capitol City. He also worked for a time in the
mines in and around Aspen.

Mr. Wilson was in Lake City when the big strike was
made in the Inez and Dupree Mines. This strike put Lake
City on its feet again after a lull in production. The Ute

and Ula, Golden Fleece and other big mines of the region
were going strong at that time.

In 1903 Mr. Wilson joined his family in La Jara, on a
big hay ranch where they lived for a year and then came
over into the western part of Montrose County, where he
was employed on the LaSal Mine at Cashin. His mother
died in La Jara in 1906 and ten months later his brother,
James O. Wilson, was killed while playing ball at Tres
Piedres, New Mexico.

Frank L. Wilson then took over his brother's store business in Tres Piedres and stayed there until he could clean
up and sold out to J. H. Elledge, after which he returned
to the Paradox country. He has operated a feed and livery
barn and hotel in Placerville, as well as taking care of his
mining interests in western Montrose County. He was in
charge of the shipping of the ore for the Standard Chemical Company for a time.

Mr. Wilson was married in 1914 to Hannah Thomas of
Mannassa, Colorado, and the couple have one girl.

Mr. Wilson has been all over the Paradox country for
many years and has worked in the oil fields near Bluff,
Utah. He has a government lease on twelve hundred acres
of government land in the Paradox Valley, which he is
holding for oil prospects.

In 1905, he discovered a salt spring near the Dolores
River that runs twenty-three per cent salt. About twenty-
five hundred pounds of salt goes into the Dolores every day
from this spring.

Mr. Wilson looks for a great development to begin in
the near future in the Paradox Valley which has vast un-
touched resources.

CHAPTER XV

HE SAW KIT CARSON

Byron Hamilton was born June 10th, 1843, in Bracken County, Kentucky, and lived in that county until he was eleven years old. He then moved westward with his father and settled in Miami County, Kansas. At the age of sixteen years he hired out to the United States Government and drove cattle from Leavenworth, Kansas, to Fort Union, New Mexico, and other points in that state. He made three trips with a wagon train and drove cattle along with the train, walking all the way. On one trip he drove mules. Altogether he made four of these trips and on one of them they had a Mexican boss who made them drive at night, sleeping in the day time. It was bitter cold on these nights on the plains and they suffered much hardship.

Mr. Hamilton saw thousands of buffalo in one herd. They encountered many Indians, but as they always had soldiers along with the train, they were not molested. The soldiers were sent to protect the government property that the train carried.

Many and varied were the experiences of the plainsmen of that day. One time they came up with a train that had been attacked by the Indians. The people of the train had all been killed or taken prisoner, many of the cattle had been killed and the wagons were still burning. The men of the second train saw a small mound in the sand, and looking into it found a small Indian boy, four or five years old. He had crawled into the sand to hide. They took the lad to the first fort and left him.

An interesting incident occurred one time when the train had stopped for dinner. The cook was preparing the meal, when a bunch of Indians came along and camped just across the Arkansas River. A big buck that had been drinking came across the stream, and, coming up to the fire, kicked the food in all directions. Of course, the cook was mad and kicked the Indian into the river.

The wagon boss said: "Well, boys, get ready to fight," and all strapped on their revolvers, and prepared for battle. They saw the chief of the redskins coming across the river, leaving behind all but two of his men and moving toward the train with a white rag, that called for peace. He asked for the man who had kicked the buck into the river. The cook came forward, and the chief patted him on the back and told him he had done just right. He saw the grub scattered around and waved the Indians back to their camp. The chief and his two men stayed for dinner and thus another situation was passed over without bloodshed.

It usually took about a year to make the trip. They went out with loaded wagons and returned empty. Each man was allowed to stay in the government pay until he got back to Fort Leavenworth or he could quit when he got to Fort Union. When they got ready to start back, they would hook several wagon together and put on two or three yoke of oxen. They would load in the men's bedding and supplies and the herders had to walk.

Fort Union was down in a hollow. Once they had the cattle down in this hollow, when the Indians came and ran the stock off. The train had just started to return to Fort Leavenworth, when the redskins commenced to shoot. The soldiers started after the savages, Kit Carson in the lead, his sword flashing in the sunshine. The men of the wagon train stopped and made camp where they were, to see what would happen. About noon the next day the soldiers returned with the stock.

On one of his trips, Hamilton had been herding cattle for a week and came into a hotel to rest. After a night's sleep, he got up and looked into the mirror and saw that he had smallpox. He promptly fainted and when consciousness returned he found that he was in an old adobe house with neither door nor window, with an old Mexican woman to care for him. However, she did take good care of him, for he never had a scar, after he recovered. When he got sick he had $100.00, but after he got well he was broke, and had to stay there eleven months before the train returned. He got work in the meantime and learned to speak Spanish and Mexican very well.

Returning home, Hamilton was married to Louisa B. Hamilton in June of 1865. In 1867 he came into Colorado and settled in the Greenhorn Mountains. He was there about a year, but the Indians were so bad that he was afraid to bring his family into the Centennial State. However, he brought them out in 1869. His first wife died in Costilla County about 1877. Mr. Hamilton was a miner and prospector. He found the Hidden Treasure Mine on Grayback in the Sangre de Christe Range, and with his brother discovered the Hamilton Mine, close to Blanca and old Fort Garland.

On May 12, 1882, he married Ida May Kile in Miami County, Kansas, the town of Paola. Since then he spent a part of his time in Colorado. He was never satisfied anywhere else. He was the father of 14 children, four with his first wife and ten with his second wife. He was a great lover of trees, flowers, and in fact, anything pertaining to nature. He was always a staunch Christian.

Five of his children are dead, nine still living. One boy lives in Denver and three in Montrose. One daughter lives in Montrose. Like their father before them, they think there is no place like Colorado.

Mr. Hamilton died at the age of eighty-three years, on August 24, 1926, and is buried in Grand View Cemetery, Montrose, which was according to his desire. He was intimately acquainted with Kit Carson and Buffalo Bill, and was in Denver when there were only three log cabins there. They traveled up and down the Arkansas River, and he has since showed Mrs. Hamilton some of his camp sites along that stream.

On one occasion they scraped the ashes away from the ground where the fire had been and made their beds down on the warm ground. The next morning there was a foot of snow on the beds.

The wagon trains always took along extra oxen, and once when one old animal had played out, they left him behind. The next morning when they went back after him, they found that he had been butchered by the Indians. The trains always had to keep men on guard, and at night the wagons were placed around in a circle with the tongues inside.

Charles Alviras Heath was born in Plainville, Connecticut, February 1, 1851. He lived until he was nine years old in that place and at Taringham, Massachusetts, then the family moved to Richmond, Crawford County, Pennsylvania, where he grew to manhood and remained until he was thirty-five years of age, operating a cheese factory and engaging in farming during that time. This was in the early days of the oil industry and Mr. Heath well remembered the first oil well ever to be brought into production. It was the Drake well at Titusville.

By 1885 Mr. Heath had lost his health and came to Colorado in that year an invalid. He first spent a few months in Denver resting and then came over to Montrose on March 13, 1885, and resided here until his death.

On coming into Montrose, after a short rest he took up the work of overseeing the dressing of the tools being used in the drilling of the artesian well near the County High School.

Mr. Heath operated a livery stable, the Magnolia Barn, in Montrose for sixteen years, being associated with George Robuck and Charlie Campbell. He also did much other work, helping in the construction of the Cimarron Ditch and many other irrigation canals in the Uncompahgre Valley. He always lived in town and took care of several ranches near Montrose. He lived in one house for forty-six years.

Two of his children, Bertie and Alviras, were burned to death when his residence near the high school was destroyed by fire. Another son, LeRoy, never recovered from his experience at the fire and died a few months later. A son, Hubert, died in 1929 and Mrs. Heath passed away in 1932.

Mr. Heath has seen Montrose grow from a small settlement of a few houses to a good sized town. He saw its buildings built up, burned down and built up again. Dave Wood had been freighting from the Magnolia Barn, and when the railroad was extended to Dallas, he moved his headquarters to that place and the barn was turned over to Charles Heath and his associates.

Mr. Heath recalled a time when court was being conducted in a log cabin, where the telephone office stands today. The court was adjourned to allow everyone to go take a drink.

Earnest A. Hale first came into the Uncompahgre Valley as a freighter or "bull whacker," in 1880. He was born in Homer, Nebraska, June 3, 1867. He lived in that town until he was about twelve years old and then moved with his brother to Colorado. He went to school in Lake City. He freighted between Del Norte and Montrose and brought in the first mowing machine and rake that was used in the valley, for T. B. Townsend. At this time there were three cabins and five tents in the town of Montrose.

He saw the LeRoy boys, stage robbers, hung in Del Norte, saw Betts and Browning hung in Lake City, he and his brother being camped only a little way from where this hanging occurred. He saw a mob hang a Negro in Gunnison for ravishing a white girl and stated that he was in the Cimarron Valley when Young Jackson was killed by the Utes.

He knew Young Jackson's father, who, it is stated, killed a man in Del Norte, with a billiard cue. Old Man Jackson was sent to the penitentiary, and Hale did not see him for many years. One day when he was working for John Ashenfelter in Ouray, Jackson was sent in to help him grease a harness, but when Hale recognized him, Jackson left and did not return.

Hale came to Montrose first with a freight outfit composed of several big teams. A man named Lowe had five bull teams, Woodey had several yoke and Charlie Hale, his brother, had five yoke, while Ernest Hale himself had three.

Mr. Hale hauled many loads of ore from the Palmetto

Mine in Lake City, in which the late Judge John C. Bell had an interest. Hale said that the Palmetto was one of the oldest mines in the Lake City region. It was located on Engineer Mountain.

One winter Hale and his brother lost sixteen yoke of oxen, which starved to death when they were snowed in on the Big Park, above Lake City. The other outfits were brought down to the lower country for the winter, but the Hale boys delayed their start for the lowlands and could not get out with their teams. That winter hay was $50 a ton.

When he first came into Colorado, Hale traded a horse, saddle and bridle for two mules and a set of harness and a wagon. In Gunnison he traded this outfit for three yoke of cattle.

He owned his own freight outfit for a time and also worked for Dave Wood and John Ashenfelter. He freighted with Dave Dillard, John Hazlett and Jesse Owen. He was with one freight outfit that belonged to Ashenfelter when the Hanging Rock snow slide at Potosi killed Hank Metcalfe, Neighbor White and John Swain. These men were not dug out of the slide until the following summer and it cost John Ashenfelter $500 to get them out. At this time there were ten six-horse teams on the road, but only four men were killed.

Another time, at Potosi, a snow slide swept fourteen pack mules off the trail and they had to be dug out.

Mr. Hale saw many exciting events happen around Montrose, and, in fact, all over Western Colorado. He recalled a tragedy that occurred the night Hugo Selig arrived in Montrose when a man was hung at the River Bridge.

Amos Augustine Frost, better known as Gus Frost, came into Colorado more than ten years before this territory became a state. He was prominently identified with its development and its progress. He made money in its industries and lost his all and started in anew. He lived on a ranch about eight miles north of Montrose and did all of his own work until shortly before his death.

Born in Ravenswood, West Virginia, on the Ohio River, he lived there for two years and then was taken to Monticello, Lewis County, Missouri, where he lived for ten years, going to the public schools of that county.

In April of the year 1865, he came into Colorado, his father being in charge of a stage station for the Ben Halliday Stage Lines, at a point about forty miles north of Denver, near Loveland.

At the age of 15 years Gus Frost went up into Wyoming, where he was employed by the Union Pacific Railroad, which was building the transcontinental line. After working at this job for two or three months, Mr. Frost joined a freighter and made the trip across the plains of Northern Wyoming to Gallatin City, Montana, where he quit this job and entered into the government service at Fort Phil Kearney, which was on the Old Oregon Trail. The Sioux Indians were on the warpath all the time he was at work there hauling logs to a sawmill. One day, while his party was eating lunch, a band of Indians charged down upon them and stampeded their cattle and horses, and shot the boss through one arm. The fight lasted for fifteen or twenty minutes and then the men all had to walk the fifteen or twenty miles into the fort.

As he was not anxious to encounter more Indians, in November of 1867, he joined five other men and started back to Colorado. The weather was very cold and it took them six or seven weeks to make the trip overland with wagons, and to make it all the more unpleasant they had trouble with the Indians all the way. Some of the members of the party had to stand guard. When they were within fifty miles of Cheyenne and food was getting low, they thought they were out of the Indian country, so they sent a man named Conrad out to the westward to hunt antelope. A short time later a party of fifteen Indians came along and asked for food. The white men had none to spare and the redskins left without molesting them. However, the party soon heard shots to the west of them and rushed in that direction to find the horribly mutilated body of Mr.

Conrad. They buried him and resumed the journey, arriving in Cheyenne, frozen, starved and scared.

It was about a hundred miles from Cheyenne to the stage station where the father of Gus Frost lived. About this time the business men of Denver started to build the Denver-Pacific Railroad from their city to the Wyoming capital. In the fall of 1859 the stock were taken off the road and the stage line abandoned. The Frost family moved south to the Divide between Colorado Springs and Denver and settled on a cattle ranch in the vicinity of Palmer Lake.

In 1870, Gus Frost joined a party from Nevada who were going to Texas to buy cattle to drive back to Colorado. They all went on horseback to Pueblo, down the Arkansas to the present site of Wichita, a distance of seven hundred miles. There were no people there at the time. The party crossed the river, went south across the Red River and to Waco, Texas, where they spent the winter buying three thousand head of steers. About the first of April, they started north with their cattle, over the Old Chisholm Trail. Here Gus first met up with Jim and Jesse O'Niell and Al Neale, pioneers of the Uncompahgre Valley, who are now deceased. On this trip, the herders had all the hardships that go with trail herding—stampedes, night riding, etc. When the steers stampeded, all there was to do was to go with them. For miles and miles, day after day, they rode through herds of buffalo. In the fall these animals moved south and in the spring returned to the northern country. When once they started stampeding nothing on Earth could stop them or turn them, it seems. They had lots of trouble with their cattle getting mixed with the buffalo, and it took six months to make the drive. They arrived on the Platte River near Denver in September. The owners sold their stock in Denver and Gus Frost was discharged and went home again.

The D. & R. G. railroad was building south from Denver, and in 1871, before he was twenty-one years old, Mr. Frost went up to the Ute Pass country and located some timber lands. He held on to these, despite his youth, and carried on logging operations, marketing nearly all the lumber in Colorado Springs. After four years at this work, he started for Califonia, stopping in Nevada, where he put in a season in the mines at Virginia City.

From Nevada, Frost went to the Sacramento Valley, in California, where he worked on a wheat ranch near Marysville for two years. He had saved considerable money by this time and, with an old man and his son, leased two hundred acres of delta land near the convergance of the Sacramento and San Joaquin Rivers, Frost putting up the money and the other two furnishing the equipment. They worked hard setting out a good crop of potatoes, tomatoes and other vegetables, and when the time for marketing the crop in San Francisco was only two weeks off, heavy rains in the high Sierras caused the river to rise and overflow their land. The early placer workings along the river had helped to dam up the main channel so that the water flowed about eight feet over their entire crop, and, although the land was protected by high levees above it, the water came over the banks and washed away everything the three men had. So this venture proved a failure and Gus started out again flat broke. He secured a job with a threshing outfit and quit in October with $300 in his pocket.

While in the Sacramento Valley, he met the girl who was to become his wife and share his experiences for the next fifty years or more. This was Nettie M. Ross, a sister to Jay J. Ross and L. E. Ross. Gus Frost, promising Miss Ross that he would return for her in a year, took his three hundred dollars and went to Leadville, Colorado, to make his fortune. Fortunes were being made there but Gus was not lucky and at the end of two years had not saved any money. Mr. Frost knew H. A. W. Tabor in the early days in California Gulch, before Mr. Tabor became rich and famous. He knew there also A. V. Hunter and George Trimble.

Deciding that he could not save any money in the frantic town of Leadville, Frost, with George Hall, bought a burro and grubstake and punched the burro all the way to Silverton, going by way of the present site of Montrose,

when the Indians still held possession of the Uncompahgre
Valley. He arrived in Silverton with four dollars and very
little grub. There his partner quit him and started dealing
stud poker, while Frost took a contract for a cross cut in
the Silver Crown Mine, at eighteen dollars a foot. This
mine was a mile west of Chattanooga, and was owned by
General Booth, who financed the work Mr. Frost was to do.
At the end of seven weeks Frost had made $1100, and de-
cided to leave the men at work, and return to California
to get his bride.

He had to go out by way of Colorado Springs, Denver
and Cheyenne. Mr. Frost and Miss Ross were married on
October 27, 1880, in Bacaville, California, and returned to
Colorado, stopping for a two weeks visit with his parents in
Colorado Springs. Ed Frost, a brother of Gus, lived in
Colorado Springs for twenty-five years and put in every
inch of the water lines of that city during that time. One
sister, Mrs. Laura Frost Staggs, died in Napa, California.
Another, Mrs. Elizabeth F. Boland, died in Chicago a few
years ago. She was a prominent musician and had sung and
played in many of the large city churches, also Madison
Square Garden.

With his brother-in-law, Jay J. Ross, Frost again turned
his face toward the San Juans, going by train to Alamosa,
and by stage through Antelope Park, Lake City and over
Stony Pass to Silverton, making fifty-five miles on foot
through the snow in two days. They arrived at the Silver
Crown Mine on Christmas Day of 1880 and found that the
crew had departed for the new town of Durango. The two
had plenty of provisions and they worked the mine until
the first of May, when Mrs. Frost came through on the
train to Amargo, near Pagosa Junction, and was there met
by Mr. Frost with a team and spring wagon.

In the fall of 1881, when the Indians were taken out of
the Uncompahgre Valley, Frost and Ross came down and
settled ranches north of the present town of Montrose. The
Indians left on the third of September and the two white
men came in right behind them. On the seventh of September, Frost started back to Silverton after Mrs. Frost

and L. E. Ross, leaving the other to hold the ranches. A man, Chas. Garten, died and was buried while he was gone. He returned to the valley in a few days with a spring wagon, coming by way of Ophir and Telluride. There was no road and it was a very difficult trip.

Arriving at the ranches, they had no money and it was twelve months before they could expect to make any from their first crop. The D. & R. G. Railroad was being built into the valley, and the three men secured work on the road. When their work was too far away from home to go there at night, a tent was secured and Mrs. Frost went along and cooked for ten or twelve of the men. They worked in the Roubideau Canyon for a time and then quit and went home with $500 apiece. They were rich for that time and were able to put in their crop. They paid $140 a ton for hay and eight cents a pound for corn. They cleared twelve acres of land and put in potatoes, corn and vegetables, raising a good crop, which was harvested and sold in the fall of 1882 for $1800.

They had all been living at the Frost ranch but during the summer of 1883, the Ross brothers built homes on their places and moved there. L. E. Ross died recently on his place and Jay J. lived for fifty years only a short distance from his original ranch.

Gus Frost operated his farm until 1883, when he entered business in Montrose. With Billy Crane, Ben Corbin and J. S. Davis, he bought out the general merchandise store of Frees, Osborn and Davis. In 1893, with J. J. Tobin, John Pelton, Elmer Young and W. T. Ryman, he organized the Montrose Fruit Growers Association.

In the panic of 1893 he lost everything, and, as there were no prospects in Montrose, he left his family, which now consisted of his wife and two daughters, and started to find a job. He was away from home eleven years, working in the mines in Cripple Creek, Gunnison, Lake City and other parts of the San Juan. He worked in the Hidden Treasure at Lake City, the Old Revenue at Ouray and was manager of the Des Ouray Mine in Poughkeepsie Gulch. He was also a boss, in charge of three hundred men at the

Liberty Bell in the Telluride district, also working at the Smuggler Union. Finally he returned home with all his debts paid, and broke again.

He made a trip to California in 1904 for a visit, returned to Montrose and entered into a partnership with E. D. Nichols, to operate a sawmill. In the fifteen years that they were together, they had mills on Sawtooth, head of Dallas Creek, Log Hill Mesa and other places. The firm made money until the lumber business became dull, and then Gus Frost established a box factory at the north end of Cascade Avenue in Montrose. Times grew worse and he lost his money again. He sold out and located on a farm he owned on North Mesa, and lived there until his death at 82 years.

His daughters are Mrs. C. A. W. Gordon, of the First National Bank of Montrose, and Mrs. Etehl O'Rourke.

Mr. Frost saw the development of Colorado from its very earliest settlement to the persent time. He saw it come up from a frontier state to a great commonwealth. He saw its towns and cities grow from sage brush flats to prosperous settlements and communities. He knew many of the famous frontiersmen of the earlier days. Buffalo Bill Cody, the Reich brothers, Al Houston, Jim Bridger, all made regular visits to his father's home, when he was a boy.

Denver was a town of ten thousand people when Frost first saw it. There was no law and crime was rampant. There were mostly tents and ramshackle buildings, with only two one story brick buildings in the entire city. There were hundreds of notorious characters, horse thieves, cattle thieves, stage robbers, bandits, tin horn gamblers. There were periodic Indian scares, when the people of all the countryside fled into Denver for protection. A Mrs. McIntyre and her son were murdered by Indians just six miles from where the post office now stands, at a point now inside the city limits.

The Vigilance Committee was organized and hangings were a general occurrence. Three men were hung in broad daylight to a cottonwood tree on Eighteenth street.

To few of us have come the early day experiences in

Colorado that Rosa Hotchkiss Osborn McCoy knew. She was born in Indiana on the eighth of March, 1863. Her mother died when she was nine months old and her father died when she was three years old. Before his death, her father had taken Rosa to Fairbury, Nebraska, where she was adopted by Roswell Hotchkiss and his wife, and immediately brought into Colorado. This state is the only real home she ever knew. She was not really adopted because her older sister would never allow the papers to be made out, but she never went back to her own folks, and knew Mr. and Mrs. Hotchkiss as her parents and always loved them dearly, and always thought of Virdie L. and Charlie, the two sons of Mr. and Mrs. Roswell Hotchkiss, as her own brothers.

The family came in nine wagons to the Cebolla Valley, where at this time, Enos Hotchkiss, a brother of Roswell, was the keeper of the toll gate at the Hot Springs on one of Otto Mear's roads. On the way into the valley one of their horses went lame and they traded the other horse for an ox and hitched it up with a cow they had with them and came on through.

They stayed in the Cebolla Valley only a few months and then came into the Uncompahgre Valley, where Roswell and Preston Hotchkiss established a store. At this time the Indians were still in the valley and were very numerous.

Roswell Hotchkiss, however, did not remain in the mercantile business for very long, but moved down near Fort Crawford and camped on the river. While at this camp, the family sold milk and butter to the officers and soldiers at the Post. As a girl of twelve years, Rosa drove a span of mules and delivered the milk every morning. She could not leave the mules unhitched or they would run away, so she had to ring a bell and have her patrons come out and get the food she was delivering.

During the time the Hotchkiss family was camped on the Uncompahgre River, the Old Agency on the present site of the Whinnerah place, was used as a distribution point for the Indian rations, and on certain days of every

week hundreds of redskins came to the Agency after their
food. Six or seven cows were butchered at a time.

Mrs. McCoy stated that the old home of Mr. Whinnerah is the remodeled gunsmith building of the agency,
and the spot across the railroad from there is the place
where the rations were handed out. At this place the
Indians had to file through a gate, one member of each
family, and receive their rations.

The Hotchkiss' were camped on the river, when Young
Jackson was a freighter. Mrs. McCoy said he was a fine
lad of twenty-one years, and often stayed at their place
over night. On every trip into the reservation he came
there after bread and milk. After he shot an Indian, he
asked to be given his gun and ammunition so that he
might protect himself. However, he was taken out unarmed and it was in a canyon near the old Son of a B - - - -
Hill, that he was taken from Captain Cline and Mr. Berry,
the Indian Agent. Mrs. McCoy also stated that no one
knows where he was killed or how. Often on his trips
from Saguache, Young Jackson would bring candy to Rosa
Hotchkiss.

She often played with the little girl, who was adopted
and later murdered by the Cudigans. Every time the family would go to Ouray to sell butter and other supplies,
the child was left at the Hotchkiss home in Portland, and
was Rosa's guest until the family came down on the return
trip.

Mrs. McCoy knew Sidney Jocknick, the author of "Early
Days on the Western Slope of Colorado," very well, and
also his brother, who often walked to school with her. In
later years, Mrs. McCoy assisted Sidney Jocknick in com-
piling certain parts of his book.

Mrs. McCoy remembered when the Indians were taken
out of the valley of the Uncompahgre. They were ordered
to go one day, but refused and were forced to make the
start the next day. One old Indian fell off his pony and
broke his arm. He came to Mrs. Hotchkiss and that lady
tore up a sheet, bound up the arm and sent him down to
the doctor at Fort Crawford.

Rosa Hotchkiss was married in 1892 to James F. Osborn, who had come into the Lake City country some time before she had come to the Cebolla Valley. The couple had three sons, Pete, of Montrose; Bill, of Wilmington, California, and Harold, of Pueblo. Mr. Osborn died December 24, 1921.

On August ninth, 1923, Mrs. Osborn was married to William C. McCoy.

Mrs. McCoy and her mother attended the sale at the time Chief Ouray and Chipeta sold their household effects, and the latter bought a window curtain and silver pitcher and sugar bowl, which Mrs. McCoy owned at the time of her death.

Miles Washington Cornett was born in Gresham County, Virginia, near the post office of North Branch, on March 15, 1852. He spent a number of years in that state, and after he was grown up he traveled over North Carolina, trading horses and mules.

In the year 1882, he came to Montrose, Colorado, which had just been moved to its new site and was being run by Buddecke & Diehl, Dave Wood, Billy and Bob Sampson, J. C. Frees, Selig & Eckerly and others. J. C. Frees had moved his store equipment from Leadville to Montrose and was established in a log shack in the old town. A man named Wright moved the Frees equipment to the new town.

At this time there was a toll gate at Pine Creek. The same year Mr. Cornett came to Montrose he helped build the old Methodist Church which has long since served its usefulness and been torn down. There was an open winter that year and the stone masons worked on the building all winter.

For some time thereafter Mr. Cornett drove a team and hauled wood, posts and various other commodities around the town of Montrose. He worked in the Montrose Flour Mill for twenty-two years, being associated with Isaac Hottell, Captain Clark, and the Diemer firm. His son, Grover, is now with the Montrose Flour Milling Company, and has held the job for over twenty years as head miller.

As Mr. Cornett recalled Montrose in the early days, it was a town of high board sidewalks, muddy streets in wet weather and gambling going on night and day. Provisions were hauled to the mining camps of the San Juan with six-horse teams of horses and cattle and ore hauled back to the railroad at Montrose.

Mr. Cornett said that wheat, although the acreage is larger now than it was when he started to be a miller, brings a higher price now than it did then. In the early days of farming in the Uncompahgre valley, there was little water for the crops and there were not nearly so many acres in cultivation as there have been since the Gunnison Tunnel has been in use. There was practically no corn raised in the valley in those days, as the farmers thought corn would not grow here. As a matter of fact, today this is a good corn country.

He also said that the Loutsenhizer addition of Montrose was first planted in alfalfa and wheat and then fruit trees were set out and it was a big orchard. Later the addition was subdivided by F. D. Catlin and building lots were sold. Mr. Cornett hauled the trees that were set out by John Ashenfelter in his big orchard on Spring Creek Mesa.

Fishing used to be better on the Gunnison than it is now and Pine Creek was good too. The horses and mules that were used here for freighting were bought and driven in from other places. The saddle horses were broomtail bronchos.

For a time Mr. Cornett burned charcoal for Buddecke, who used it for toasting meat. He had two kilns burning coal. The hotel burned and he lost his market for charcoal in Montrose, so he hauled what he had on hand to Ouray and sold it, also taking some to Telluride, where it was used for sharpening tools.

For fifty years John Virgil Lathrop has been identified with the business life of Montrose, Colorado. He was born in Sprague, New London County, Connecticut, on December 5, 1855, and lived there for sixteen years, going to school at that place. About 1872, he moved to Cawker City,

Kansas, where he spent seven years on a ranch and then became connected with a hardware store in that town.

Coming to Colorado in October of 1890, he became associated with the firm of Frees, Osborn and Davis, buying a one-fourth interest in the store from Davis. The store was later changed to the Montrose Mercantile Company and was operated as such for twenty-eight years, after which it was incorporated as the Lathrop Hardware Company. This was about twenty years ago. Mr. Lathrop is still connected with the store, although not active in its management.

Mr. Lathrop's life has been a more or less quiet one, as he has gone about his own affairs. One of his outstanding experiences was a buffalo hunt in 1873. In the early days when he was in Kansas, there were no bridges and they had to ford the Solomon River. He was in Montrose when the Lot and Belvedere Hotels burned. He states that hardware prices are higher today than they were when he first came to Montrose.

Daniel Morrison Kelley was born in New York City on November 7, 1865. When four years old he went with his parents to Fall River, Massachusetts, where he attended school until the family moved to Longmont, Colorado, in 1879, where he continued his education in the Longmont schools.

At this time the country around Longmont was rather well settled. He worked on a farm with his uncle, William Leach. In March 1883 Kelley came to Montrose, which was a little town of log buildings. He went to work for Mr. Cushman, helping with the construction of the Cushman Ditch on California Mesa, which takes water from Dry or "Chapparal Creek."

After the ditch was finished Kelley put in a summer crop for Cushman. Owning two span of mules, he started to freight and for some time hauled supplies between Grand Junction and Glenwood Springs, before the railroad was built, and when there was only one small town, Newcastle, between the two points.

In 1887 he went to Glenwood and engaged in the build-

ing business, after which he came again to California Mesa
and took up land. On this place he lived for twenty years.
He now resides in Montrose.

Joseph Henry Meyer was born in Wilkesbarre, Pennsylvania and lived in that city until he had grown to manhood. He came West to Denver in 1880 and cast his first
vote in that city. He worked in a machine shop in Denver
until the spring of 1885, when he came over the Continental Divide to Montrose, settling on a farm on North
Mesa a few miles north of the town.

Mr. Meyer says that at the time he came to Montrose it
was composed mostly of saloons. He was married to Mary
Albert in Montrose in 1887 and they raised a family on
the North Mesa Ranch, living there for thirty-seven years.
Four sons and two daughters are living now. They are:
Chester P., Joseph H., William A., Albert G., Mrs. Louise
Brady, and Mrs. Minnie Heald.

Mr. Meyer recalls the Chinese riot which took place
while he was in Denver. It seems that the Chinamen had
been taking the work from the white men. They had been
shipped in by railroad companies to work on the new
grades and stayed on to work cheaper than the whites
could do it. In this riot, the houses were burned and looted
and the yellow men handled very roughly. The firemen
turned the hose on the mob and its frenzied members cut
the fire hose to pieces with axes.

Th life of Mr. Meyer has been a rather quiet one. He
has gone his own way and raised his family.

Luther Cassell Kinikin was born near Columbus, Ohio,
September 5, 1866, leaving there with his parents when
he was three years of age for Missouri and Illinois re-
spectively. He came to Telluride, Colorado, in 1891 as
stenographer for Judge Gabbert and when the latter was
elected district judge in 1933, Mr. Kinikin became official
stenographer until 1897 when he was admitted to the bar
of Colorado and to practice in the federal courts.

December 28, 1892, Mr. Kinikin and M. Gertrude Bar-
rick were married at Sedalia, Missouri. They have lived in
Telluride and Montrose since their marriage. Mr. Kinikin

was official stenographer of the People's Party national convention at St. Louis in 1896 when William Jennings Bryan was endorsed for president and Tom Watson for vice-president. He served as city attorney of Telluride for several years, up to and including the period of the Tellurid strike and boycott over the miners' demand for the eight-hour day and the resultant martial law.

In 1910 he engaged in farming for a short period on what has since been called Kinikin Heights, and served as county judge of Montrose County from 1924 to 1932. Before and after being elected county judge, Mr. Kinikin has practiced law in Montrose and adjoining counties.

Lyman Beecher Harsh was born in Havana, Mission County, Illinois, on December 18, 1868. His father had come into Colorado in 1859 with the Pike's Peak gold rush, located two quartz claims, and operated a sawmill for a man named Copeland. Then he went to Iowa to winter his stock, planning to return the following spring. But he did not get back until after the Civil War, when he came out with his son in 1880. The elder Harsh had been in the Central City district, but on his later trip the family settled in Pueblo first, and then went to Silver Cliff.

Lyman Beecher Harsh states that as a boy he made as much as seven dollars a day shining shoes and selling papers on the streets of Silver Cliff and Rosita. At that time, he states, the Sangre de Christo Range was like a pepper box, it had so many prospect holes in its mountain sides.

The father, Alexander, had many experiences with the Indians in the early days. As a boy in Wood County, Ohio, he was stolen by a bunch of Indians and was held from eight o'clock in the morning until eleven at night, when he was rescued by his father. In 1860, Alexander's father started out to Colorado to join his son. At the river crossing between Denver and Loveland, the wagon train he was with met up with another train in which was an old school chum of Mr. Harsh's. The two met and were scuffling in fun. An hour and a half later, the elder Harsh died. He was the first person buried in the big cemetery near the crossing now.

Alexander Harsh built the roof on the Wells-Fargo Building in Denver in 1859. L. B. Harsh went to school with the girl who later became Mrs. Parrish, whose husband was killed a few years ago by the Fleagle gang of outlaws, in the Lamar Bank robbery.

Harsh worked in the mines around Silver Cliff and Rosita, and spent four years in a grocery store. He went to Cripple Creek in 1903, where he also worked in the mines.

He was in the Hole In The Wall country when Marigold was a town and states that cattle thieves were very busy in that country at the time. Almost every hole in the ground had a cow skull in it. One outfit killed a cow in the owner's yard and hung the hide on the fence.

Coming to Montrose in 1905, Harsh settled on a ranch in Spring Creek Canyon, where he has lived since that time.

He recalls many stories his father told of the Indian days on the plains. Once, the wagon train his father was with encountered another train which had been taking whiskey to the Mountain regions. All the white men had been killed by the Indians and there were about three hundred drunk Indians lying around the ruins of the wagons. The men of the last train broke up seven barrels and let the whiskey run out onto the ground and left the drunken Indians where they lay. Indians then followed them for miles begging for more whiskey.

He also recalls an experience he had near a blockhouse at Central City. He was panning gold in a gulch and saw his partner who was working near him start back to the blockhouse. An Indian raised up from hiding nearby and started after the partner. So Harsh followed the Indian. When the partner entered the blockhouse, the Indian turned away and Harsh took a shot at the ground behind the savage. The Indian let out a yell and made tracks for parts unknown.

The elder Harsh told his son that at the time he crossed the plains first, there were thousands of buffalo and they had to drive through the herds.

CHAPTER XVI

CAME TO COLORADO IN '73

Although James Henry Hill has spent much of his life out of the State of Colorado, he is a pioneer of the great Centennial State, for he came into Denver on the Fifth day of July, 1873. Born on the Ohio River near Steubenville, Ohio, in the same house where his father was born and died, and which had been built by his grandfather in 1806, he went to school near there and attended a college at Newmarket for two terms and another college at Hopedale two more terms. After leaving school he worked on the farm until he had grown to manhood, then joined the Westward trek. He rode on the recently-completed Union Pacific Railroad to Cheyenne and the Denver Pacific into the little town of Denver.

The day after his arrival in that city he went to an employment office, or "intelligence office" as it was called then, and secured a job for the Phelps-Biggs Lumber Company, and went up the Platte River about thirty miles and helped build a "bum" dam to impound water to float logs down the river to Denver. This work was completed in October and he returned to Denver. Then with three other men, John Brooks, an old timer who had taken part in the Battle of Sand Creek; J. C. Smith and Ed Briggs, a Wisconsin lumber jack, he returned to the vicinity of the dam and chopped ties until June, getting out about 7400 ties, which they had hauled to the river. They threw the ties into the water above the logs back of the dam and let them go. A log jam occurred at the mouth of the Platte Canyon and they spent two months taking their ties out onto the bank to wait for the high water in the spring. John Brooks died and Ed Briggs went to work in the Pollack Livery Stable. Here Hill stayed until November, when he rolled his blankets and with Smith walked to Empire City, a town of a dozen houses, and chopped cordwood, which they hauled to Georgetown to be sold. While at this job, Mr. Hill cut his ankle rather badly and was on crutches all winter. They secured a contract to deliver wood to the Conqueror Mine, to be used in the boiler fire, and run the timbers down a chute that extended a quarter of a mile down the mountain side. They also worked in the mine and mill and stayed there until the spring of 1876, when they started for the Black Hills by wagon. At Old Fort Laramie they joined a train of 12 wagons and 19 men. The Custer Massacre, which occurred on June 25, 1876, was consumated while they were on the way to the Dakotas.

A band of Indians raided the camp at Hat Creek, attempting to drive away the horses. However, the white men were prepared for them and fired a volley immediately. At Indian Creek, they made a dry camp on an open plain and the Indians attacked again, first shooting at the four scouts who were ahead of the train, and killing one man. The horse was shot from under another and he lay beside his horse until after the fight and escaped unharmed.

Mr. Hill shot one Indian, coming out of an arroya, and probably got others in the course of the battle.

After the battle was over they buried the dead man in the road and drove their teams over the grave to keep the Indians from finding it. However they learned later that the redskins found it, disinterred the body, and in their frenzy, literally cut it to pieces.

The day before this fight the caravan had met Captain Egan and his command mounted on two hundred grey horses. Sitting Bull had boasted that his Indians would soon be riding these grey horses, but they never did.

The men of the wagon train decided that it would be folly to attempt to get into the forbidden territory around the Black Hills, so turned back to Fort Laramie, where Mr. Hill's partner, Smith, enlisted as a packer for General Reno.

With Fred Howe, Hill again returned to Colorado and mined until 1879, then returned to his old home in Ohio, where he spent ten years firing and acting as locomotive engineer, after which he farmed for a while. He spent the years of 1893-94-95 operating a big grain ranch near Los Angeles, California, returned to Ohio in 1895 and was on the farm again until 1911, when he came to Colorado again and settled on the ranch on High Mesa, near Montrose where he has since resided. In Ohio he was bothered by severe hadaches, but has never had one in Colorado.

He was married in 1881 to Lilly R. Neff, and has one daughter, Mrs. Clyde MacGregor, and two sons, Fred and Kenneth.

Mr. Hill recalls a Mrs. Casey, who owned a small ranch in the foothills, near the Platte Canyon. Often, when on his way to Denver after mail and supplies, he would stop at this ranch and listen to Mrs. Casey tell of Davy Crockett. She would say: "Davy and I were little fellows together."

The first cabin he built on the Platte was where Gunbarrel Creek runs into the river. Mr. Hill named the creek, when one of the men with him found an old muzzle-loading gun barrel there, and it has since retained that name. John Muir built the first cabin in that vicinity and Hill helped in the construction of the second, third and fourth houses to be built on the river thereabouts.

Robert McKeen Ormsby was born on the banks of Cherry Creek, near Denver, Colorado, on the thirteenth day of June, 1868, the son of McKeen and Mary Adeline Ormsby. For several years the family lived on Cherry Creek and Mr. Ormsby recalls two different times when there were Indian scares and the whole family was bundled up and hurried into the little city of Denver. The elder Ormsby then returned alone to do some scouting. However, these were only scares and the Indians never molested the family.

In 1874, at the age of six years, Mr. Ormsby went with his family into the Wet Mountain Valley, which at that time held three post offices. One of these was at Ula, another at Legert and the third at Colfax. Today there are no towns on the sites of these old settlements. McKeen

Ormsby established the first saloon in Ula, and during his residence there he held the offices of constable, sheriff, and deputy sheriff. In later years, he received a pension from the State of California for his activities as an Indian scout.

Those were exciting days in the Wet Mountain Valley, and Mr. Ormsby recalls seeing a mob kill a man named Graham, riddling the latter's body with a hundred and twenty-five shots. Graham was mobbed for holding a mine on a bogus deed. The same day the town of Rosita was cleaned out by a Vigilance Committee. Two bankers, Boyd and Stewart, and about forty other citizens were run out of town. That night a woman named Her held off the mob with two six shooters while her husband made his getaway. This same woman, as a girl, had discovered the Pocahontas Mine.

Another time, Ormsby saw a man named Amison killed by one Jim Moore, in a fight over a Little Topay stove. He also recalls an Englishman by the name of Whuert, who left a thousand dollars with Ormsby's mother one night, as he was afraid he would be robbed. The next morning he started out to return to England to claim an estate and got as far as Boneyard Hill, and was never seen again, although years later a skeleton was discovered near there, and was thought to have been the unfortunate Englishman, who was probably murdered.

Mr. Ormsby worked in the ore mills at Bassick and at one time, he states, was receiving $125 a month and board.

He was in Leadville before the railroad was built to that place. For a time he waited tables in the camp at Leadville. Once, here he saw a marshal shoot two men in three minutes. Another time, he went on the gold rush to Williams Creek, where thousands of people stampeded when false assay returns were sent out. Finally, one of the miners ground up and mortared a water jug and sent it to the assayer, who reported that it would run $150 to the ton in gold. Thus were the false reports run down, and a mine sale of $150,000 halted.

Mr. Ormsby says that every time he went to Salida he saw some excitement. One time in that town he saw five men killed, four of them being members of a gang of desperadoes and the other a town marshal. Six months later, to the day, he was in Salida again and saw Baxter Stingley, another marshal, shot by Frank Reed, who was a member of the same gang of outlaws that had killed the first marshal.

Another time, while in Salida with a freight outfit, he saw a man, while drunk, kill a twelve year old boy. The man was caught by a mob and thrown out of his bedroom window, with his head tied to the bedstead, so that his neck was broken.

Robert McKeen Ormsby was married in Folsom, New Mexico, to Miss Minnie Donnell and to this union nine children were born. Seven of these are still living and they raised one grandchild. The living children are: Mrs. L. Seevers, Mrs. John E. Smith, Mrs. Cleo Culver, Robert, Vernon, Cecil and Oliver and the grandson is Harvey Dopp.

Together, Mr. and Mrs. Ormsby have driven four times across the plains of New Mexico and Oklahoma in a covered wagon. Once in Kansas, when one of the little girls was sick with whooping cough, Mr. Ormsby had to use a shotgun twice to force the farmers to sell him some milk. He was working in a store in Folsom when the outlaw, Black Jack, was killed, the latter being hung after a train robbery. He recalls that once he sold the same Black Jack a mule and immediately after the sale, the desperado hit the mule in the head with an axe.

While herding cattle on the South Canadian River, a herd of 4000 head stampeded and were scattered in a storm. Ormsby came in with thirty head alone, hours after the stampede. The foreman of the ranch carried twenty-seven notches in his gun. This man was named Cook and as a U. S. marshal, together with another marshal named Zeb Russell, attempted to run the Mexicans out of the Maxwell Grant on the Colorado-New Mexico line. Cook and Russell had worked on the Jinglebob Ranch, where Billy the Kid and Sam Bass got their start years before.

In earlier days, while in Westcliffe, Ormsby was a deputy marshal, and in two years, while he was in office, there was one man in jail. A while before this there were on an average of two shooting scrapes a week in the same town.

In 1910 he moved to Montrose and has lived in this town since that time. During his residence in Montrose, he has engaged in concrete work, and at the time of this writing is living a retired life with his family.

John William McCaw was born in Pike County, Illinois, January 30, 1855, and lived in various parts of that state throughout his childhood. His mother was a widow and her son had to forego the advantages of education and work to help support the family. He engaged in team work, farming, etc. He has always been an enthusiast over good race horses and has owned a few himself.

In September of 1879, Mr. McCaw came west, settling for a time in Longmont, Colorado. There he met Dan Kelley, who is now located in the city of Montrose. The two have been friends for more than fifty years. Together, they hauled baled hay for Alf Cushman, prominent rancher of the Longmont district.

In 1908 John McCaw came into the Uncompahgre Valley and secured one hundred acres of land in the Pea Green district. Nine or ten years of his life were spent in the San Luis Valley. Part of this time, he drove a freight outfit between Villa Grove and Saguache and the rest of the time he operated a butcher shop in the latter town.

He was married to Mrs. Alice Buchanan and the couple had no children. Mrs. McCaw died in April, 1933, leaving her husband, a son in New York and a daughter in New Jersey.

Once while hauling flag stones from Lyons to Longmont to be shipped to Denver, he met a woman on horseback who was riding furiously to give the alarm of Indians on the warpath. The redskins attacked a schoolhouse, killed one little girl and ravished the school teacher.

In the boom days of Leadville, McCaw hauled bailed hay from Longmont to that city, and sold it for $100 a ton and sold oats for six and eight cents a pound. At this time there were thousands of teams and freight outfits, and a police patrol man was engaged to guard the immense piles of freight that were hauled into the famous camp.

The policeman once entered the board bank at eleven o'clock at night and cashed checks for $150 for a man who was in a hurry to get his money. Dogs and deer and other animals ran at large in the streets of Leadville and McCaw once saw a dead man lying in the road where he had been shot—and most of the people thought he was asleep or dead drunk.

He recalls that once in Saguache, he and his brother had a mean mule, which they were attempting to ride. The animal ran down in front of a church, where services were in progress, and fell in the street. For half an hour they tried to get the beast onto his feet and finally the sheriff came and told them they would have to move on as they were getting a larger crowd than the preacher, so they hitched a team of horses to the mule and dragged it away.

On a ditching contract with one G. T. Hansen, McCaw was sent into the mountains to haul wood, which was placed on the line of the ditch and burned to thaw out the frozen ground.

James Francis Walsh was born in Quincy, Massachusetts on January 6, 1848. There he attended school, and then entered the Hinckley & Williams Locomotive Works as a machinist. In 1872 he took a job in the Lake Superior Iron Mines, as a locomotive repair man.

When the panic came in 1873, Walsh went to Old Mexico, where he helped build the first American Experimental Copper Smelter, for the Butcher & Campbell Drug firm of Philadelphia, then the leading druggists of the United States. With the smelter they were only able to get two and one half pounds of copper from a twenty-five hundred pound charge, and they had to haul their coal seventyfive miles, and burn mesquite timber also. The smelter was abandoned and in 1877 Walsh came north to Denver, and then came over to the LaSal Mountains, where he has spent much time prospecting and locating mines. Mr. Walsh said that he located the Cashin Mine and the Big Indian on LaSal Creek, and sold them to the Mormons.

When Lemuel Hecox was murdered at the Cashin in about 1920, he took the watchman's place at the mine.

Walsh worked in the machine shops of the iron mines at Sunrise, Wyoming, and helped keep five engines in commission to haul the ore to Pueblo. He also worked for John I. Mullen in the Marvel Mine of the Standard Chemical Company. He stated that he engaged in simple, ordinary successful mining. He is now deceased.

Sterling Samuel Sherman was born October 22, 1852, at Hebron, New York, being in his 84th year at the time of his passing. His ancestors came to America in 1732 and he was one of the same line of Shermans that produced the famous General Sherman of the Civil war, being a distant cousin of the general.

Judge Sherman was the son of Jesse Seeley and Lucinda Woodard Sherman. The father was a farmer and in 1858 moved to Monroe's Meadows, taking his family with him. In 1868 the elder Sherman traded his farm there for another near Salem. This farm had 265 acres of land, a sawmill, flax mill and potato starch mill.

Sterling went to school in North Hebron and Salem and attended the Washington county academy from which he graduated in January, 1872. He took a year's postgraduate course there. He had a desire to become a civil engineer and his father sent him to Zurick, Switzerland, where he went to school for nine months. Then a number of young Americans at the school decided to move to Karlsruhe, Germany, for further study. Here Sherman attended the Polytechnic university, studying civil engineering. He was a classmate of Marion Crawford, the writer, and others who became famous in various lines, including Theodore Brintana, who was a prominent Chicago judge for 20 years and at one time American minister to Hungary.

He returned home in March, 1875, taught school for a year and then went into the law office of Judge James Gibson where he studied law for three years, took the bar examination and was admitted to the New York bar in November, 1879. In December of the same year he came to Lake City and went into the office of Judge N. B. Gerry

and was with the judge for a year and then practiced alone
for a time. When he came to Colorado, the railroad was
built only to Alamosa and Sherman rode astride a pile of
mail on a sleigh from Alamosa to Lake City. They arrived
in Lake City December 30, with the thermometer at 40 below zero.

Judge Sherman was admitted to practice law before
the Colorado Bar association in January, 1880. On October
27, 1882, he was married to Mary Elizabeth Masters, of
Schaghticoke, New York, at Del Norte.

Lake City was a boom mining town then. The late John
C. Bell was practicing law there. With the decline of that
camp, Sherman moved to Delta in 1884 where he practiced
law and was mayor of the city in 1887-88.

A son, Sterling Samuel, was born in Lake City September 22, 1883, but died in Montrose, January 17, 1890.

Judge Sherman moved to Montrose in December, 1888,
and went into partnership with F. C. Goudy. The year
1888 saw Judge Bell elected as district judge and his retiring from the firm of Bell and Goudy left a vacancy. Sherman was invited to become a partner of Goudy, which he
did. The first year after coming to Montrose, Mr. Sherman
and family lived in the W. O. Redding house on Main street
but in 1889 he bought the place where he resided until his
death, at Uncompahgre and North Third St.

Judge Sherman was connected with a number of law
firms in Montrose. He was with Goudy for eight years.
Then when Goudy went to Denver, Sherman took L. F.
Twitchell into the office. Later Twitchell joined Goudy in
Denver and Ben Griffith became the partner of Mr. Sherman. This partnership existed for three years and Griffith
moved to Grand Junction. Frank Ross was his next partner and he also went to Denver. The next partnership was
consummated in 1907 when Judge Sherman met a young
attorney, just out of college and looking for a location.
Sherman invited him to share his office in Montrose. C. J.
Moynihan remained with Judge Sherman three or four
years and then embarked in the law business for himself.

In 1908 Judge Sherman's son, Edward M., having finished his law studies, became associated with his father. They were together until the retirement of the elder Sherman in 1916 when he became county judge, being re-elected four years later, serving altogether eight years.

Judge Sherman is survived by two sons, Edward M. Sherman of Montrose and Henry S. Sherman of Denver. He also had three sisters and two brothers: Mrs. D. R. Haskins, Granville, N. Y.; Mrs. William M. Brown, Starkey, Idaho; Mrs. John M. Flack, Omaha; William A. Sherman, Salem, N. Y., and Daniel E. Sherman.

Judge Sherman was a member of all the Masonic bodies in Montrose and also Denver Shrine. He had held offices of master in the Blue lodge, high priest in the Chapter and Commander in the Commandery, the latter for seven years in succession. He was a 32nd degree Mason, being a member of Denver Consistory No. 1.

Judge Sherman was signally honored by his fellow men, having held many offices of trust and responsibility. He was elected county judge in 1920 and 1924, president of the Montrose County Bar association continuously from November 1888 to 1916—28 years; attorney for Delta and Montrose Canal Co. for 20 years; attorney for First National Bank of Montrose in 1920 and from 1924 until he retired; served as mayor of Delta, city attorney, county attorney and county judge of Montrose. He was a member of the legal advisory board for Montrose during the war, member of selective service board for Montrose and chairman of the Liberty Loan committee of Montrose.

Judge Sherman lived a long and useful life. He was an able and capable attorney and took part in many important cases. He was a man of high convictions and ideals. He was always dignified and an honor to the bar. However he cared little for show and abhorred sham and ostentation. It was fitting that the funeral rites were held at the Addington Mortuary chapel in the very building in which he spent most of his life and on the very site where he did spend most of his time in Montrose as he had an office in a small building for years before the present Sherman building was erected.

Frank Warmand England was born in Pittsburg, Pennsylvania, on August 4, 1859. He lived there for seventeen years going to school at the Iron City Business College and Duff's College. He came into Denver in 1879, went from there to Leadville, then to Gunnison and Crested Butte, where he lived most of the time for the past fifty years. He engaged in the painting and paperhanging business and indulged in a little mining.

He made a trip to Leadville, Grand Junction and Montrose in 1909. He was in Ouray when the Indians were taken out of the valley, and his first recollection of Montrose is of a bunch of sod houses up by the railroad wye.

He remembered that on a trip from Gothic to the Muddy country he and his companions met a bunch of Indians, who asked them if they had seen "any cayuses" (horses).

The first saloon in Crested Butte was built while he was there. There were three pine trees, where the freight wagons unloaded. One of these was felled and split to make a bar, and the men pulled a barrel of whiskey off the wagon, and all hunted cans to drink out of. The drinks were sold at 25c each.

He remembers also when a snow slide killed the two Welch brothers on "Oh Be Joyful" Creek. The men of the community moved tons of snow in an attempt to find them, but they were not uncovered until the following summer. The slide occurred in December, on Christmas Eve, and the two men were found together on the 26th of July. When they were buried the workmen had to dip the water out of the grave, and it ran up over the coffins as soon as they were placed in the grave.

When Eaton was running for governor, England was working on the new railway to the Smith Mine at the Mouth of "Oh Be Joyful." The governor received 450 votes from one community, and it was discovered that the bartender was the only man there.

When they were building the railroad to Irvin, two Italians were warming some dynamite in the blacksmith shop. The stuff exploded and all they found of the two

Italians was buried in a cracker box. This was in 1883.

Mr. England was married to Mary Swan in Crested Butte in 1886. He has one son, Howard Arden England, living in LaGrande, Oregon. He has seen the "jack whackers" or "burro punchers" come into the town of Crested Butte and shoot out the lights. Once when this happened he and another man crawled under the pool table and then went out the back door so fast that they both went into the creek, which ran very close to the building.

One bad man had a habit of walking up the street shooting at other people's feet. Someone shot him from across the street once, and no one ever found out who did it. They probably did not want to know.

Once when he was on a scaffold, painting the city hall, this same bad man shot up "White Dog Lizzie's" place, across the street. England climbed down off his scaffold and fled into a saloon for protection from flying bullets.

Micky Hampton is not a pioneer of Western Colorado, but since coming here in 1911 has won considerable local fame as a hunter and trapper. He was born in Cherokee County, North Carolina, on January 20, 1879, lived on a ranch there until he was seventeen, going to school at the Belleview High School.

When he was seventeen he went with a colony of North Carolinans and Georgians into Missouri and farmed near Springfield for nearly three years. Then he returned to North Carolina and brought his mother and father back to Missouri. He lived there for four more years and came to Montrose, Colorado, June 25, 1911. The day he landed here he got a job at the Wiggins Ranch in the Uncompahgre district. He pre-empted a place near there, under the proposed extension to the Hairpin Ditch, but it never materialized and Hampton spent two years irrigating on the home ranch of W. P. Price on Bostwick Park.

In 1914 he took up a place at the Cimarron headgate and rode ditch for the Cimarron Canal and Reservoir Company, making the trip on horseback between the headgate and the reservoir on Cerro Summit. He became a hunter and trapper in the year 1916, and killed his first bear near the Hampton Lake, which received its name at that time.

The day he killed this bear, he was hunting with Roy Atkinson and Erdie Heyden. They separated and in about fifteen minutes, Hampton surprised a bear and shot it at a distance of about two hundred yards. The wounded animal rolled down the hill and Roy Atkinson came near running into it. The latter's hound was afraid of the bear and beat it over the back trail. It took them about twenty minutes to find the dog and get it back onto the bear's track, but after he regained his nerve, he chased the bear up onto a big boulder and Micky shot it. Heyden then said: "We'll call this Hampton Lake," and this name it has kept since that time.

A while before he had this experience, he shot at a bear with a six shooter. He had come upon the bear suddenly and the animal had reared up on his hind legs and charged him. He stunned it with the first shot, and the bear rolled down the hill scratching the aspens as it went. It landed against a tree, coughed, and got up and ran. The next day Micky tracked it for seven hours, but never did find the brute.

The largest bear he ever shot weighed about eight hundred pounds and was killed two miles southeast of the headgate of the Cimarron ditch. Coming upon an old carcass that had been freshly eaten on by the bear, he took up its trail and shot the animal after a short chase.

Micky had quite an exciting time with another bear on the Cimarron. He had set a trap in a sheep camp, attempting to get the animal that had been killing sheep. He caught the bear and Bruin dragged the log that was chained to the trap up into a tall tree, and fell out of the tree. When Hampton arrived on the scene, the bear made for him with a snort, swinging the trap from side to side as he came. The peep sight on the man's rifle was out of line and the first two shots missed. He pulled down low and saw the hair fly from the top of the bear's head. So he pulled the gun down some more and, when the bear was about ten feet away from him, shot it in the tip of the nose.

Micky Hampton says that the female bears are worse

to handle than the males. They are meaner. Many times he saw signs of a big grizzly that spent the winters on the Cimarron, but never got a shot at him.

'He was after a bear one day and came to a boggy place. He got off to lead his horse across the bog and as he climbed up onto a big log, he almost laid his hand on Mr. Bear, who was on the opposite side of the log. He turned, grabbed his gun out of the holster on his saddle and shot the beast dead.

In the years he has been trapping, Mr. Hampton has killed six hundred coyotes and wildcats, the coyotes bringing an average price of $8 a hide, and the cats $4 apiece. He has killed 125 marten, which averaged about $30 each. The marten are coming back, but are in the high mountains where trapping is extremely dangerous, and a man would have to average $80 or $90 a day to make it pay.

Miriam White Gravestock Loper was born on a farm in Galia County, Ohio, on April 30, 1860. She lived at home and assisted with the farm work until she was nineteen years of age, when she came to Colorado with her uncle John Weed.

She lived in Canon City from 1880 to 1884. She was married in 1881 to John G. Gravestock, who was a farmer in the Canon City district and owned thirty acres of what is now the town of Canon City. The two had seven children, two of whom are still living. They are: Thurston, of San Francisco, and John Edwin, of Amarillo, Texas.

In 1885 Mr. and Mrs. Gravestock settled on a farm on Spring Creek, near Maple Grove. They owned the ranches now belonging to Squirrel and Sherman. They built a house on Spring Creek. At one time, while they were building the house, Thurston, then a small child, fell through the ice into Spring Creek and his sister, Bertha, sat down on the ice and held on to him, all the while screaming for assistance. The father and uncle, George White, came running and pulled the lad out of the creek.

Mr. Gravestock died in 1901 and his widow was married to Eli Loper in 1903, and they had one son, Wesley, now of Montrose. Mr. Loper is now deceased.

An incident that Mrs. Loper recalled is the death of thirteen cows and a bull, which occurred on the ranch, the deaths being due to eating poison weeds. They had just paid $250.00 for the bull so the loss was felt keenly.

Mrs. Loper died a couple of years ago, in Montrose.

CHAPTER XVII

EARLY DAYS

Edward A. Krisher came to Leadville, Colorado, in 1882 and worked for a time in various mines of the district, the Robert E. Lee, the Evening Star and others. He says that at that time, Leadville was a wild, wide-open, crazy town. One of his outstanding memories of the Leadville days is the hanging of Si Minick on February 5, 1886. Minick had murdered a fellow and robbed him so that he could buy seal skin coats. His wife married another man a half hour after her husband was executed. Thus she had a bunch of new clothes and a new husband so all was well.

Everything was wide open and all the people wanted to spend their money, and there were plenty of professional gamblers to take it away from them.

In 1886, Mr. Krisher went to Kingston, New Mexico. In August of '87 he came up to Silverton and then climbed over the mountains to Telluride. Then in the fall of '87 he went to Ouray, where for many years he was connected with the mining game. For seventeen years he was foreman of the Revenue Mine, above the Camp Bird. He states that the mine produced in the neighborhood of $14,000,000 in silver and lead, but that it was worked out some years ago. The Revenue was a very deep mine, the depth being about 3500 feet from the highest to the lowest workings. It was owned by A. E. Reynolds, Thatcher Brothers, and the Havemeyers and was a closed corporation, no stock being put on the market.

Mr. Krisher was in many rescue parties seeking to recover the bodies of snow slide victims. One time, an Irishman named Billy Maher was killed by an explosion at a cabin at an elevation of about 13,000 above sea level. The rescue party had a very difficult time getting the man down from the mountain. Four men were sent from the Virginius Mine to assist in getting him down, and they were swept to their deaths by a slide. They were found standing with their arms held up in the air.

Mr. Krisher tells us that Gene Perroti and another man were swept a thousand feet down the mountain side, and lived to tell of it. A number of men were killed in the same slide and were not found for two years, although two men were sent from the Virginius Mine to look for them every day. He says that a mail carrier was swept down by a slide, and dug himself out. He was carrying a shovel when he was struck and he held on to the tool and was able to dig out. Joe Emerson was suffocated by a slide in Yankee Boy Basin.

Krisher remembers the slide that killed twenty-eight horses and five men. One horse was thrown thirty feet, but was found standing on the slide, still in harness.

He also recalls the time when five Swedes were dropped 1100 feet to their deaths, in an accident in the Virginius Mine, when the cage was dropped down the shaft, without being hooked to the reel. Their bodies were terribly crushed and jammed and Krisher was the first man to reach the scene.

A slide swept a cabin down at the Ruby Trust Mine. The men in the cabin escaped but the cat went down with it. Thirty-two days later, when the snow had melted, the cat walked out alive, somewhat lean, but otherwise none the worse for the experience. A similar accident occurred in Aspen, when a dog was under a slide for thirty days and came out alive.

The three Hotchkiss brothers came into Colorado at a very early date. They were in the Lake City region as early as 1874, when they discovered the Hotchkiss Mine, which later became the Golden Fleece. Enos Hotchkiss was in Lake City, and in about 1873 or 1874 Preston came over and established a store in the town of Portland a few miles below Ouray. There his brother Roswell joined him and there on the ninth of July, 1876, was born Edgar Alvinza

Hotchkiss, the son of Preston, who was the first white child born in Ouray county.

Besides his store, Preston Hotchkiss was engaged in the lumber and cattle businesses. He furnished the first lumber for the buildings in Ouray. He had sawmills in Happy Hollow, south of Ridgway, and on Horsefly. E. A. Hotchkiss went to school one year in Portland and lived in the sawmill camps in the summer time. He has lived in Colona since 1883.

E. A. Hotchkiss and his brothers are famous as bear and mountain lion hunters. One winter they caught thirty-six mountain lions. They got two in one day, just four miles from home.

William Rathmell of Ouray was a teacher in the Portland school, as were Hilliard Smith and a man named Higgins.

Bessie Allen Bickford Meyers was born in Lepolorita, New Mexico, and when she was five weeks old her parents came into Colorado by ox team. She was born on April 25, 1880, and was the daughter of Charles W. and Sarah Deval Allen. First coming into Pueblo, they stayed there a short time and then came over to Montrose in 1882.

Arriving in the Uncompahgre Valley, the elder Allen cleared away the sage brush to make a place for his tent, on the place that he later homesteaded near Happy Canyon. Mrs. Meyers stills owns forty acres of this ranch.

Fort Crawford was in its heyday at this time and all the settlers went there to celebrate the fourh of July and other occasions.

Mrs. Meyers was married first on September 26, 1900, to Albert C. Bickford, and to them four children were born. These are: Allen, Clarence, Morris and Mrs. Heman Getty of Montrose. Mr. Bickford was an engineer on the Rio Grande Southern Railroad and was killed in a railroad wreck, three miles from Telluride, when the train he was driving went through a bridge.

Mrs. Bickford was later married to Louis Meyers and they have one daughter, Miss Phyllis, who was born in the old Chief Ouray adobe house on January 20th, 1918, before the old house was torn down to make way for the present home of the Meyers family. The old adobe barn still stands on the place today.

Jack Scates was born in Tyrone County, Ireland, September 9, 1871. The family came to America when Jack was a small boy and arrived in Colorado Springs on June 16, 1873, going from there to Leadville and then Fairplay, where the father operated a store in 1875. Jack went to school in the South Park. He remembers when the Indians killed Mr. Marksbury and also Old Man Elliott, when the Utes were on their last buffalo hunting expedition on the plains.

During his lifetime, Scates has worked in the mines in Cripple Creek, Leadville, Telluride, Creede, Ouray, Silverton and other camps in the state. He was in Cripple Creek when there were only two cabins there.

Peter A. Hiebler was one of the early sawmill operators of southwestern Colorado, having operated sawmills in various parts of this section. He spent most of his time around Montrose, although the family spent twelve years in Montezuma County, near Mancos. He operated retail lumber yards in Mancos, Montrose and Denver.

He also spent some time in the mining game, near Ouray, where he had a lease on the Old Governor Mine, which was owned by an English company.

Thomas John McKelvey was born in Ontario, Canada, April 1, 1870. He lived in Canada for twenty years and attended the public schools of that Province, also attending high school in Calcedonia, Canada.

He came to Denver in 1890 and states that at that time one could see the Albany Hotel from the depot. He worked in the accounting office of the Union Pacific, and then took a position as telegraph operator for the Denver, Fort Worth and Texas Railway, working at this for four or five months. He also held the position of telegraph operator at the station on LaVeta Pass the same year where he was also the station agent.

Coming to Silverton in November of 1891 he was operator for the D. & R. G. Railway and also worked in the office in Red Mountain, being connected with Otto Mear's Red Mountain Railway at this place. This line was long ago abandoned. McKelvey was well acquainted with Otto Mear's superintendent, Moses Liverman, who died and was succeeded by Alec Anderson. The Red Mountain Railroad was built in 1888, and was one of the highest railroads in the World. It was a very difficult road to keep in operation because of the deep snow and snow slides in the winter. Some of the big mines that were operating at this time were the Yankee Girl, the Guston, the Silver Belle, and at Ironton the Genessee-Vanderbilt.

Mr. McKelvey remembers when the whole town of Red Mountain burned. Every building in the town was consumed by the fire. Some of the merchants in Red Mountain at this time were: Humphries and Green, clothiers, Frank Roper, who operated a restaurant. George Seaman was operating the Red Mountain Journal. There were the usual saloons, hotels, restaurants, etc., that make up the business section of the mountain mining camp.

The big fire in Red Mountain occurred about 1905 and after that Mr. McKelvey worked for a time in the General Office of the D. & R. G. in Silverton until the railroad was started to Animas Forks. This camp had been built up considerably in the past, but at the time McKelvey went there most of the buildings were deserted. He established a store in the best of these and ran it for five years. Bill Kinney of the Gold King Mine at Gladstone built a million dollar mill for the Gold Prince at Animas Forks and built a tram line from the mine to the town of Animas Forks. Rasmus Hansen was operating the Old San Juan Chief Mine at this time. Mr. McKelvey said that Animas Forks was a nice little village and a pleasant place to live.

In 1910, in company with Al Sams, Ben Pond, Herman Stroble and Ned Carmichael, McKelvey went to Salmon City, Idaho, and bought a big ranch, where he lived until 1912, when he went to Great Falls, Montana, later going to Judith Pass, where he worked on the railroad for six months.

Coming to Montrose, Colorado, in 1913, he became a

part owner in the Lathrop Hardware Company with Bert Nymeyer, Herbert Ross and I. O. McIntyre. He was connected with this firm until 1927, when he sold out and went to Buffalo, spending five years in that city and various parts of Canada. He returned to Montrose in 1932 and until his death was connected wtih the Rose-Arctic Ice Cream Company, in the capacity of bookkeeper.

March Addington was born in Gainesville, Georgia, in 1840. He came into Colorado and settled at St. Mary's, Huerfano County, shortly after the Civil War, in 1869, and for years took an active part in affairs in Southern Colorado. He was in Walsenburg, before the railroad was built to that point. He had served under General Robert E. Lee in the Confederate Army in the Civil War, and was married in Gainesville, in 1866, to Sarah E. Butts.

Mr. Addington passed away December 26, 1927, at the age of eighty-five years. However, the family still holds the memory of some of his deeds. He had many battles with the Indians in the early days, having been a mail carrier in 1870, and carrying mail between Walsenburg and Gardner. One time he encountered Chief Ouray, when the latter came into Gardner with a bunch of other Indians. The famous chief told the white settlers not to be afraid as his tribe was peaceful.

When March Addington came to Denver first in 1869, there was no town at the present site of the city, but only a small settlement on Cherry Creek nearby. He went into the Wet Mountain Valley in 1872, when Rosita and Silver Cliff were booming. The latter town had about 30,000 people and was about to become the capital of the State of Colorado.

Mr. Addington helped dig the first grave in the Gardner cemetery. It was dug for one Grandma Hudson. He was carrying mail during the smallpox plague, in which several hundred people died. For a time he operated a livery stable in Rosita. In 1885, Mr. Addington killed Huerfano's worst bad man, Toll Caldwell, for insulting one of Addington's daughters at a dance. The man was killed with a fifteen cent pocket knife.

William Fenlon Diehl was born November 28, 1847, at Hartleton, Pennsylvania. His wife, Anna Johnson Diehl, was born July 19, 1864, at Three Rivers, Michigan. She was taken by her parents to Lewistown, Pennsylvania, at a very early age and there lived until she had gone through school and married. She came as a bride to Montrose in 1888, arriving the day before Christmas. Her husband had preceded her to Montrose in 1885 and then returned for her. Mr. Diehl, better known as "Studebaker Bill," established a blacksmith shop on what was then First Street in Montrose.

R. C. Diehl, a brother of William F., had come into Montrose in the early eighties. He had planned on going to Grand Junction, but, arriving in Montrose, he was offered two lots, where the Busy Corner Drug Store and Warner's Variety Store are today. So he stayed in Montrose. His wife homesteaded the Jim Brown ranch at the north edge of that town. R. C. came in by wagon before the railroad was built and shortly after the Indians were taken out of the valley. His wife was one of the first twelve women in Montrose, some of the others who can be recalled being: Mrs. Willerup, Mrs. George Smith, Mrs. Bowersock, Mrs. Charlie Zaun, Mrs. Fendel and Mrs. Gus Frost.

On establishing himself in Montrose, R. C. Diehl sent back to Hays City, Kansas, for his partner, A. E. Buddecke, who then came here. The two men bought the stock of A. E. Reynolds in Lake City and established a store in a building which they constructed on their corner lot. They did such a heavy credit business that in 1886, the grocery department failed and was taken over by W. W. Robinson, while Buddecke and Diehl kept the dry goods department.

This firm also carried on a rather extensive freighting business, hauling supplies to Telluride. They built the Buddecke & Diehl road over Log Hill Mesa.

For a time R. C. Diehl was assistant postmaster at the log cabin post office near where the Catholic Church now stands. At this time the soldiers were at Fort Crawford and the money for their pay was sent in by Thatcher

Brothers. This was in bills, rolled up with an envelope around them and tied with string. On these occasions, Mr. Diehl had to stay up all night and guard the cash.

When Mrs. William F. Diehl came to Montrose there were no sidewalks and when she went out in the mud she often lost her shoes. There were no electric lights and the water was taken from ditches running from the river. There were street lamps but the man in charge often forgot to light them. Chris Henderson, former Montrose blacksmith, came into Montrose on foot and worked for Wm. F. Diehl, as did H. M. McCafferty, father of Dr. Ross C. McCafferty, of Montrose, who later invented the McCafferty Marker now widely used by the farmers.

William F. Diehl dug the second well in Montrose near his home, which, incidentally, was on First Street but was nearer to 22nd Street than it was to Third Street, according to an old map of Montrose. At this time the water from the Uncompahgre was filthy with sewage, mine tailings and alkali.

R. C. Diehl owned the Opera House, which is now the State Armory. The first show presented there featured Effie Esler, one of the famous actresses of the day, and the tickets were five dollars each.

Once when Joe R. Brown and William F. Diehl were irrigating a piece of ground, Rev. A. D. Fairbanks came along and shouted at them: "My God, we'll all be in jail. You are washing out the railroad."

W. F. Diehl dug the ditch and put in the first pipe line down Cascade Avenue to North Third Street, and also owned the first bath tub, built of tin and wood, which was in popular demand at the time.

Mrs. Diehl had come from a modern home and wanted luxuries and this first bath tub was a luxury. Half the people in Montrose came to the Diehl home to take baths. She also had the first rubber-tired baby buggy for her son, Charles W.

For many years Wm. F. Diehl had a big business in blacksmithing and the sale of Studebaker wagons and carriages. People would come all the way from Paradox and Moab, Utah, to do business with him. His old blacksmith shop still stands near the old home where the widow and Charles live today.   Mr. Diehl died April 24, 1925.

A. E. Buddecke and R. C. Diehl got out the timbers for the big flume built by an English syndicate below the Club Ranch on the San Miguel.

There were at one time five Diehl brothers in Montrose. R. C., Wm. F., Caleb, who operated a grocery, bakery and meat store, Sam, a carriage painter, and Henry, a tinner, who was town marshal in 1886.

Charles W. Diehl, son of William F., is in Montrose at present with his mother.   He is a graduate of the Dunwoody Industrial School of Minneapolis, Minnesota, where he took a course in scientific cooking and baking.   He has been head cook and baker at some of the largest mines in the San Juan, including the Sunnyside, Tomboy, Atlas and Smuggler.   He was also a student in the Bernarr McFadden Physical Culture Training School in 1908 and 1909, and trained with Jack Dempsey, when the former champ lived in Montrose.

No two citizens of Western Colorado were more prominent in the development of the cattle and sheep industries of this great section of the state than Jesse and Jim O'Neill. These two brothers passed away a number of years ago, but the accounts of their lives have been preserved in newspaper clippings, taken from the Montrose papers at the time of their passing, Jesse in 1921 and Jim a short time thereafter.

Apparently the birthplace of these two pioneers has been lost to us, for the clippings do not tell that, nor do they tell when the brothers were born.   However, their early lives were spent on the plains of Kansas.   As a boy Jesse O'Neill joined the United States Army and became a bugler in the commands of General Nelson A. Miles and General George A. Custer, and took part in various engagements against the Sioux Indians in the seventies.   It was Jesse O'Neill that led the regular army, as a scout, onto the battlefield to recover the body of General Custer, after the famous massacre in 1876, in which the general and his entire command lost their lives.

In one of his Indian battles, Jesse O'Neill fell severely

wounded. He was taken to a hospital boat frozen in the
ice in the Missouri river. He lay for weeks without medical aid, for the army was badly scattered and demoralized.

In the last days of his life, Jesse O'Neill told many interesting experiences of the days of the Indian wars. He
gave a good description of the battle of the Little Big Horn.
He had been shot by the redskins many times. Once he
was shot in the hip and his leg broken. The outfit was far
from any medical aid and he was strapped to the back of
a mule, where he lay suffering untold agonies for forty-
eight hours, until they reached headquarters. Then he lay
in stick splints for weeks before the bones had knit together so that they could be removed. Then for a long
time he was on crutches. Always thereafter, Jesse O'Neill
walked with a limp. He never received a pension for his
services in the army.

Jesse O'Neill also spent some time as a buffalo hunter
and frontiersman, as well as a freighter. Jim, his brother,
was a freighter hauling supplies from Dodge City to Adobe
Walls and Camp Supply, and other points farther west. It
was in 1878 that the two brothers came into Colorado.
They freighted the supplies for the building of the railroad
to Salida, then to Gunnison, then hauled supplies from the
end of the railroad to Montrose, Ouray, Telluride, keeping
ahead of the rails, until the tracks reached the last out-
posts. Then they went into business in Ridgway, later selling out and acquiring extensive cattle holdings. They were
successful in the cow business and emmassed considerable
wealth.

They sold out their cattle and bought sheep, which they
held for some time, later selling these and retiring from
the active business of stock raising.

CHAPTER XVIII

THE STORY OF YOUNG JACKSON

Young Jackson was a freighter who drove a freight team into the Uncompahgre Valley from Saguache. At the age of twenty-one years he met a sad fate at the hands of a bunch of renegade Utes. The mystery of his death is still unsolved.

It seems that Jackson had made many trips into the valley and often stopped at the Hotchkiss home to get fresh milk, butter and bread, and on these trips he always brought some candy for the little girl, Rosa Hotchkiss.

On one of his trips, in fact, the last trip he ever made into this valley, he had just arrived at the Government Springs and was unhitching his tired mules. Some Indians came into his camp and insisted on Jackson giving them food. He had just enough to last him for the trip and was not much in favor of feeding a bunch of hungry Utes. However, he told them to wait until he had the team cared for.

One of the Indians started to climb into the wagon and Jackson told him to get down. The redskin said: "Me shoot." But Jackson beat him to it and shot at the Indian. The bullet struck some part of the wagon and glanced, wounding the Ute in one hand. This made the rest of the Indians mad and Jackson leaped onto his saddle mule and made a dash for Fort Crawford, arriving there just ahead of a band of furious Utes.

Under the protection of the soldiers, the young man was kept at the Post for several days, and then Captain Cline and Indian Agent Berry started for Gunnison with him. However, they would not allow him to go armed. Jackson said to them at the time: "Give me my guns and ammunition and I will fight my way through." But the agent, evidently fearing a general uprising of the Utes, would not give the youth a chance to defend himself.

Taking only a few soldiers, the party proceeded toward Gunnison. As they came into the canyon near the famous Son of a B - - - - Hill on the Blue, the Indians, probably by prearrangement, swooped down upon the little party, took Jackson from them and left the others unharmed.

There are many different stories of the murder of Young Jackson. The one here related is by Mrs. McCoy, who was at Fort Crawford at the time, she being the adopted daughter of Mr. and Mrs. Roswell Hotchkiss. No one knows what really became of Jackson and no one knows where he was left, after he was killed. He was probably tortured considerably before he met his death at the hands of the bloodthirsty Utes.

Frank Wheaton Clarke was born in Fort Leavenworth, Kansas, on the second day of February, 1861. He went to school in the town of Leavenworth and at the age of 14 went into the printing office of the Leavenworth Times, where he worked for three years, acting first as devil and then as press boy. Following this he worked in the Post Trader's Store at Fort Leavenworth until 1886, when he came to Colorado and entered the store operated by his brother-in-law, James A. Fenlon, at Fort Crawford. The Indians had already been taken out of the Uncompahgre Valley when he came and only a few were left about the Post. He remembers playing baseball with the Fort Crawford soldiers, and making trips to Gunnison, Ouray and Montrose.

In the year 1899, Frank Clarke followed the call of gold and journeyed to the Yukon Territory, where he spent thirty-one years. He lived for a time on Bonanza creek and knew the man who made the first big strike there—the strike that started the great rush into the Yukon gold fields. From 1899 to 1915 he worked in the store of the Cudahy Company and then went into the placer mining game for himself. He states that the best day's work he did was the day he found six ounces and eight pennyweight in gold in one pan, taken from bedrock.

Elbert Lewis Hayes was for two years a teamster at

Fort Crawford, the Army Post on the Uncompahgre in the eighties. He was born in Homer, Calhoun County, Michigan, eighty miles from Detroit, on September 19, 1852. He went to the country schools of that state and attended the Hillsdale College, a Baptist institution. After finishing his schooling he took a position with the Chilson Brothers Nursery in Battle Creek, Michigan.

An older brother of Mr. Hayes' had gone to Missouri and settled, and the latter went to that state for a visit. Finding that young steers would bring a good price there, he went back to Michigan, resigned his position at the nursery, bought one hundred and three head of steers and brought them to Missouri, where he sold them the following year. Then he returned to Michigan again and bought one hundred and forty head of steers, which he also fattened and sold in Missouri. These animals he took to Linn County, which at that time was all prairie land.

In the year 1879, Mr. Hayes came to Colorado Springs, where he spent a few years as a cowboy and at driving freight teams for Cal Houston, who operated a sawmill. He also bought cattle for the North End Market for a couple of years, after which he came to Montrose in February of 1884. He came in on the railroad and says that the new road was a little shaky at that time.

Arriving in Montrose, he preempted one hundred and sixty acres of land on Log Hill Mesa, on McKenzie Creek, near the site of General McKenzie's old army camp. At that time the pole and brush shelters built for the horses were still there as they were left by the soldiers who spent the summers at this camp.

Mr. Hayes spent two years as a teamster for the Post at Fort Crawford. He and the late Thomas H. Dougherty hauled water in tank wagons for the use at the Fort, bringing it from the Uncompahgre River. Hayes also drove the officers' ambulance. The Fort was a good sized one, and had many buildings, only two or three of which remain in existence today. One wing of the hospital is the residence of the T. M. Reynolds ranch near Riverside, and was purchased and moved there by E. L. Hayes, who bought the place from Richard Dunn in 1888,

and Charles Raish bought the rest of the hospital, tore
it down and rebuilt it on his home ranch, also in the Riverside country.

Jim Fenlon operated the Settler's Store and Bar. There
were officers' buildings, bakery, quarters for married soldiers, guard house, large hospital, mule corrals, etc. The
old parade ground can be seen on the Fenlon ranch, with
its border of stately trees, today.

One summer while Mr. Hayes was working for the
Post, the soldiers went on a two weeks camping trip to the
San Miguel River below Telluride. Hayes was driving a
six-mule team, when the officers passed them, riding in
buckboards. The mules of his team recognized their
friends and commenced to bray, all at once, and the soldiers who were riding with him had to get off the wagon
and hold them to keep the teams from running after the
officers' teams.

Life for the soldiers at Fort Crawford was very mon-
otonous, as the daily routine was always the same. There
was nothing much to do, as the Indians were gone and
never came back. However, the government left them
there because there were good quarters already built and
the United States was saved the task of erecting suitable
buildings elsewhere.

After the Post was discontinued, Mr. Hayes moved to
his ranch, which he had rented to George Taylor. Later
he sold the place to T. M. Reynolds, who still owns it.
Before selling this place, he purchased a ranch from Mrs.
Herman Vachman, near Happy Canyon, lived there two
years and bought a house in Montrose into which he
moved his family. This house was purchased from Charley Ryan and later sold to Mrs. Emma Stites.

At the present time Mr. Hayes owns two ranches on
Spring Creek Mesa, two on California Mesa, one at Crawford and one east of Montrose. He also owns several houses
in Montrose and two buildings on Main Street in that town.

During the past fifty-three years Charles Henry Fosdick
has worked on various jobs throughout Southern Colorado.
He was born in Waverly, Ohio, on January 23, 1862. His
mother died when he was two weeks old, and his father

took him to Granville, Ohio, where they lived on a farm.

In the spring of 1880 he came into Pueblo, Colorado, and secured a job digging for the laying of the ties for the first street car lines in that city.

After three months work in Pueblo, Fosdick went to Silver Cliff, where he worked in the mines and freighted from the Wet Mountain Valley to Canon City, Coal Creek and Pueblo. He says that on these trips he saw plenty of wild game, especially antelope.

The jail burned while he was in Silver Cliff and two men were cremated. On day, Fosdick bought a five dollar meal ticket and started to eat his first meal on the ticket. A fire started across the street before he finished his meal and burned up half the town. He never did get the rest of his meals on that ticket.

While in the Wet Mountain Valley, he worked in various mines and mills, doing all kinds of labor. He says that at that time they were finding silver at the grass roots.

During the summer of 1882, Fosdick, with Charley Phelps and another man whose name he does not remember, made a long horseback trip over the Western Slope of Colorado. The railroad had been built only as far as Sargents, and that town was a settlement of tents. On this trip they passed through the towns of Villa Grove, Saguache, Del Norte, Durango, Farmington and Ophir.

In 1885 Fosdick returned to Montrose and has been around this vicinity since that year. He has never been married and has lived his own quiet life. He has worked in the mines around Ouray, grubbed cedar and pinyon trees for Jim and Joe Calloway in Dry Cedar Basin and has otherwise helped in the development of Western Colorado.

Mr. Fosdick remembers that when he came to Montrose there were many saloons, one being in the basement under the present location of the Western Furniture Co. And Ouray was a lively town, too. He recalls the experience of opening the road to the Camp Bird Mine after heavy snow storms.

Everett Hooker Miles was born in Grant County, Wisconsin, on the Fourth of September, 1860. He was five years old when his father came out of the Civil War, with a shoulder nearly shot off, after four years of service.

After the war the family moved to the town of Waverly, Bremer County, Iowa, by wagon. The father, a carpenter, built the town of Plainfield, employing about thirty-five men. In those days there were many Indians but Mr. Miles stated he was never molested by one of them.

He moved to Mitchell County, Kansas, the town of Beloit, and in 1881 came to Gunnison, Colorado, which was a lively town, with gambling, freighting and stage lines running out of the town.

He did not stay in Gunnison long, but came into the Uncompahgre Valley and settled on a farm near Colona, just above Kelly's Trail on the Montrose-Ouray highway. For this land he paid the government $1.25 an acre. He stayed on this ranch until his death.

One of his most exciting experiences was when he helped the Hotchkiss boys, Bill and Uri, capture a huge mountain lion alive, after treeing it six times. They finally killed it and Uri took the hide, giving the other two men the bounty, which was five dollars apiece.

George Washington Robuck was born on February 18, 1855, in Macon City, Missouri. He attended school in that town and grew to manhood there. On May 4, 1885, he arrived in the town of Montrose, Colorado, at midnight, on the train, flat broke. He says that, after one look at the adobe hills to the east of Montrose, if he had had the money he would have left the town and never returned. However, fate had not decreed that he do so, and he was here until he died—and glad of it.

Shortly after coming to Montrose, he went to Telluride, where he ran a livery stable for Ike King for a year and a half. Returning to Montrose, he took up eighty acres of land in Floral Valley, about eighteen miles northwest of the town. He lived there for ten months and then sold the land to Dave Wood, or rather he traded it for the Magnolia Livery Stable, which was located where the Rhodes Blacksmith Shop is now.

After disposing of the Livery Stable, Robuck conducted a second hand store for seventeen years, or until 1930, when he retired and later passed away.

Mr. Robuck was married in 1876 to Mary Jane Smiley, and to this union was born five childern, all of whom are still living. They are: Mrs. C. C. Dole, of Portland, Oregon; Lester, of Montrose; Mrs. H. H. Ender, of Los Angeles; Mrs. Gertrude Davis, of Portland, Oregon; and Mrs. W. H. McCarthy of San Diego, California.

In the years he has spent in Western Colorado, Mr. Robuck has done a good deal of hunting. Some of the old timers he especially recalls are: J. V. Lathrop, Abe Roberts, J. C. Frees, O. D. Loutsenhizer, and Walter Musgrave.

The family of Gerhardt and Wilhelmina Jutten have been prominent in the development of the Uncompahgre Valley since the white man first came in. They were Germans and their first son, Henry, was born in Germany on May 16, 1874. Henry was eight years old the day he landed in New York City. Three girls were born to the family in Germany. One of them, Ida Waugh is the wife of Clark Waugh and lives on the original Jutten homestead. Two more sons, John B. and Joe, live in the Colona district, near where both were born. Each of the boys owns three ranches and together they have about 11,000 acres of grazing land on Sawtooth and near Craig's Point in the Hanks Valley district.

Henry Jutten was married in 1902 to Cora Brower and they have a daughter, Aileen. Joe was married to Daisy Kittleson and they have two children, Billy and Joan. Johnny was married to Avah Humphrey in 1916 and they have five children.

Henry remembers when the soldiers were at Fort Crawford. The cavalry used to bring in supplies on pack mules. At that time the grass was good and the cattle grazed all over the valley. There were no fences and the big cattlemen ran the country. Some of the prominent cattlemen of the day were Billy Moore, Jim Fenlon, Clarence Knight, Oscar Smith, Jim Kettle, Paul Gere, Preston Hotchkiss, W. T. Ryan, Schwend and Mostyn and Tom Moody.

Joe and John Jutten have about three thousand head of

sheep and 1,000 cattle. One of the old Dave Wood stage stations was on the present ranch of Henry Jutten.

Mr. Jutten remembers the shooting matches that were held at Fort Crawford. The target pits were about where the Edgar Williams ranch is now located. Everybody in the valley was invited to the dances.

Ed Ryan was on the water wagon with E. L. Hayes, Will Sigafus was the butcher. Mock Skeen, of Ouray, was a soldier and Charley Arndt was a sergeant, who had won many medals at Fort Leavenworth. On receiving his discharge, Arndt took up a ranch near Uncompahgre and married Henry Jutten's sister, Ida. They went to Oklahoma and were living on a farm, when Arndt accidentally shot himself to death. Clark Waugh was working for Henry Jutten, and the latter sent Waugh to Oklahoma with a bunch of horses, and instructions to assist Mrs. Arndt in the operation of the place. Later the two were married and returned to the Uncompahgre Valley where they have since resided.

The soldiers of Fort Crawford secured their coal from the Old Miller Mine on Sawtooth. One of the officers of the Post opened the Taylor Mine and later sold it.

John Rottemacher, an uncle of Henry Jutten, cut wild hay on Gere Flats and hauled it to Montrose, about twenty miles away, and sold it for $80 a ton.

Deer were so plentiful that they could be shot from the highways, and the soldiers used to seine the fish from the Uncompahgre River. Once Henry Jutten hauled a large sum of money to the bank in Montrose in a seamless sack.

Hugo Selig was born in Ostrowa, Prussia, on the twenty-fifth of December, 1864. In 1872, when he was eight years old, he came to America, going first to Baltimore, Maryland. Mr. Selig is a nephew of the late Joseph Selig, founder of the town of Montrose. Joseph Selig died at the age of thirty-eight years, while on a visit with a sister in Baltimore, and is buried in the Hebrew Friendship Cemetery at that place.

From Baltimore, Leopold Selig, father of Hugo, took his family to Wheeling, West Virginia, and later to Parkersburg in the same state. Then they went into Ohio, where they settled in Adams County, near the postoffice of Selig. The father was in the leaf tobacco business, buying tobacco from the producers.

Hugo Selig received the first part of his education in Germany. He later attended school in the towns where he lived in America, and finished a Normal course. He taught school for a time in Adams County, and was a candidate in the primary election for clerk of the common pleas court. The man who defeated him appointed Selig as his deputy.

Joseph Selig died in 1886 and Hugo's father was executor of the estate, and the family came to Montrose, Colorado, in 1887. Mr. Selig took the bar examination the same year and has since practiced in Montrose, serving as deputy district attorney under Hershel M. Hogg. He was in partnership with Judge John Gray in the firm of Gray & Selig. Gray was then district attorney, and they were the county attorneys. Hugo Selig served as deputy district attorney from 1890 to 1898, and in 1908 was elected district attorney for the Seventh Judicial District of Colorado.

He was district attorney at the time of the Western Federated Miners strike following the Peabody regime in 1905. He prosecuted Steve Adams and Vincent St. John on a change of venue case to Mesa County from San Miguel, in 1905 and 1906. The two men were acquitted.

Mr. Selig tells many interesting things about his uncle, Joseph Selig, the founder of Montrose, and has many newspaper records of early day events that Joseph Selig took part in.

Joseph Selig was president of the Original Townsite Company and negotiated with the government and platted the town of Montrose and Selig's Addition. Patents were issued to him, and town lots were purchased from him. He was the first mayor of Montrose, and was appointed as the first county clerk by Governor Pitkin.

In 1893, at the time of the Cripple Creek strike, several hundred miners came down from Rico and Telluride and took possession of the town of Montrose. They captured the east bound train and commanded the engineer and conductor to take them to Cripple Creek. The train was ditched at Cedar Creek to await the arrival of two companies of troops from Pueblo and sixty deputy U. S. marshals from Grand Junciton. The miners learned of the coming of the government men and fled into the hills.

At that time L. F. Twitchell was mayor, Dr. J. F. Coleman was county coroner. These two organized a posse to keep the miners out of town, but the county government was in sympathy with the miners. John Gray, as district attorney, and Ben Dillon, sheriff of the Populist Party, joined the strikers and took possession of the saloons and eating houses. They kept possession until the train from Grand Junction, then a narrow gauge, came in. The train crew was forced to take the miners to Cedar Creek, where they received secret orders to hold it until the arrival of the troops and deputy U. S. marshals. But the secret leaked out and the miners fled.

The narrow gauge railroad between Grand Junction and Montrose was changed to a standard gauge in 1892.

On election night of 1904 an armed mob forced Dr. Schermerhorn and Dr. Coleman to go to the jail and perform a surgical operation on one H. F. Allen, who had been accused of attacking a little girl. The two doctors were indicted, together with Marshal M. F. Tillery, on a charge of mayhem, but before the trial, Allen was taken from the county hospital by the mob and was not heard of again. So the case was dismissed for lack of evidence. Hugo Selig was district attorney at this time, and called the grand jury that indicted the three men. A petition, signed by most of the citizens of Montrose, was brought before Judge Theron Stevens and he excoriated the citizens thoroughly for their stand in the matter.

In 1889, a mob of five hundred people came from Delta to lynch one Mark Powers, who had killed Chas. A. Bear in Delta County. Judge Bell on the district bench appointed forty or fifty Montrose citizens to protect the man. These Montrose men went to the rear of the jail, while the mob was storming the front door and tore a hole in the rear wall and took Powers out to safety to Fort Crawford, where he was under federal protection.

Notable cases that Hugo Seilg has been connected with

are the case of Henry Young, plaintiff in error, vs. the People of the State of Colorado which was tried in district court when Selig was district attorney; and the case of the People of the State of Colorado vs. John Jasper Baker, in which case Selig was one of the attorneys for the defense.

The Henry Young case was tried in district court in 1907. Young was convicted of the murder of Charley Wilkinson and sentenced to serve twenty-five years in the state penitentiary. He was incarcerated and later escaped. T. J. Black and H. M. Hogg were the attorneys for the defense.

Selig was one of the attorneys for the defense, together with M. D. Vincent and S. N. Wheeler, in the case of the People vs. John Jasper Baker, on trial for the murder of James Kelley. Baker was found guilty and sentenced to a term in the penitentiary.

Mr. Selig has been connected with several law firms in the years that he has practiced in the state of Colorado. The first firm he was connected with was Gray & Selig, then Selig & Blake, Selig & Crose, Black, Selig & Stivers and Selig & Cox.

Selig was prominent in law affairs in Montrose for many years and maintained an office here until retirement. He has made Montrose his home for a long time and is highly respected as a citizen.

For more than fifty years Harry Vorhees Monell was connected with the affairs of Montrose and the Uncompahgre Valley. He was born in Dunkirk, New York, on September 25, 1880, and at the age of eight months, he was brought to Colorado Springs, where the family resided for two years, coming to Montrose in 1882.

He attended the old four-room school, the first built in Montrose. The graduating class he was in was composed of Lester Robuck, Burrell Hitchcock, Stanley Sherman, George Abernathy, Harry Monell, Leonora Pelton, Alma Dole (now Mrs. Onias Skinner), and Mary Imes. The principal was Prof. Rhodes, who was also a Methodist preacher, and one of the best history teachers that ever came to Montrose. Their first teacher was Clara Land, who later became Mrs. Charles Ryan, and who is the mother of Archie Ryan of Denver and an aunt of Chas. A.

Lindbergh, the famous flyer, and Rear Admiral Emery S. Land of the U. S. Navy. A Miss Giffen taught them for the biggest part of three terms. The principal taught most of the classes. Two grades were taught on the corner where the post office is now, and before the class was graduated two more rooms were added to the north and two to the south of the old building. All the classes finishing before 1895 were graduated from the upstairs north room of the old building.

When the Monell family came into Montrose, Mr. Monell was connected with the Weir sawmill, which was located on McKenzie Creek on Log Hill Mesa. The lumber yard was at the wye, where the town of Montrose was situated at that time. In 1885 the yard was moved to the new town, across the tracks from the main part of town. The father, P. B. Monell, was a carpenter and constructed many houses in this city. He built the house on the corner of South First and Selig, now belonging to Mrs. Estep, for Dr. Ashley. He built the Cleve Brown house on Main Street and several other residences, being assisted in the work by John Elliott, father of Charley Elliott, long superintendent of the Uncompahgre Valley Irrigation Project.

The Monells were living across the tracks when McClease was hung to the big gate at the stockyards. Harry and his brother, then only small boys, were going home with the milk in the early morning. They saw the dead man hanging there by his neck, and dropped their milk and ran for home.

Harry Monell saw the Main Street of Montrose come from a muddy mire to gravel and thence to pavement. He saw most of the old business buildings burned to the ground. The night the old Belvedere Hotel burned, he and Burrell Hitchcock were selling flowers at the Fireman's Ball, which was held in the hotel.

When the old Methodist Church was built, Harry and his brother hauled the rock for it. The Monells farmed under the Loutenhizer Canal, long before the Gunnison Tunnel was built. This canal was the first one built to carry water to the farms on the east side of the Uncompahgre River, and the farmers under it took turns riding ditch. Some of these farmers were: Col. Phil. Peters, P. B. Monell and Henry Wilson, father of Lisle and George Wilson of Nucla.

Harry Monell's brother Tony, now postmaster of Montrose, was for twenty-five years or more county clerk of Montrose County and Harry spent many years in this office. For several years past he has been the county assessor. For six years he was the secretary of the Western Slope Fair association.

He was married in 1904 to Minnie Meyer and they have four children: Minnie Fender, of Long Beach, California; Harry, Jr., of San Diego, California; Margaret Browning, of Montrose, and Lloyd, of Montrose. They also raised a granddaughter, Patsy Jo Monell.

Mr. Monell saw the range country turn from cattle to sheep. The 640 acre homestead law put the finishing touches on the old time cowmen of Western Colorado and they have almost passed out of the picture. He saw the time when thousands of head of cattle ranged all over the higher parts of the valley. There would be sixty or seventy cowboys, each with five or six horses and pack animals, to ride the range every summer. They would start in the Roubideau country in June and end up on the Blue Mesa in late August. He rode with the roundup when he was thirteen years old, and at nineteen cooked for an outfit of thirty men, assisted by Pete Shrock. That was in 1902, and they started on Larue Creek, near Cow Creek and worked over to the Blue.

Old time cattlemen who were in the busienss then were: Dick Collin, Verdie and Uri Hotchkiss, Jack Tripler, Billy Harris, Billy Moore, Russell and Wold, George Truesdale, Stillman Schildt, Bill McMinn, Dutch Veo, the Bill Boot outfit, Pat O'Brien, Frank Hovey, Ed Garrett, Tom Nutt and Johnny Whittingham.

Cowboys who rode the range with these old time cattlemen were: Frank and Fred Hotchkiss, Ned Tripler, Jim Cairns, Lewis Mitchell, Bill Schildt, Lou Loback, Harry Russell and Chet Moore. It was nothing to drive in 500 to 1000 head of cattle a day. They would brand all the new calves and take the strays back to their own ranges.

It the early nineties the country from Montrose east to the Gunnison was mostly open range and was used as the winter feeding ground, and only the poorer cows were fed. Bostwick Park and Kinikin Heights were a part of the range, and the cattle were not taken into the higher hills until the middle of May.

Ed Shinn, who was later one of the biggest sheep men in the valley, started out with a buckboard to move camp with and by feeding twenty bucks on the Monell ranch, just east of Montrose. H. E. Perkins, another of the successful sheep men of an earlier day, started with a saddle horse and a pack burro, for a camp moving outfit and sold out for a large sum of money.

One of the most noteworthy projects that Harry Monell has been connected with was the original Rainbow Route Highway from Montrose to Sapinero. Before it was built, it was necessary to go around by Grand Junction, Leadville, Buena Vista and Salida to get between these two points by automobile. Nick Krohn was the superintendent of the project, appointed to this place by the county commissioners of Gunnison and Montrose Counties, and the project consisted of building the road from Stumpy Creek to Sapinero. L. T. Morey was the foreman of the rock crew and Harry Monell was the foreman of the grading crew, and the construction of this piece of trail paved the way for the present fine highway between these points.

CHAPTER XIX

THE REAL DISCOVERER OF RADIUM

From 1887 until his death in December, 1939, Thomas Michael McKee was identified with the interests of Western Colorado. Not being a man who craves publicity, Mr. McKee went about his work and pleasure quietly, and said little to anyone about anything, unless approached for certain reasons.

Mr. McKee was one of the first men in the world to carry on experiments with carnotite ore and radium, some of his discoveries leading up to the general use of radium throughout the world today. In the early days of his experimenting he used carnotite ore as a means of furnishing light for photographic work.

He was also one of the first men in the world to think of the commercial possibilities of the oil shale that is found in abundance in Western Colorado and Eastern Utah.

He was one of the first photographers to visit the Mesa Verde region and make a photographic record of the extensive prehistoric ruins to be found within its borders.

He had a collection of relics, photographs of early day scenes, and material collected among the Ute Indians and a wealth of information on general topics that a king's ransom could not buy.

He was an accomplished artist and portrait painter and an authority on fossils and paleanthology, on archaeology and Indian lore, and knew more about the Ute Indians than any other man. His collection of Ute bead work and baskets, on exhibition at the Fox Theatre in Montrose, is worth $10,000 and will increase in value as the years go by.

Thomas Michael McKee was born in Scary Creek, Putnam County, West Virginia (it was then Virginia) on March 17, 1854, and was but a baby when his parents took him down the river by steamboat to Louisville, Kentucky, and then by stage coach to Nashville, Tennessee, where he spent his boyhood days and attended school. He studied portrait painting and in succeeding years traveled over much of the South pursuing this work. In 1877 he was in St. Louis for a time. Along with his portrait work, Mr. McKee studied photography and took a course in anatomy, so that he would be better able to do portrait painting.

He watched Nashville grow from a small town to a city and watched the construction of some of her famous buildings. For years he traveled over Texas and adjoining states as an express messenger. He went into the city of El Paso on the first train run over the Texas & Pacific, and was employed by the Texas Express Company when it closed its business.

Mr. McKee was married in 1885 to Amanda S. Kauffman, and to them three sons were born. One son died in infancy, the eldest, Mizner, was drowned in the Gunnison River and the other, John, was long in the asphalt business in central Cuba, but now lives in Montrose.

In about 1887, Mr. McKee started from Texas to Sitka, Alaska. He had written to A. E. Buddecke of Montrose and learned that there was no photographer in Montrose, so he changed his plans and came here, the trip to Montrose costing him fifty dollars more than it would have cost to go to Sitka.

During the many years that he was in and around Montrose, Mr. McKee took thousands of photographs. He had photos of the old Post at Fort Crawford, with the soldiers on parade. He had pictures of all the early day events. He spent several years as the official photographer for the Denver & Rio Grande Railroad for Western Colorado.

While a messenger on the Rio Grande Southern Railway, he became interested in the prehistoric ruins in Lost Canyon, between Mancos and Dolores, and photographed them. Then, in 1896, he took an expedition into the Mesa Verde, where, at that time, there were no trails. He had a great deal of difficulty doing his photographic work in this great canyon country. He had to dig out the old

springs of the cliff dwellers to secure water for his work
and camp use. He had his dark room in some of the inner
rooms of Spruce Tree House and Cliff Palace, and had to
carry his large plate cameras over the cliffs and through
the almost impenetrable oak brush. But he secured a
wonderful bunch of photos, which were partly responsible
for the Mesa Verde being set aside as a great national
park. His guide was Stearl P. Thomas, sheriff at Cortez,
for whom he named a small Cliff Dweller village west
of the hotel in Spruce Tree Camp, an uncle of Ranger
M. M. Guillett of the Black Canyon National Monument,
and a Mr. Keely was his guide, and showed him the ruins
in the Yellow Jacket and Ruin Canyon districts of the
Montezuma valley.

Mr. McKee's photographs are now the prized possessions of many museums, and others are clamoring for
them.

Before radium was considered a commercial possibility,
Tom McKee was carrying on experiments with it, and it
was largely through his efforts, together with Onias Skinner and Lynn Monroe, publishers of the Montrose Enterprise, and Gordon Kimball, Ouray citizen, that it has come
into general use. Carnotite, the ore from which radium
is taken, was discovered in Montrose County by an Irishman named Duling, who sold his claims for $10,000. This
county has since then produced many, many times that
amount in radium ore. Mr. McKee used nitrates of uranium instead of gold, in his photographic work.

From 1906 to 1920, Mr. McKee spent most of his time
in Utah in the Ute reservation, to which the Uncompahgre
Utes were taken after being removed from this valley.
Here he learned to know the Utes, their language, their
ways, their dances and their customs. He was well acquainted with Chipeta for sixteen years, and she often
came to his home. Here he secured his famous collection
of bead work and baskets. Here he took time off from his
own business to show the oil-bearing stratas to men who
were interested in the study and development of oil shale.

Mr. McKee took some of the first X-ray pictures ever
taken in the West. He has always been an enthusiastic

trout fisherman and has secured a Colorado fishing and small game license every year since they were first issued.

He was always much interested in paleanthology, and has collected many fossils and showed others where to find them. This was merely a hobby and he never commercialized his knowledge.

In the early days Mr. McKee maintained a studio in Ouray and one at the town of Old Dallas.

Truly Thomas Michael McKee greatly aided the development of this empire that is Western Colorado. He enriched the town of Montrose by his presence there, and won a place in the hearts of his fellow citizens that will always be his.

Mr. McKee brought the first motion picture outfit into Western Colorado. It was a Kinetoscope, and he exhibited it in every town in this part of the state.

Bert Albin was born in Copenhagen, Denmark, May 29, 1867, and when two years old was brought to America by his parents, Mr. and Mrs. Andrew Albin and settled in Topeka, Kansas, where they spent two years, before going to Wabaunsee County in the same state where the family lived in the town of Alma, and where Bert went to school. The father died while there and then Bert and his mother came to Montrose, Colorado, in 1888.

At this time, Montrose was the distributing point for the San Juan mining district and there was much activity here in the way of freighting supplies in to the mines. Mr. Albin spent several years working in various mines in the district, being employed at the Tomboy, at Telluride, the Jumbo and Enterprise mines at Rico and spending three years at the Ute and Ulay in Lake City.

In the year 1897, Bert Albin quit mining and became engaged in the stock business, handling cattle until 1913 and then selling his cattle and buying sheep.

In the days of his cattle experience the roundup would last almost all summer, and the chuck wagon moved around with the herds. The horses were run into a rope corral every morning, after being night herded. Each outfit had its day and night herders, and men to round up the strays. Mr. Albin had about four hundred head of cattle which he ranged in the Horsefly country, shipping every fall to Denver or Kansas City.

He remembered many of the real cowboys of the past. Mid Hampton, Burt Fraiser, and Dewey Greagor worked for him and others who would ride anything with four legs were: Harry Watt, Quint Sullivan, Don Robinson and Joe Gray.

Married in 1891 to Emma Hampton, Mr. Albin has two sons, Alex, who operates the Texaco Service Station and Hotel at Placerville, and Clarence, who was associated with his father in the sheep business at the time of the death of the elder Albin.

Mr. Albin stated that in the twenty years that he was in the sheep business he made lots of money and lost lots of money so that it was about a standoff.

He well remembered the Lambert-Young feud, and was in town when the Youngs were brought in and disarmed by the officers. Then, when they started back home, they were waylaid in the river bottom by the vigilance commtitee, who commenced shooting. Old man Young jumped out of the wagon and in the face of gunfire, took George Booker's gun away from him.

Then there was the time when old man Young waylaid a man named Ainsley, at his home on Spring Creek and shot him. Then later Ainsley waylaid Lambert, shot him and left him in Dry Creek for dead. Coming into town he gave himself up and said he had killed Lambert. A posse started out after the body and met Lambert riding in on his mule.

He well remembers the time young Dick Netherley shot Johnny Wilson in the latter's saloon on Main street in Montrose. Dick was shot at the same time, but recovered and was sent to the penitentiary at Canon City.

Those were exciting days in the Uncompahgre Valley and no one recalled more interesting events than Bert Albin, who for years was a prominent citizen and stockman. Bert was killed in an auto accident in 1934.

Lewis Emerson Ross was born in the North Woods, north of Grand Rapids, Michigan, on April 3, 1856. When he was six weeks old, the family moved to Ionia, Kent

County, and in May, 1864, set out for California, going to
New York by rail, and down the Atlantic coast to the
Isthmus of Panama, across the isthmus by rail and up the
Pacific coast on a windjammer.   The vessel soon ran out
of water and they had to condense ocean water for domes-
tic use. They carried their livestock on foot and killed the
animals as the meat was needed. Lew said about all the
meat served was rotten.

Mr. Ross was eight years old on this trip and one thing
he remembered was when a passenger died and they sewed
him up in canvas and pushed him over the rail, assigned
to Davy Jones' locker.

The Ross family settled first in Humboldt County, moved into Salano County in 1867 and in 1878 moved to Sacramento County. While there, there came a serious drought
and the people prayed for rain. It rained for six weeks
straight, and almost floated the whole country down to
the sea.

Jay J. Ross, brother of Lew, and Gus Frost, his brother-
in-law, had gone to Colorado in 1880, and six months
after they departed, Lew sold the farm and joined them in
Silverton, making the trip via Denver, Colorado Springs,
Alamosa, and Durango, and taking three weeks for the
journey on the train.

When the Indians were pushed out of the Uncompahgre
Valley, Gus Frost and Jay Ross settled on farms in the
Menoken district, then the former returned to Silverton
to get his wife and her brother, Lew Ross. They bought
a spring wagon and drove to Ophir over a new road. Here
the road ended and they came to Telluride over a burro
trail and had a hard time getting through. Once they unloaded all the stuff they had in the wagon except a big
trunk. Going down a hill the trunk jumped right over
Frost's head, leaped over the team and catapulted down
the hill.

Lew Ross was the only man in the lower part of
the Uncompahgre Valley who lived on the ranch he
located in 1881 until his death about three years ago. His
place was the site of the old supply camp of General Mc-
Kenzie, who removed the Utes from the valley. He also

stated that there used to be deep trails from Shavano Val-
ly down to the agency, near Colona, where the Indians had
gone after their rations.

A man named Garten died and was buried on the flat
just west of the Lew Ross ranch in 1881. Shortly thereafter, Jay Ross and Gus Frost went to the Roubideau to
work on the railroad. Before Garten died, he made the
men who buried him promise that they would not let the
coyotes pick his bones. So when the two men departed for
the lower valley, they left instructions with Lew Ross to
watch the grave. He had to re-cover it twice after the
coyotes had dug into it.

Lew Ross spent ten years on the Menoken school board
and for eight years was president of the county high
school committee. He was for some time fruit and weevil
inspector for the Montrose district. The first day's work
he did in the valley was spent riding a plow beam on the
Menoken switch. The Ross brothers and Frost were offered town lots free in Montrose, when the town was started,
but refused to take them, preferring to raise vegetables
and sell them to the townspople. Lew Ross was still in
this business at the time he died. The last year from two
acres of land he made $264.00, selling $52.00 worth of tomatoes from a sixteenth of an acre of ground, or an average of $800.00 an acre. From a quarter of an acre of land
he sold $80.00 worth of potatoes.

John Edwin Ballew, for years a road overseer in San
Miguel county, was born April 8, 1845, in North Missouri.
He served in the Confederate army in the Civil War and
took part in many small engagements. He was with Gen-
eral Banks in the expedition up the Red River. His outfit
met Jim Lane, the Kansas Jayhawker, in a battle in
Jackson county, Missouri, and took part in General Joe
Shelby's raids, which were running fights most of the time.
They met the federal General Sheagle in battle at Carthage,
Mo., and fought at Fort Camden and also met Steel at
Washita.

After the war, in 1867, he came to Nebraska before that
state was admitted to the union, when the Union Pacific
railroad was just being built. There were forts all along

the Platte river, Fort Kearney, Fort McPherson, Fort
Morgan, Fort Lupton, Fort Collins, Fort St. Vrain, with
Fort Laramie on the North Platte. Mr. Ballew freighted
from Sidney, Nebraska, to most of these forts during his
first year in Colorado and said Indian fights were a part of
the daily work. They always had to stand guard at night.
The freighters were never allowed to leave a post without
a sufficient number of men to protect the wagon train.
They were held until there were 50 men, and then allowed
to proceed. However, the emigrants traveled faster than
the freighters and they separated soon after leaving a fort.
Ballew drove a freight team from Julesburg to Chasewick
as it was called, then to Denver. He made one trip with
mules to Deadwood, S. D., where he spent only a little
time, returning soon to Colorado. He delivered supplies
on this trip to Fort Robinson and the Spotted Tail agency.
He was in Deadwood when the Custer massacre occurred.

Coming over into the western part of Colorado, he
lived in Telluride for 30 years and spent 20 in Naturita.
He was a road overseer for San Miguel county for 17 years
and worked for the U. S. Radium Corporation near Naturita for ten years. He did work on all the roads of San
Miguel county. Mr. Ballew was married in 1885 to Fanny
Esther Feary and two children were born: Logan O. Ballew
of California and Mrs. Mae Ficklin of Spokane, Wash. Mr.
Ballew always worked hard and had little time for recrea-
tion.

CHAPTER XX

IN THE OLD DAYS

(Copied from "The Montrose Messenger," Sept. 20, 1922.)

"I came to this country in 1876 in a prairie schooner with a grasshopper brake. In 1883 I was working in the Nevada mine at Ophir. On December 22 it started to snow and did not let up until the 27th. A snow slide on that day covered the mouth of the tunnel and trapped the miners so that we had to tunnel through 19 feet of snow to get them out.

"Two ore sorters were carried down the mountain side and killed. We found one the next day and the other the next July. I was laid up with a bad cold at the time of the slide or I would have been with the two men who were killed."

—Joseph Macaw.

"I came here in 1884 on the Denver and Rio Grande. We were lucky enough to have the track clear through in those days."

—Benton Blackburn.

"As a young chap I married and lived in Missouri and in 1884 I wanted a new location so I started westward, coming into Pueblo by train. From there I started out afoot and walked practically all over Colorado before I landed in the Uncompahgre Valley in May of that year. My wife came out in September.

"Two things about the country interested me in those days. One was irrigation. I had lived in a state where crops just burned up so that irrigation farming certainly went well with me. The other was the number of saloons in the town. Main street was lined with them and I used to go in sometimes and watch others get fleeced out of their money. I wasn't for saloons then and am against them today; in fact I do all I can to fight the moonshine stills.

"I am 70 years old and have never had a doctor, which I think is a record hard to duplicate. I underwent an examination for the army in the World War and passed it but of course my age barred me out. I attribute not a little of my hardihood to the climate."

—W. R. Blackburn.

"I came into the valley in 1883, November 3, having come from Sapinero on the train. I had been in Lake City.

"The winter of '83 had one snow and that came in March. The people all got out their sleighs and went sleigh riding and all returned in the mud. I worked on the Montrose and Delta canal, when it was being constructed and secured a ranch on Spring Creek mesa, which I later sold."

—N. O. K. Lamb.

"I arrived in the Uncompahgre valley on a freight train in '84. My first work here was whacking bulls for Dave Wood. I was later owner and driver of a stage coach. The stage ran between Silverton and Ouray for many years."

—S. T. Norris.

"I can't quite recollect whether or not we came into the valley with a team or on the train in the spring of '83. But at any rate I recall that we drove with a wagon from town to California Mesa, where we took up life on our ranch, and my, but the roads were awful! It was all we could do to keep our places on the wagon seat.

"Years of the hardest kind of work followed but we were young and full of ambition and didn't mind. In later years we have been repaid for all our toil and hardships for after developing our ranch from a sage brush tract to a high state of cultivation, sold out and since then have been able to travel around and look at the country from Canada to New Mexico and from the Atlantic to the Pacific."

—Mrs. J. Bagley.

"I was only sixteen when we came over to Ouray in 1881. On our way there we passed through the old Indian agency near Colona, Colorado, and on that day the Indians were getting their rations. It was the first time that I had ever seen any real Indians and I'll never forget it. It made the country look pretty wild."

—James S. Osborn.

"Over the range on snowshoes is the way I came into this valley and the year was 1877. Came in from Lake City. I placered for gold near Ridgway and was ordered out every day by the Utes, but did not leave until I found it didn't pay. Then I went to California and later returned."

—J. Hale Brown.

"It was early in June of the year 1880 that I first saw the Uncompahgre. I came from Lake City by stage and buckboard.

"I conveyed the survey party that laid out Montrose township. We left town and went out into the country several miles. Then we camped until about midnight when the surveyors got their directions and locations from the stars."

—Jack (J. B.) Pool.

"In the early '80's I was drifting around Colorado from one mining camp to another. I had been freighting near Dillon, Colorado, and in '83 I quit my job and went to Leadville. From there I went to Salida and then to Gunnison, later coming to Montrose. In Montrose I met Jim Donnelly, whom I had known in Leadville, 'pullin' the buckskin off'n 'em on the Ouray run.' I have drifted in and out of Montrose a good many times in the past years, and just now I am 'Dad' at the Montrose fire station."

—P. C. Wills.

"The first child born in Paradox was William Huff, born in August, 1882, the second was Blanch Nyswonger, March, 1884, third S. H. Waggoner, October, 1884.

"The first marriage was that of Mennie Nyswonger and Curtis Eustice, Feb. 5, 1885, with Eugene C. Hamilton officiating and Wood Galloway and Delia Webb attendants.

"The first death was Mrs. Cotherne Talbert in the autumn of 1881. John Prentiss was murdered July 11, 1885.

"The first settlers were Riley Watson and Thomas Gashorn, fall of 1879, James Huff, summer, 1880, S. T. Talbert, 1881, Richard Netherly, 1881, Thomas Bradley, 1882; J. P. Gallaway, G. N. Barret, E. C. Hamilton, J. Q. Waggoner, and Monte Leach, 1883."

—Mrs. J. Q. Waggoner.

"We came over in 1883 driving a team and a few cattle. After we reached the valley we kept right on over the old Ute trail making the first road into Paradox. In some places where the road was exceptionally steep we had to let the wagons down by using a block and tackle."

—J. Q. Waggoner.

"I came here first in September, 1880, then I left and in 1884 returned from Buena Vista with a team. With my brother and George Sanborn I located what is known as the Felton and Sanborn road. I was a civil engineer on the D. & R. G. and later went to Mexico."

—Joe Felton.

"I packed my blankets on a burro and hiked into the valley from Silverton and I got stuck on the shoveling of mountain scenery on the toll roads we had here then. If I remember right I noticed there were more people living in Chicago at that time than there were living in Montrose."

—Edward Finnegan.

"In 1878 I came into this valley from Texas behind a yoke of oxen and I liked the country better than any I had seen so I stayed here. I recall the excitement caused by the murder of Young Jackson by the Indians."

—J. W. Campbell.

"I came to Colorado in 1880 and first landed in this section in 1882. I've seen quite a few exciting times that I'll never forget, but the main things were not adventures with bad men but the development of the valley. I helped survey the Moffat road and assisted by Dick Whinnerah made the pioneer survey of the Gunnison Tunnel. I was superintending engineer of the Cimarron ditch and believe that I was the original author of the present waterworks system."

—Walter H. Fleming.

"Ive been in the Uncompahgre valley for 38 years now. It was August 17 of '84 that I first drifted into the valley from New Mexico coming with my partner, the two of us riding and walking as we drove ahead of us a bunch of cattle. I'll say stranger, that we did far more walking than riding and there were days when we didn't see our horses from morning until evening.

"I finally got hold of the ranch I still own on Coal Creek and in due time I married and took my wife out there to live. We bought a big six-hole range from the Frees-Osborn store and started out to our place with it but the roads were so fierce that we lost every eye before we got to our destination. Then the door of the cabin wasn't big enough to admit the stove so we had to cut a hole in the doorway to get it in. I might say in passing that it was a mighty fine stove and we used it until three years ago, when we turned it in on a new one.

"I had vowed I'd never work indoors. The outdoors was what I loved and it seemed to me I could think better on horseback smoking a good cigar than anywhere else. But after I've been here a while I was prevailed upon to go into the First National Bank and there I have been for 33½ years. I've no complaint with the way the affairs of the bank have gone but just the same I wish I'd never gone into the business.

"As I said before, the outdoors is what I love and I've never ceased to regret that I chose a profession which took me away from it."

—C. B. Akard.

"I landed in Lake City in the early days pretty much of a tenderfoot, coming from the state of Tennessee.

"The day I arrived in the town I stepped into the bar room of a hotel and a well known citizen of the place had just about three sails to the wind, stepped up to me and said: 'I have a match, who has a cigar?'

"It was impossible to ignore the hint so I gave him a cigar which he lighted and then inquired, 'Partner, what kind of a ship did you sail in on?'

" 'A double decker,' I replied.

"He took me by the lapel of my coat, whirled me around before the bar and said, 'Cast anchor, sir.'

"I set him up to a drink and after disposing of it he trailed out muttering to himself, 'One cigar and one drink. Didn't pay a cent and a damn poor day for suckers.'

"This man was a well known Lake City wit. On another occasion when he was about half intoxicated, he came my way and I asked him to go to the hotel to lunch with me. He accepted and we were placed at a table with the Rev. Alexander Darley of Del Norte.

"On learning of Mr. Darley's profession my guest remarked to the parson, 'You might save poor Joe (himself) if you could only get the prejudice out of his mind against water but ever since his mother had him read that little chapter in Genesis about the great deluge, water has always tasted to him like drowned sinners.'

" 'Nevertheless,' replied Mr. Darley, 'I have come to stake this town for Jesus Christ.'

" 'Well, that's all right,' answered poor Joe, 'but I'll give you fair warning. If you don't get your assessment work done by spring the devil will jump your claim sure.' "

—John C. Bell.

"I came into the valley in 1883 on the railroad but coming over Marshall Pass I actually got sorry for the engine which seemed to be having a very hard time of it and so I got off and walked and I could have made much better time afoot than on the train.

"The main events of my early life as well as of my later days have been connected with my efforts in my chosen profession of the ministry. Locally, in pioneer times, it was in dealing with the people in the terms of the gospel while others dispensed intoxicants without stint.

"One time in the second floor parlors of the Loutenhizer hotel I preached the funeral of a woman who had been brought down from Ouray and at the same time carousal and festivity proceeded noisily below the stairs on the first floor.

"Another time I saw a young man of the town tear up a twenty dollar bill piece by piece in payment for drinks until the bartender finally had the whole bill. I am thankful that I had something to do with changing the sentiment of the town to where it would not now countenance two such proceedings as those cited."

—Rev. A. D. Fairbanks.

"After driving a bunch of horses and cattle into this valley in 1879, I waited four years for the Indians to leave so I could settle in the valley. At the time of the Meeker Massacre in the fall of '79 one of the settlers on the Dallas thought he saw Indians around his cabin and walked or ran barefooted into Ouray. I was detailed as one of the scouts but the Indians proved to be burnt stumps, which he had mistaken for redskins."

—W. O. Brower.

"In the fall of 1877 I came in from Pueblo by mule team. I carried mail from Barnum to Cimarron until June, 1878. In the spring of '80 I started punching cows in the Paradox country and had some exciting experiences.

"I remember one time I was helping Fred Mayall and his boy drive a bunch of cattle through Gypsum valley. One evening we camped at the head of Jack creek. I started to get supper and Fred and the boy went up to help a cow out of an alkali spring where it had become mired down.

"Suddenly a fusilade of shots was heard down on the other side of the cattle. I looked in that direction and saw about 20 Indian bucks riding pell mell through that herd shooting cattle right and left. They must have killed about a hundred head.

"Fred and his son ran down to where I was and when the Indians arrived in camp the leader got off his horse and came to us. He was very mad for some reason. Reaching down he grabbed up a weed and thrust it into Fred's mouth, saving 'Eat this, you Melican . . . .'

"I also remember when Al and Isadore Wilson and Jim Higginson were massacred by the Indians. Al had my spurs at the time, having borrowed them from me.

"Charley Ouray, nephew of the famous chief, was my chum for a long time and we used to have some great times together."

—J. H. Hafer.

CHAPTER XXI

WHEN I FIRST CAME HERE

(Individual experiences of Pioneers, as chronicled in the issue of "The Montrose Messenger," published by the Author for the Pioneers' Reunion, Sept. 20, 1922.)

"The roads over the Cochetopa Pass were very bad when I first came over in 1884, and the first year the valley did not look so good. There was only one store, one mill and six buildings here then. I lived in one house on Shavano Valley for 36 years before I moved to Montrose."

—Carrie Bever.

"I arrived in this valley December 25, 1881, having driven four mules down from Lake City. Had no roughlock and it was a slick trip. Most of my early experience was in building ditches to get water on California Mesa to raise crops and after the crops were raised there was no market for them. This country always suited me so I stayed here."

—D. H. Roatcap.

"Our party landed in Montrose the second day of July, 1882, having come in on foot. Four of us traveled through the White River and Grand country. We passed through the Black Canon to Currecanti creek the fourth of July and settled on Crystal creek."

—Paul Kruemling.

"At the age of seven years I arrived in the valley in a camp wagon. I have always liked the country because of the climate and because the crops hardly ever fail.

"When I was eight years old I used to herd the deer out of the field to save the crops. At nine I helped to plow. My father and I bought a Walter A. Woods mower, the first on California mesa.

"One night when father and I returned from a trip to town, we found our tent had been blown down and covered with snow. We crawled under the canvas and stayed there till morning."

—Daniel Rowan.

"It was June 25, 1880, that I arrived in Gunnison County, having come from Winfield, Kansas, in a prairie schooner. I helped to build the road from Crested Butte to Gothic, also organized school district No. 10, north of Montrose, helped build the house, put in desks in 1885 and taught the first term."

—Charles T. Baker.

"One time when I was driving a large bunch of cattle from the Tabeguache basin to Montrose, we ran into a severe snow storm. During the night we lost the trail. We were three hours trying to keep the cattle from drifting, and trying to find out where we were. It was a hard cold night but the next morning we reached Montrose without any loss."

—J. W. Tripler.

G. H. Rawson, who drove two burros over here in '82 and who spent his first winter in the roundhouse at Cimarron, has an interesting experience to tell.

On the road out of the Black Mesa out of Currecanti Creek, his two burros lost their balance, and the load and all began to roll down the hill. Rawson had given up all hope of ever recovering them, when, to his surprise one brought up against a tree, and the other was stopped by a large rock. After he had succeeded in getting them back on the trail he found that the packs had been tied on so securely that it was not even necessary to stop and relash them. The next day, October, 1884, he located at Maher where he lived until 1906, when he moved to Olathe which is now his home.

"I first came into the Gunnison country in 1884. I was with the railroad company having started working for them in 1879. Once while I was on a switch engine on the stock yard switching in Montrose, I saw a man hanging

to the upper beams of the yard.   He had been lynched the
previous night."

—Hugh Gallagher.

Sam Busha (Frenchie) spent the year 1880 as interpreter for Chief Ouray.   The government then transferred
him to the Red Cloud reservation in Wyoming where he
was interpreter for the Sioux Indians until 1889.   As soon
as he was released he returned to Montrose.

"We remember watching A. E. Buddecke drive six yoke
of oxen with a wagon and a trailer behind loaded with
lumber and turn them around in the public square.   It
always seemed wonderful to us."

—Mr. and Mrs. W. S. Pool.

"I came to Gunnison county in 1880, coming by rail as
far as Canon City, stage to Silver Cliff and then with a
prospecting outfit through the mountains into Gunnison
county.   Have been in Montrose since 1885.   For the past
thirty years I have been a preacher of the gospel.   Once in
the early days I escaped being carried away by a cloud-
burst by moving my camp just two days before the flood
came."

—Wilson Hampton.

"In 1876 I came in by wagon.   My most interesting
experiences have occurred while hunting bear and lions in
Ouray County."

—Uri Hotchkiss.

"From Del Norte, via Lake City and behind an ox team
was the way that I came over into this valley.   I remember
principally the high water in the spring of '84 and the
Indian raid on the Blue mountains in Utah that summer.
In those days I was helping Al Neale bust bronchos."

—A. W. Galloway.

"The most striking thing I remember on coming into
the valley was its absolute barrenness and the lack of trees.
The sun shown down on the bare yellow adobe and reflect-
ed back with a glare.   There was not a tree or any shade
to be found."

—Emma Willis.

"The Barlow and Sanderson stage carried me from Gunnison to Lake City in 1882. It was a six-horse stage and four changes of horses were made. Every horse used was a white or dappled gray."

—C. A. Mendenhall.

"I came in my wagon from Canon City in the summer of 1881. We passed through Saguache and I first saw Indians in war paint. The first school was built in the old town. It was of logs, with a dirt roof and floor, slab door and one small window. Dry goods boxes were the seats and desks and at recess we played in the old Armory. After that the old central school was built on its present site and had such loyal teachers as our John Tobin and others, who made our valley what it is today."

—Mrs. Laura Denning.

"I was born in Portland, Colorado, near Ouray, in 1876, and was the first white child born on the Uncompahgre. I have never left because this is my home.

"My brothers and I have spent much time capturing lions. One winter we caught thirty-six of the beasts and many times have caught five or six bob cats a day.

"When I was a small boy in Portland, one day a bunch of Indians chased me home. I ran into the house and crawled under the bed. Mother ran out into the yard, picked up a neck yoke and made the Indians clear out."

—E. A. Hotchkiss.

"I came over here in a prairie schooner in 1878, and about the first thing that I did was to get married. I have spent most of my time since, building the trails for the tenderfeet and getting the roads open for them."

—W. P. McMinn.

"In October of the year of '83 while I was on my way to the Uncompahgre valley from Lake City horseback and leading two pack horses, I lost my grub in the Lake Fork. There was ice on the edges of the river and the water was cold. I rode into the water and one of the pack horses jumped astraddle of the other one and knocked

the pack into the water, losing all the grub I had. I had to
go on and I got some grub at a cattle ranch at Cimarron."

—J. S. Hogan.

"I came over into the valley behind a team of oxen and
the date was 1877. We camped for a while very close to
Portland and near a camp of Indians. We got along with
them fine except for one thing—we had to feed them
whenever they wanted it and they sure could eat. There
were four or five hundred of them and they almost ate us
out of house and home in the few days that we were there.
One day about half a dozen came into our cabin and ordered supper. We got it for them without much argument
and after they had eaten, they informed us that they had
decided to stay all night. There was nothing to do but
permit it and soon they all piled up and were sound asleep.
We didn't sleep much ourselves but the next morning they
thanked us and left. In return for our enforced hospitality
whenever we lost any cattle, they would find them for us.
Those were exciting times but our biggest adventure was
in making the valley what it is today."

—Mrs. W. B. Phillips.

"It is hardly necessary for me to mention what the
W. C. T. U. has accomplished in Montrose, but it is very
interesting to note how they made their first dollar. When
election time came, we secured a large tent and placed it
near the polling place. Among ourselves we solicited provisions and decided to serve a lunch. Father Young made
the coffee and settled it with a dozen eggs. After we had
served lunch, we had a lot left over and so we decided to
serve supper. We were almost rushed to death and kept
open until 10 o'clock that night. When we counted our
money, we had $75.25. The effort proving a great success,
we were greatly encouraged to keep up the work. We did
and all of you know the wonderful result."

—Mrs. Anette Fairbanks.

"I came into the Uncompahgre valley by wagon in February, 1884, and have stayed here. While a boy in Lake
City, before coming to Montrose, I remember watching my

father and brother at their sawmill on Slumgullion saw the
scaffold on which Packer, who was supposed to have killed
and eaten the flesh of his three companions near Lake
City, was to hang. Packer's sentence was later changed to
life imprisonment so the gallows was not used."

—Archie H. Roatcap.

CHAPTER XXII

WHAT THE PIONEERS SAID

(Items taken from the issue of "The Montrose Messenger," published
Sept. 20, 1922, for the Old Timers' Reunion.)

"We came in from Alamosa in the fall of '79, making
the trip with mule teams and covered wagons. We came
with the intention of making our homes here and have
since done so.

"I don't recall any very thrilling experiences although
the Indians were among us a great deal. We first located
in Uncompahgre park near Ridgway and when the reservation was thrown open for settlement we moved to our
present home. This was September 2, 1881. My son,
James Arthur Smith, was the first white child born on the
Indian reservation, October 5, 1881."

—Mrs. Oscar D. Smith.

"In the year 1872 I was with Geo. M. Wheeler's U. S.
geological survey party when they passed through this part
of the state. Many of the towns that had been in Colorado
were in New Mexico after the correction lines had been
made. Our party laid out the corners of the state.

"A few years ago I wrote the book—'Early Days on
the Western Slope of Colorado'."

—Sidney Jocknick.

"I had never been out of the south until I was married
and went to Lake City as a bride.

"Having been in the town only a few weeks, I was
thrown into a great state of excitement one night when
Mr. Bell, together with other members of the Pitkin
Guards, was called out to capture a pair by the names of
Betts and Browning, who ran a dance hall and who had
shot and killed the sheriff after the sheriff and the mar-

shall hid in the Englishman's house which the pair had come to rob, not knowing that their intentions had been discovered.

"The two were captured toward daylight. The miners, to whose calling the sheriff belonged, swarmed into the town from every hill and the next night they hung Betts and Browning to the bridge across the Lake Fork.

"Mr. Bell and Mr. H. J. Alexander, who will be recalled by the Lake City pioneers, were out all the night of the hanging while Mrs. Alexander and I huddled in the house, frightened half to death.

"In the early hours of dawn the men came home and invited us to go for a walk. We went and they solemnly marched us down to the bridge, where the two bodies still dangled at the ends of long pieces of rope.

"It was a terrible sight. I didn't sleep for a week but the horror of the occasion was mitigated somewhat for me by an amusing angle of it which came up in my home.

"Gov. Pitkin had been expected in Lake City the night of the hanging and Mr. Bell was to introduce him. It was to have been my first opportunity to hear my husband address a public gathering and I was naturally looking forward to it.

"But because of the hanging the meeting was abandoned to Mr. Bell's enormous relief for the simple reason that he was in exquisite dread of having me in his audience for the first time."

—Mrs. John C. Bell.

"For 11 years from 1873 to 1884 I lived on the Dolores river at Rico. In 1884 however, I moved to Montrose, finding this country so well fitted for stock raising that I have been here ever since. I located and proved up on what is now the Rolla Butterfield ranch on Spring Creek mesa. For the past 25 years I have resided at my place near Uncompahgre."

—William T. Ryman.

"We came into this valley on the train in October, 1883, and have always liked it. I saw many interesting things while I was with the Mears hotel which my father, the late

Colonel Phil Peters, and James F. Kyle operated at that
time."

—Mary E. Sawyer.

"We came in covered wagons from Alamosa in the
fall of 1879. There was no Montrose then. At Uncompahgre stood the post which was occupied by United States
soldiers and the Utes were camped up in the valley a short
distance. They lived in wigwams. Indians often visited us
and were always very friendly."

—Mrs. Alice Middleton.

"I came to Colorado in 1875 to regain my health and
swore that if the country treated me right I would not
leave it. In September of 1884, I came to the Uncompahgre valley in a wagon and bought 80 acres of land (near
Riverside) for $750. This place is now valued at $17,000.
I was one of the first to get water out of the river on the
reservation land, having helped to build the Logan ditch.
I was taking water from the river when the Loutsenhizer
was a mere ditch and before there was a crop on Spring
Creek mesa, but now am number 37 in the line of priori-
ties."

—A. C. Freeman.

"I shall never forget the time that a band of Indians
got drunk up at Ouray, Colorado. They had been having
some trouble with one of their chiefs and chose this time
for their revenge. By the time they got through there
wasn't much left of the unfortunate leader. There was
still a little life left in him however and the important
thing to do was to get him away from the Indians until he
had a chance to recover. My parents' ranch was in Ouray
County, and it was decided to take him there to recuperate.
So an Indian chief spent a few weeks on my father's ranch
and we are still alive to tell of it."

—S. J. Phillips.

"In August of 1881, I came in with the railroad grading
gang. I drove four horses. I don't know why I stayed
though I always liked it here. I helped to build the railroad from Gunnison to Utah and saw a great deal of the

rough side of life. I have ridden across the desert between Delta and Grand Junction when one's hand went to his gun when a stranger was sighted. There were bandits galore until instinctively each man went for his gun at sight."

—M. F. Tillery.

Frank Teachout wandered into this country behind two stubborn animals that continually rebelled against the hard journey. In some places while crossing the Black Mesa he found the road so steep that it was necessary to rope, chain and pole the load but at last he got here. He discovered Montrose to be a group of log cabins and ten houses.

"One of the most interesting and at the same time dangerous experiences I had in the early days was when there was no road between Silverton and Red Mountain and we were making the trip through the mountains with pack burros. We were caught in a snow storm and had a hard time getting through. This is the best place to live that I have ever found."

—William Williams.

Elmer E. Young arrived in the valley of the Uncompahgre by the way of the D. & R. G. coming all the way from California. Colorado looked good and he stayed and helped build the town of Olathe. He was a member of the board of trustees when that town was organized and was on the first board of directors for the Gunnison tunnel.

"In the spring of '77 when Will and Henry Ripley were moving their newspaper plant from Canon City to Ouray they passed through what is now Montrose, there was no bridge across the river. Chief Ouray told them where to cross the river to escape a big hole. A short time after this a man, who had not been advised, was drowned in trying to cross at this place. Near Ouray the river bed was the only road.

"To have ridden in the old stage coach to have been here before the first ditch or the first plow was used or the first fruit tree was planted—causes a feeling of pride to come as one beholds the growth and development of today."

—Mrs. Henry Ripley.

"I just drifted into Colorado and the Uncompahgre valley.

"In '76 I came in first on horseback with a bunch of cattle and as I was always broke in those early days I had to stick around because I couldn't get away.

"Of course I had lots of thrilling experiences. I remember getting so scared once at the Indians that my hair rose up so straight and stiff that it took my hat up with it and I had to pull my hat down on my head again. Fact.

"Then once I was almost put out of my misery by a mob that took me for another fellow.

"It happened this way:

"I had been given a fancy gun which had an ivory handle and was trimmed with steer horn so it was easily identified. Over at Chalmers a fellow named Johnson borrowed it from me and then he went out and got drunk and began shooting all around and just naturally sent a bullet through a tent killing a man on the inside of it.

"It wasn't any time at all until a mob formed and started out after Johnson. Happened they came across me and I looked like their man and had the gun which did the killing. They'd have got me sure but that Jack Knous, father of Lee Knous, struck the leader down with a neck yoke that happened to be handy. Then the woman who ran the eating house came out and told the mob they had the wrong man and they believed her, so I got off that time. Later Knous and I rescued Johnson and took him out of the country."

—Al A. Neale.

"In 1883 I drove in the first herd of cattle from Antelope park. There were 800 head of cattle in the herd and we experienced many difficulties. Came in over the Stony Gulch road from Silverton. I came to Colorado in '73 and settled at Del Norte. Later I went to the Antelope Park country and drove a pack train to Silverton for three years.

"In 1877 there was a serious famine in Silverton. The

only way any food could be sent in was by mail and the
mail was taken in on a pack horse, so not much food could
go that way. I have seen the people of Silverton go to a
snow slide and dig out the bodies of mountain sheep in
order to keep from starving to death."

—L. W. Galloway.

"Three days after I arrived in this country in March,
1882, two men, Betts and Browning, were lynched and
hung near Lake City for killing Sheriff Campbell at that
place. I made my first trip to Montrose in '83 and later
came here to locate."

—Jesse Bell.

"I drove cattle over here in 1884 and I remember
starting to school here when I was 18 years of age. When
I was 20 I voted for woman suffrage in the straw vote
they had then."

—George Richards.

"When I was still a small boy my sister and I used to
go horseback riding. I remember several times the Indians
scared us quite badly and I can still remember the first
train that came into the valley."

—Milton E. Rewalt.

"In '84 I and Henry Allerton rode in from Lake City
on horseback. We came here to make our homes. That
winter we went to Utah and purchased about 500 head of
cattle, which we wintered there and drove here the following spring, and ranged on Horsefly. We located in
Happy Canon at the crossing of the old Indian trail. I
bought a ranch in the valley in 1885 and lived there until
1896, when I was elected county treasurer. I have since
lived in town."

—John Deeble.

"Arriving in Montrose on the train in 1884 I took up
my residence here and have remained since that time a
resident of Montrose which was then a hustling metropolis
of the western slope. I recall the time Jack Watson shot
Bob Murphy, city marshal, in the heel and also shot Justice
of the Peace Sol Edwards. I was impaneled on his jury

and the case was heard before Judge Gerry and the defendant acquitted. I have stayed here because this is the best country on earth."

—Joe L. Atkinson.

"When I came here from Gunnison in 1884, there were no sidewalks, no trees and I surely thought it was the jumping off place. I did not expect to remain but after I got acquainted the longer I stayed, the better I liked it. I have never regretted that I remained in Montrose."

—W. A. Cassel.

"The valley was dry and barren when I first came here in 1884. We lived on the Dallas and at Telluride for a time and later moved to Coal Creek where my father located one of the first ranches in Floral valley."

—Mrs. Leila Everett.

"The first trip I made into this section was with a freighting outfit and I made the trip from Canon City to Ouray in 1877. We had to unload the wagons to cross the river. The last trip made that fall it took us a month to come from Canon City, six days from the mouth of Stumpy creek and two days over Cerro. At this time the Los Pinos Indian agency was being moved from the Cochetopa country to Colona. I hauled the paper to Ouray for the early publications of the Ouray Times published by Mr. and Mrs. Henry Ripley.

"I do not think the hardships of the pioneer were so great as the ones some of us are going through now."

—Richard Collin.

"In the year 1881 I rode over from Gunnison horseback, driving a mule team. I camped the first winter near where Olathe now stands. It did not freeze that winter and it snowed only two inches. Frogs were alive in the pool near my camp all winter.

"I hauled in the first grocery store Buddecke & Diehl had in Placerville. I used to haul in provisions and take out deer hides."

—J. S. Duncan.

"We camped on the present site of Montrose for two days in 1877, when there was no town here. We came in with ox teams. Going down the Indian trail from Log Hill to where Ridgway stands, we had to cut big trees and fasten them to the rear of the wagon to keep from going too fast and poles were fastened to the upper side of the wagons and held to keep from turning over."
—Mrs. C. E. Comstock.

"When I was coming into this country in 1881, we came through the Big Bend country of the Dolores river. The morning after the Big Bend Indian Massacre, as we passed the scene of the battle there were the bodies of about 25 Indians and several whites strewn over the ground. I found cattle to be a good paying business in this section."
—W. E. Impson.

"I came into this valley via the Stork route, Oct. 5, 1881, being the first white child born on the reserve on the old home ranch at Colona."
—J. A. Smith.

"In the early days I helped to build the Uncompahgre Canal and while working for Dave Wood as check clerk, I helped train John J. Tobin so that he could handle the older boys in the school. Since then I have degenerated into a locomotive engineer and have worked for the D. & R. G. for over thirty years."
—Charles C. Ervin.

"I will never forget the strenuous times that we went through during the time of the Meeker Massacre. I spent most of the time cooking for the men cleaning and loading all firearms, and sharpening bowie knives. We were all determined to sell our lives as dearly as possible if the Indians came our way, but luckily they didn't."
—Mrs. Jennie H. Foster.

"I first saw the valley of the Uncompahgre in 1876, when we came in by wagon. I like it better than any other place. I have left but I always come back.

"Have spent my time hunting, stock raising and farming, and have had many experiences with wild animals. One winter we caught 30 lions, nine of them alive. Several years ago we brought one to Montrose in an automobile alive. The animals we caught alive were treed first and then one of us would climb up and hog-tie them.

"Once forded the Gunnison river at Delta with a plow engine where the river was seven feet deep."

—W. R. Hotchkiss.

"I came over here in 1881 with a bunch of stage horses for Dave Wood and didn't stay long, but soon left. In '84 I came back, like the bad penny. This time I was driving cattle for Jack Tripler. Again I left but at last I returned to stay."

—Charles E. Neale.

"I came to the U. S. in 1859 from the Isle of Man and to Colorado in 1861 with my brother, Captain William McClain of the Colorado 2nd Infantry, opening trails and roads as a prospector. I later became interested in the sheep business and stayed here on that account.

"When we came here we saw nothing but Indians on the warpath. They all wore paint and red blankets to keep out the whites. I am one of the last of the fifty-niners now living. I spent my tenth birthday on Cherry Creek and helped roll the first log for the Denver post office. The other men there at the time were 25 to 40 years old at that time and I was seventy-two last August so I think I am about the only one left here."

—Isaac McClain.

"I remember that I was terribly afraid of cowboys just after we first arrived here, and it was some time until I got over it. One day two of them rode up to me and asked for a drink. I was terribly frightened but I gave it to them. They seemed pretty jolly and gave me a nickle. I hurried to the house and told my mother, still half afraid, but as they hadn't hurt me, I gradually overcame my fear of them."

—Grace Foraker McKelvey.

"I was running a cattle ranch in western Kansas when I heard that the Indians were being removed from this valley. I sold out and came to the Uncompahgre with Charlie Diehl by train and team, arriving here from Gunnison in February, 1881. I had the second store in the old town up near the present high school. There was a livery stable, two stores and three saloons. Selig gave me my choice of four corners at Main and Cascade to move to the new town. I ran a store where the Busy Corner now is."

—A. E. Buddecke.

"Came from Alamosa on the train and then to Ouray by stage in December, 1880. In April, 1882, I came to Montrose and started a shoe shop, the only one there at the time. Moved to Dallas March, 1889, and was there until Ridgway became a town in 1891 and have since lived there."

—N. L. Quist.

"I came by rail in 1882. I came here to take charge of the freight house and yard for the D. & R. G. and kept my job till '87, when I took up ranching, which I have since followed."

—William Sampson.

"May 15, 1887, came in with eight head of burros loaded for prospecting. Camped on the ground where Montrose now is. Only three Mexican cabins were in evidence. Went into the San Miguels to prospect."

—Chas. Saunders.

"We came to Ouray in July, 1881, coming up to Poncha Springs on the train and the rest of the way in a wagon. I was the 11th woman in Montrose and my son C. E. Quist was the first boy born in that town. He was born July 13 and is now an engineer on the R. G. S."

—Mrs. N. L. Quist.

"Will say that I arrived in Gunnison Sept. 5, 1881, it then being the 'end of the track,' and the freighting point for 'the reservation' and all points west. I was in business at Gunnison until Sept., 1885, when I went to Montrose, where I resided until 1906, when I came to Denver. Mr. S. E. Dawson was my uncle, and I was instrumental in the laying out of the Fair Ground or Loutsenhizer addition to Montrose, where I have a street named after me. I have been a taxpayer and property owner in Montrose continuously since 1885, as I still own property there, and still have many friends among the old timers. I was married there and our only child was born there. If eligible under the rules, I would be pleased to have my name among the other old timers in Montrose."

—Geo. A. Stough.

"In 1876 I was in Hinsdale County, at Lake City. Several of us set out with our packs on our backs to walk to Ouray over the mountains. This was the month of April, and the snow was still deep and snow slides were numerous. As we walked along the trail, suddenly just ahead of us a part of the trail broke away and went crashing down the steep slope into Bear Creek way below. We were scared that it would start a snow slide and you can bet we went mighty careful over that place one at a time. That was in 1878. Aside from two years spent in Oregon, I have lived on the western slope since '76."

—A. M. Comstock.

CHAPTER XXIII

HEY! HEY! OLD TIMER!

William Zillmer came into the valley with General McKenzie's expedition as a wagon master in 1880, having joined the supply train at Saguache. The cavalry had to go to Grand Mesa in order to find feed for their horses, as the valley was practically a desert. They built the first road up the mesa.

According to Zillmer, who was with Gen. McKenzie's expedition, the lattered ordered the Indians to move out or fight and the Indians chose the latter, having three days in which to pack up and move out.

When General McKenzie was taking the Indians out of the valley he was camped where the L. E. Ross ranch now is. Two of his soldiers who died at the camp were buried on the side of High Mesa west of the Ben Parrish ranch. The bodies were later removed. Another man, Chas. Garten, who died there, still lies buried on a terrace of the mesa where the two soldier graves had been.

Zillmer tells of the Indian camp at the Buckhorn Lakes, while he was chief cook for the supply trains at the Post (Uncompahgre). Every Saturday the government would bring in 25 head of cattle and drive them into a corral for the Indians. The Utes rode down from the lakes and the chiefs would kill the cattle, and at a given command the crowd of Indians waiting outside the corral fence would make a dash for the carcasses and a wild scramble ensued as each sought to cut out his favorite slices of beef for the coming week.

May 2, 1882, was the day the town of Montrose was born. It was then a part of Gunnison county. May 2, 1922, just forty years after its incorporation saw Montrose the thriving metropolis of the Uncompahgre Valley.

W. Cummings was the mayor of Montrose with A. E. Humphrey, R. C. Diehl, T. R. Hiebler and William Wilson, trustees. Moses Liverman was town attorney, Solomon Edwards, police magistrate, and Robert Murphy, city marshal.

When Hans von Hagan came into the Uncompahgre valley with his father and brother, there was not a bridge between the Lake Fork and the settlement at Ouray. The water was so high and swift that the wagon boxes were floated off and carried down the stream by the water. At this time the only whites in the valley were at the Los Pinos Agency (Colona).

Al Neale drove a herd of horses into Colorado in 1873. He then gathered steers on the Picketwire range near Trinidad and loaded at Las Animas, which was then the farthest western loading point. He herded mules for Carlisle, Orman and Cook, while they were doing the construction work on the D. & R. G. and drove beef to market at Silverton and Lake City in 1877.

J. C. Frees tells us that in December, 1878, he was returning to Leadville from Ouray. As they came down the river below Ridgway, a party of Indians, who were going on the warpath, could be seen having a big war dance around an immense campfire just across the river. Mr. Frees states that his party was lucky to get out alive. The people who could not barricade their homes fled to Ouray.

In the very early '80's William Zillmer and Tom Nutt were given permission to cut hay inside the reserve. They found high grass in clearings in the bottom lands. One time while Chief Shavano was on a hunting trip, he stopped at their camp and fed most of their hay to his horses. Shortly after this Mr. Zillmer located the ranch where he lived near Menoken.

Soon after Francis Kelly brought his family into the valley he bought a grocery store, which he operated at the present location of the King Cole Bakery. Later he bought the improvements on what is now a part of the Ashenfelter ranch from Rev. Wright, pastor of the M. E. church. He sold his property to Ashenfelter in 1891.

From what was originally school district number two in Montrose county there have since been formed sixteen smaller districts. The district took in the country north of Menoken and west to Paradox.

It is said that in the year 1883, there were only two baby buggies in the valley. One belonged to Mrs. Markely and the other to Mrs. Alice M. Reynolds. Many people were then seeking only land and gold, but no where in the valley were there two more envied possessions.

Gus Frost and J. J. Ross were said to have picked cucumbers off vines at the Chief Ouray place when they first came into the Uncompahgre Valley.

Ross Brothers and Frost are also said to have sold the first spuds raised in the valley to a Kannah Creek man for three cents a pound in the bulk.

Francis Kelly, together with a number of others, had to walk from Sapinero to Montrose in the early eighties. They came to Sapinero over the railroad, which had just been finished and found the track in Black Canyon under water, so they were compelled to continue their journey on foot.

CHAPTER XXIV

JOSEPH SELIG, FOUNDER OF THE TOWN OF
MONTROSE

(From "Montrose Messenger," Sept. 20, 1922.)

Joseph Selig was the man who saw far enough ahead to see a bright future for the valley of the Uncompahgre. He was the real founder of the town but did not live to see his fondest hopes of its development realized.

Born in the Province of Posen, Germany, of Jewish parentage in the year 1859, he grew to manhood in that country, being conscripted into the Prussian Army at the age of 18. However, at first opportunity he left the land of his birth and came to the U. S.

He drifted westward and engaged in mining and lumbering in Utah for several years. In 1880, when the Utes were still roaming the Uncompahgre Valley, Selig came into the reservation.

He immediately saw the possibilities of this country. He met Otto Mears, the pathfinder of the Rockies, and they became warm friends. In 1881 the firm of Joseph Selig and Co. was formed with Mr. Selig and William A. Eckerley as partners. This firm was continued until 1886 when Selig's life was brought to an untimely end at the age of 36 years by the ravages of cancer of the stomach.

The company incorporated the town of Montrose in May, 1882, naming the place after the Duchess of Montrose, a character found in one of Sir Walter Scott's novels.

Selig located the Selig Ditch, added an addition to the town and gave various sites for streets, parks, churches and schools.

In 1883 he was appointed county clerk and recorder. He originally owned the old court house building, then used as a skating rink, now the Goodwin Hardware store.

Selig died before he was able to help develop the town and country as much as he desired but he started the ball to rolling and if he could be here today, he would no doubt be proud of the great Uncompahgre Valley and the town of Montrose, which he fostered in its infancy.

CHAPTER XXV

OTTO MEARS

(Copied from the issue of "The Montrose Messenger," published by the Author on Sept. 20, 1922, for the Old Timers' Reunion.)

The Greatest Pioneer of Them All.

Otto Mears, the famous "Pathfinder of the San Juan," who was in this country in 1865, and who was one of the great pioneers of the Western Slope writes as follows from California:

Mr. W. D. Asbury, Secretary,
Western Slope Fair,
Montrose, Colorado.
Mr. Dear Mr. Asbury:

I am just in receipt of your kind invitation to be present on Pioneer Day of the western slope fair and I thank you very much for same and regret that it will be impossible for me to arrange matters to be present, as my wife here is in bad health and I cannot leave California.

I certainly would enjoy meeting some of the old settlers but as far as I know I am the only survivor of the boys of 65 when the western slope was a part of Saguache and Conejos counties, and as Indian commissioner I helped to remove the Indians from the western slope and later as a member from Saguache county to the Colorado legislature and as chairman of the committee on county lines, I assisted in passing the bill making the three new counties of the western slope.

While I am 82 years young, I hope to be able to attend your next meeting if the invitation is again extended and thanking both the committee and the many citizens who have not forgotten me, I am,

Sincerely yours,
OTTO MEARS

The following is an excerpt from "The Handclasp of the East and West" by Martha and Henry Ripley:

In the opening of a new country, wagon roads are indispensable, and more especially in as rough and rugged one as this. When the mineral wealth of the country was discovered by the early prospectors, the nearest town of any size was Saguache, and between the new discoveries and this place there was no road. Roads there must be, burro transportation being too slow, and Otto Mears and Enos Hotchkiss undertook to build a toll road to Lake City. The need was urgent and no pretense was made of building a finished road. After locating the route, the immediate object was to build the trail, and finish it up as soon as possible. This being done, quite naturally the first to pass over it was not especially outspoken in their praise of it, in fact the tenor of their remarks were in the other direction.

One day Mr. Mears passing over this road in a buggy, met a couple of unfortunates with their wagon stuck fast in a mud hole, with which the road was abundantly supplied. Accosting them cheerily he asked them what the trouble was, and received in reply such an impassioned description of the character of the man who would collect a toll for passing over such a road, and what ought to be done with him, that he immediately fell in with their views. Asked if he had seen this man, Mears, he replied that he had passed him some distance back and that they would soon meet him. With this assurance and a cordial wish he hurried on.

One day, being the only passenger in the coach over this road, the driver took special care to hit every bump, stump and rock in the road and gave him a good shaking up. Arriving at the station where they were to change horses, Otto crawled out, yawned and stretched himself and said, "Oh, but I had such a beautiful sleep."

No sooner had one road been made passable than the necessity for another became apparent and Mears built a road from Indian Creek to Ouray. Then one down Leopard Creek and up the San Miguel. Later still he built the road over Marshall pass. We believe he built every road into the country.

In building these roads, Mears contributed a great stimulus to the country. His work probably did more toward this end than that of any other. Otto Mears the Road Builder and the greatest Pioneer of them all.

CHAPTER XXVI

DEVELOPMENT OF THE UNCOMPAHGRE VALLEY

(Written by J. J. Ross, for the "Montrose Messenger," published
Sept. 20, 1922, for the Old Timers' Reunion.)

General McKenzie got behind the Uncompahgre Utes on
Sept. 3, 1881, and told them he was here to remove them
peaceably if he could and forcibly if he must, and they
were taken to the Uintah reservation in Utah. The settlers were allowed to follow up on Sept. 4, 1881. The writer
arriving Sept. 7, 1881. The entire valley was dry and barren save along the banks of the streams with chico, sage
brush and grease wood and the sparse growth of mesquite
and gramma grass on mesas. The first settlement was
along the river bottom, that being covered in the first few
days rush save for a few small patches here and there.

The land was not surveyed by the government until
about two years later. Every settler was compelled to set
the corners of his 160 acre tract to suit his own taste, and
the next fitted his farm up against the other fellows' as
best he could and when the land was finally surveyed,
every settler was supposed to go to his nearest lines. This
caused a great deal of dissension, some of them losing
some of their choicest holdings and sometimes part of
their cultivated land.

There was no market for our produce save the limited
demand of Ouray and Telluride. Fortunately for the early
squatter the D. & R. G. W. R. R. was being constructed in
the fall of 1881 and the Mormon contractors, Hammond
and Hendricks, gave employment to the ranchers at $1.75
per day and board. Dave Wood delivered all supplies
from Gunnison at that time.

The mesa land was not taken up until along in '83 and

'84. There was no hay raised in the valley for the first two years. The first settlers attempted to squat on all the grassy spots along the river bottoms which proved later to be poor soil and inclined to seep.

The ranchers work teams, which consisted of oxen, mules and bronchos were compelled to graze on the mesas and river bottoms. All grain was freighted from Gunnison, costing the rancher 7c per pound. The D. & R. G. contractors fed their teams grain shipped from Gunnison and night herded them on the mesa for roughness. There were no roads nor bridges in the valley save the old government trail claiming them to be laid out by the U. S. outfit in their early western exploring. There was marked and well improved difference between the roads of 1922 and 1881. When we look at the fine graveled roads and splendid bridges with all steep grades having been cut down making travel a pleasure instead of a task.

School district No. 1 was organized in the fall of 1882, it being then in Gunnison county. It took all the children of school age in the town of Montrose and three Mormon children eight miles below town on the place which was later proved up on by I. N. Loper to make the required 10 pupils of school age. Rev. Wright was the first teacher (he now resides in Southern California).

The following fall of 1883 the writer circulated the petition which created school district No. 2 striking about two miles north of Montrose, running east and west taking in all the north end of Montrose county, including Paradox Valley. It required all the children in the north end of the valley to make the 10 pupils of school age. These pupils consisted of the Foster, Brown, Platt, Church and Ross children. The first school was held in Chep Church's log cabin residence and was taught by Chas. Young (laid to rest in Cedar Cemetery some 34 years ago).

The first literary society on the western slope was formed in the same old cabin, a few of us got our early training in parliamentary usages from Cushing's manual at these meetings. Hod Corey got up the first literary paper for this society. Some of the items were very amusing as well as interesting.

Many districts have been created from these two old ones with wonderful school development, splendid school buildings, surpassed by none, including our high school system. We point with a great deal of pride to our schools of today, hoping that within a short time consolidated schools will be a predominant feature.

The first business house in Montrose was J. C. Frees' store, a 10x10 picket log cabin. Mr. Frees ate and slept in this building and sold us anything from a knitting needle to a threshing machine, delivering same from forwarding station at Gunnison. But many other business adventures followed in quick succession, such as Buddecke and Diehl outfitters, Barney Wolfe wholesale grocer, C. E. McConnell Banking house, the Montrose Messenger, saloons and barber shops. Joe Selig and Eckerley, the founders of the town, were dissatisfied with the central location of the city so they purchased a squatter's claim and created what is now known as Selig addition and gave to each business firm a corner lot in consideration that they move their place of business.

These places were designated as follows: first four corners; Messenger, C. E. McConnell (bank), Dr. Cummings (mayor) and Roberts and Frees. Next four corners, Mears hotel, Barney Wolfe, Stewart Bros., and Buddecke & Diehl outfitters. Next and last two corners, Hammond Livery Stable and Tom McCaffrey Saloon. Fire has destroyed all these buildings save Frees store and Barney Wolfe building, both having been moved to other locations. Montrose has never had a boom but has always enjoyed a steady and substantial growth.

The first fair was held in the fall of '83. Vegetables and other produce were exhibited in the old skating rink, now the present Goodwin Hardware.

Races were by good local horses owned by Roberts Bros., D. Nichols, and others. The races were run on the southeastern part of town. We now put on as good a fair (Western Slope Fair) as any in the state.

The early settler knew nothing about modern modes of irrigation. Many attempted to flood this adobe soil and a great many met with poor success. They later learned the corrugation system with the result, together with fertility of soil have produced some marvelous crops in grain, hay, vegetables and fruit. We challenge the world on these productions. Fortunately our early settlers were an energetic class of people who came into the valley to build up an empire. For example one of our early lady teachers (who came from Pennsylvania) and expected to see cowboys with horns, upon being introduced to five different cowboys at the log school house opening found them to be graduates from five different colleges in the east.

The cowboys often appeared at social gatherings in chaps and spurs, high heeled boots and with large bandannas around their necks. The ranch men in overalls and jumpers with gum boots. The ladies wore long dresses with immense trains with waist line no larger than a man's hat band and large flowing sleeves. (What would the lady of yesterday say were she to meet Miss Today?)

We travelled on horse back, ladies on side saddles, also in farm wagons on boards and spring seats.

Montrose county was created by the state legislature on March 12, 1883, the governor appointing A. E. Buddecke, O. D. Loutenhizer and S. H. Nye board of county commissioners. After 50 years watching the country grow from a small pioneer town, the writer is convinced 'tis a privilege to live in Montrose County, Colorado.

CHAPTER XXVII

THE MONTROSE MESSENGER

(Copied from the issue of "The Montrose Messenger," published by
the Author on Sept. 20, 1922, for the Old Timers' Reunion.)

THE MONTROSE MESSENGER is published as a souvenir on the occasion of the First Annual Old Timers' celebration on Pioneer Day, being observed at the Western Slope Fair, Montrose, Colo., Wednesday, September 20, 1922.

Th Montrose Messenger had its origin in the spring of the year 1882 when Abe Roberts, who had been publishing the "Mountaineer" at Colorado Springs, moved his plant to Montrose and launched the "Messenger." Mr. Roberts had heard much about the Uncompahgre Valley and was a firm believer in its future prospects.

The first paper was run off on a Washington hand press May 23, 1882, and was purchased by Joseph Selig for $10. The second went to William Eckerley, for $5, etc., the first two dozen bringing in over $200 at auction. This was a great day for Montrose and at the time created considerable enthusiasm.

In 1884, W. A. Cassel, who had been working at nights for a couple of years on the Gunnison News-Democrat, took a position with the Messenger. He was tired of working at nights and came down here for a change. At that time he had no intention of staying in the valley; however, in 1885 he leased the paper from Mr. Roberts, who took up ranching.

Mr. Cassel employed Tony Monell to furnish the power for the Washington hand press he used to print the papers. The next fall, Mr. Cassel, together with Fred J. Land, purchased the paper, which was later merged into the Messenger Publishing company. At a later date Cassel and

Monell leased the paper for a year and before the end of the year relinquished the lease on the paper to I. G. Berry and J. W. Callaway, who changed the name of the publication to the Industrial Union.

This was the history of the old Messenger until it ceased to be and the Industrial Union replaced it.

CHAPTER XXVIII

HOW JOHN F. ROPER TOOK THE NAVAJOES OUT OF WESTERN COLORADO

By JOHN F. ROPER

About 1887 I took a long needed rest from the hotel business, which I had engaged in for four prosperous years at Red Mountain, Ouray County—an exciting mining camp of about 1000 population at that time. Few of us old timers are here today to tell of that wild and wooly camp in the eighties, the Red Mountain brass band, Fire Company, the Red Mountain Journal (the first daily paper), the grand balls, etc. This and the many accidents in snow slides and in mining are things that cannot be forgotten.

During the year silver was demonetized, the mines began to close down—the town burned down, and was partly rebuilt, and later went down to what it is today— nothing left but the reservoir and water works as a marker to show where the town was located.

It was during those depressing times that I outfitted with thirteen burros and five horses, a dog, guns and ammunition, to go prospecting, trapping and hunting. We camped one night in Montrose, put up at the Chas. Heath livery stable. There were but a few business houses in town. I recall Buddecke & Diehl, grocers, Getz, the druggist, the Belvedere Hotel and others. The well was at the corner of the Belvedere Hotel and quite a mud hole around. During my stopover, a Mr. Bretherton was game warden, and he and many others visited the corral to see my outfit.

From here I went over to the head of the Plateau River and prospected old supposed Spanish diggings. Thence to Rangley on White River, some ninety miles from Grand

Junction. This trip leads to incidents which prompt me to relate experiences that perhaps will prove of interest.

On these rounds, Berry Thomas, my companion, son of Captain Thomas, both of whom are now deceased, accompanied me and we pitched camp for the winter on what is known as the "Rabbit Hills," where game was plentiful.

After setting traps and dressing deer pelts into buckskin, from which we made our hunting suits, we frequently met Indians, among whom was one Augustus and Chipeta, the former a chief or leader of the hunting parties and the latter the wife of Chief Ouray. I met these several times during the winter and often traded eagle feathers for their buckskin. Upon asking the question: "Gus, what do you do with those feathers?", the Indian replied: "Huh, me two-three boys—heap like 'em," and he pointed to the top of his head.

Later, we found several squaws in teepees all around us, and, after a visit or two, I was surprised to learn that I had caused them to "vamoos" to the reservation, leaving the good hunting grounds for us. Now, I shall try to explain how this came about. Before leaving Grand Junction, I tried to find suitable buttons for a buckskin suit. Failing in this, I then accepted an offer of police buttons, which a merchant had on hand. These were strong, brass buttons with the word POLICE on them. They were on my hunting suit. The Indians had some one among them who could read and gave the alarm to others—calling me the "Buckskin Police," (meaning the game warden).

Following their departure, a very cold spell came up and we were short on supplies, so, I saddled up two burros and a pony, donned my buckskin suit, and went down to the White River, stopping at Johnson's ranch. This man had the reputation of being off in the head at times and when I appeared at his door, I surely thought he was crazy. For, he spied my buttons and began to laugh "ya, ya, ya," etc., until he ran out of breath and then began holding his side. I was very much put out by his action, and blurted out: "When you get through laughing, I'LL TALK BUSINESS WITH YOU." He finally asked me to come in and offered a chair, and still he kept laughing, until he could laugh no more, and then pointed to my buttons, saying: "You are the one that run all the Indians out of this country; you see, they all stop with me coming and going—and as they went out I asked them why they were going and they answered: "Huh! Buckskin police."

After a very successful winter in trapping and hunting, I made up my mind to move to the San Miguel River in Montrose County, where placer mining was booming. In trying to round up my burros, I found that they had been killed by lover wolves. So I had to buy more burros. My next camp was at Roc Creek, on the Dolores River, a few miles below Hydraulic—a gold camp. In prospecting around there, I discovered a grave among the boulders, and I wondered how this man met his death. I asked the foreman of a Utah cattle company, which was located near —how that man died. His answer was: "Oh, he was a fellow mavericking here."

Not finding any good prospects, I learned that the 47 Cattle Co. had sold out and abandoned their winter quarters. So I moved to this place and made a nice little home.

While living here the Navajo Indians ventured into Tabeguache Basin and were slaughtering deer for their hides. The white people decided to drive them out and were making ready to start, when someone said:

"Let's get the bear hunter to go with us."

So they sent for me and when I was informed about the Indians, I told them my experience on White River, and said that I would make it work here. All I asked was for someone to drive me up to the Cross Camp. John Blake volunteered to do this, so with my buckskin suit and police buttons, I represented myself as "game warden" and succeeded in moving them out without any difficulty.

This was prior to the start of the C. C. Company. All the old time cowboys—the Rays, Galloways, Bood Moore, Chas. Reed, Brammiers, Blakes and Payson, and many others will verify my statements above.

CHAPTER XXIX

EARLY HISTORY OF THE UNCOMPAHGRE
NATIONAL FOREST

(As compiled by Ranger Keep, of the Uncompahgre National Forest,
and copied by Arthur W. Monroe, field survey worker for the
Colorado Historical Society.)

After the establishment of the Uncompahgre National
Forest, Dr. H. K. Porter was appointed as forest supervisor. Mr. Porter was a local resident, as well as being
established in the cattle business. Shortly afterward,
Charles McMullin, who is now a resident of Olathe, was
appointed as forest ranger to assist in the work. The first
supervisor's office of the forest was maintained at Dr.
Porter's residence, located on Garnet Mesa, Delta. Shortly
afterward, the office was moved south near the top of the
present 4th Street hill, in that town. It consisted of a
frame shack, and the office equipment consisted of card-
board filing cases, one typewriter, and a couple of home
made chairs and tables. This headquarters was maintained for the transaction of business on the then existing
Uncompahgre, Ouray, and Fruita forests. Ranger Mc-
Mullin took the first grazing applications for the different
forests in June, 1906, at Whitewater, Delta, Olathe, Ridgway and Montrose.

During the summer of 1906, Thomas Jacques was also
appointed as ranger of the forest, and shortly afterwards
Henry Spencer as ranger on the Ouray reserve, with headquarters at Ouray during 1907. He was transferred back
to Delta in the fall, and Ranger T. J. Watkins was appointed as ranger, with headquarters at Lake City, during
July of 1907. In November, Mr. Watkins moved to Ouray,
establishing this as his headquarters, for work on the

Ouray reserve. Ranger Watkins was in charge of the Ouray district until the spring of 1926. Ranger William Doran was the ranger for the Ouray district for many years. Ranger Spencer is at present the ranger at Crested Buttes on the Gunnison Forest.

As the work was gradually laid out and expanded, hundreds of cases coming up and needing attention, the forest force was gradually increased, until in the year 1911, there were employed a supervisor, deputy supervisor, clerk in the office and nine rangers in the field.

However, even though the service was firmly established during the years of 1906 and 1907, much local prejudice still existed against the establishment of the forests, with their existing regulations. On March 22, 1909, Gifford Pinchot, forester, along with Messrs. Kneipp, Potter, Riley, Leavitt, Zon, Pollock, Moore and Cavanaugh, visited Delta, and held a public meeting lasting three days. This meeting was held at the opera house on the corner of Third and Main streets, or what is now known as the Delta Hardware Co. The purpose of the meeting was to better acquaint the local community with the aims and policies as well as benefits derived from the forests, and to overcome, if possible, the antagonism and criticism of the service by the local people. It might be well to state that Mr. Pinchot was driven from Grand Junction in Mr. Dave Clark's automobile. This trip of this car was the first to negotiate the trip from Grand Junction to Delta, over the then existing wagon road between the two towns.

However, by straight dealing, tact, judgment and foresight on the part of the field officers, this opposition has been overcome, and the part played by them in laying out the foundation of the work, will be largely responsible, more than anything else, for the giant strides which will be made in the work in the years to come. The field man had laid out the foundation, so that today the forestry idea is completely sold, and their connected policies are not merely accepted, but demanded by the people.

Ranger McMullin had no summer headquarters on the forest. It was necessary for him to camp at whatever place became most handy, or where it was possible for him to obtain quarters. The users were not always in accord with existing regulations, and at times openly defiant and antagonistic. The stockman was particularly so, because up to this time he had free access to the ranges, ranging his cattle where he pleased, following his own methods of procedure. To have a government officer, one of inferior knowledge, according to his line of reasoning, dictate to him and tell him how many cattle he should run, where to salt, methods of handling and above all demand a range fee, seemed to him all out of reason. This obstacle had to be met by the field man, and the education of the public has been a long and tedious process. Happily the efforts and the labor expended along these lines are beginning to bear fruit, and today the cattleman is the strongest agitator for the continuation of existing policies.

The Silesca ranger station site was selected as the first summer headquarters on the plateau by Ranger McMullin. This camp was originally called the colony, and was used at the time when a movement was on foot to colonize the country around Nucla and the San Miguel River valley. The improvements being abandoned, Ranger McMullin took them over, repaired the cabin and barn somewhat, in order to make them habitable.

CHAPTER XXX

PIONEERS OF THE CATTLE INDUSTRY OF
WESTERN COLORADO

(As compiled by Ranger Keep, of the Uncompahgre National Forest,
and copied by Arthur W. Monroe, field survey worker
for the Colorado Historical Society.)

The pioneer cattlemen of the country acquired the luxuriant summer ranges in the surrounding hills, along with the valley lands, after the Indians were removed from the country. Usually each man held a particular territory which was favorably situated from his home ranch holdings. Although he acquired no titles to the vast public domain, it was conceded to him by the residents of the community, that each individual controlled his portion. It was his as long as he could defend himself from all comers, and many fights and arguments, and sometimes killings took place, resulting from disputed rights. Most of the time, might was right.

At this time, it might be well to dwell upon Professor Hayden's report of the Uncompahgre Plateau, taken during the year 1875, at which time he was making an extensive survey of this country. "Nowhere is the influence of elevation on the character of the vegetation more plainly marked than on this plateau. In the interior near the crest, the land is to the Utes, one flowing with milk and honey. Here are fine streams of clear, cold water, beautiful aspen groves, the best of grass in the greatest abundance, and a profusion of wild flowers, wild fruit and berries, and the country is a perfect flower garden. This extends as low as 7,000 feet (which is about the present forest boundary), below which the scene changes to one in all respects the reverse. Aspen gives way to pinion and cedar. The grasses, fruit and flowers to sage, cacti and bare rock. The game changes. Black tailed deer give way to the white tailed specie. Grouse disappear, while rattlenakes and centipedes assert their proprietorship. In the place of an open rolling country, we enter a district traversed by deep gorges, and often high, precipitous slopes, a country difficult in the extreme to traverse without knowledge of its few trails."

The first stock cattle brought into the valley were driven in from the Gunnison Valley in the summer of 1875, by Alonzo Hartman, Jim Bishop, George Beckwith, Jim Kelley, Antonio Madrill and Sidney Jocknick. They were Ute cattle and were brought in to supply beef for the men who were getting out the lumber and building material for the construction of the Indian Agency, which was soon to be removed to the valley of the Uncompahgre.

It is also reported that Pumphrey and Loutsenhizer, upon securing the contract from the government, drove in 5000 head, trailing them from the San Luis Valley. After the Utes were removed in 1881, they went out of business, and sold small bunches of breeding cattle to the mines and railroad construction camps. Also from this first outfit, many of our present day herds of cattle are built.

Thus the cattleman came into his own, after the removal of the Utes. Vast territories of luxuriant feed and succulent grasses awaited his cattle, as is evidenced by Professor Hayden's report of the country. The railroad just entering the virgin territory, insuring the cattleman of transportation to market and the outside world. Plenty of winter range, spring range, the best of summer range. No crowding, no private land holdings, nothing to interfere with the handling of his stock, a virgin country. Is it any wonder that the cattleman of today still considers himself as being a distinct part of the community, considering the above? Why should it not be hard for him to give up the country which he originally acquired, to others, when at one time it was his, held either by force or community proclamation. The cattleman has had his day, and his period is practically over. He is at present fighting the battle of existence, but without doubt a losing one, as too many present day factors and obstacles are in the way or against him. He has abused his privileges in the past, ruined his summer range, gradually been crowded out of his winter and spring range, and is now faced with the problem of feeding his cattle high priced hay, while they are not on the forest ranges. His days are numbered, unless economic conditions are adjusted in such manner that it will be possible for him to compete and survive.

The Roberts brothers were pioneers of the cattle industry around Delta. Besides being cattlemen, their business consisted of breeding and raising race horse stock, and many fine horses were produced from their herds. They commenced their operations in 1882, and constructed a trail up Cottonwood Creek, and up to the top of 25 Mesa, what is now known as the old Roberts trail. Their camp originally is what is known as 25 camp on 25 Mesa, and occupied at present by Russell Davis. 25 Mesa was originally called Home Mesa. The name was changed later to 25 Mesa by Mr. J. D. Dillard, the leading cattleman of the country, from the presence of the 25 cow brand being run here, and also the cow camp being located in section 25. A great many of the present day names of the different creeks and mesas, of the Delta district in this vicinity, originated from this early outfit.

Smokehouse spring near the divide north of Columbine Pass, was named because of a smokehouse being built at this point by the Roberts brothers. In the early days they killed and smoked quite a lot of deer meat at this point.

Monitor Creek and Monitor Mesa received their names after a famous stallion, which ran on this mesa with his band of mares.

Potter Creek was named after the stallion "Potter," also owned by Roberts Brothers, as was Little John Mesa and Springs, named in honor of another stallion.

Each of the above stallions maintained leadership of his own band of mares, each one king over his portion of the range. Many the wild rides and furious chases on the part of the cowboys to corral these bands of horses, in order to pick the likely ones for breaking and sale. How-

ever, the race horse game broke both of the brothers, and
their outfit gradually disappeared to be replaced by others.

John Love brought cattle onto the plateau in 1885. He
maintained his rights and holdings on Love Mesa, which
still retains his name.

Criswell Creek was named after Al Criswell, who
brought cattle into the Criswell Creek and Basin country.

A Mr. Wanamaker brought the 7N brand into the
country. He maintained his holdings on what is now
called 7N Mesa, the mesa still bearing that name.

Sawmill Mesa was originally called Briggs Mesa, named
after another of the famous Roberts stallions. It was later
changed to the name of Sawmill Mesa, from the presence
of a number of sawmills.

Goddard Creek and Goddard Basin were named after
Ed Goddard, who brought cattle into that country in 1885.

Pool Creek received the name from the establishment
of a camp on this creek, a short distance above Roubideau
Creek. The camp was established for the purpose of having a community camp and pooling all of the cattle in this
section. The remains of the old cabin are found along the
creek bank.

Socks and Dan Mesa on the head of the Escalante receives its name from two old pensioned saddle horses,
owned by Mr. Sam Maupin, which when turned out in the
spring, used this mesa for their range.

Traver Creek and Traver Mesa received the name from
Ike Traver, who established himself in the cattle business
in this vicinity during the year 1884. He controlled this
portion of the range.

Johnson Springs—a spring along the Montrose-Horsefly
road—was named after Mr. John Johnson, who settled
on this land on August 22, 1889.

Ashley Point, or Ridge—Named after the Ashley Cattle
Co., which was the first outfit to run cattle in this vicinity
after the Indians were removed.

Davis Point or Ridge—Named after the Davis brothers,
who were the first to run cattle in this vicinity.

Cabin Creek—Named from the fact that Henry Paine,
for whom the Paine Mesa is named, constructed a cabin on

this creek, which is on the west side of Paine Mesa. The remains of the old cabin can still be seen.

Jacksonville—An old settlement on the Big Cimarron River, was named after Captain Jackson, whose old cabin

CHAPTER XXXI

EARLY ROADS OF THE UNCOMPAHGRE VALLEY

(From data compiled by Ranger Keep, of the Uncompahgre National
Forest, and copied by Arthur W. Monroe, field survey worker
for the Colorado Historical Society.)

One of the first roads constructed in the valley, was laid
out and built by Jay J. Ross, who lived where Spring
Creek empties into the Uncompahgre River between Olathe
and Montrose. He laid out a road from Montrose to
Brown, later named Colorow, and still later changed to
Olathe. The original road through the valley was laid out
by Hayden in 1875. The route commenced at Old Fort
Crawford, and kept on the west side of the river, across
the mesas, crossing Spring Creek Mesa, Ash Mesa and
California Mesa, finally crossing the Gunnison River just
above the mouth of Roubideau Creek, continuing down
the east side of the Gunnison to the ford on the Colorado
River at Grand Junction and thence on to Salt Lake City
and Utah.

The first road through the forest was laid out by Dave
Wood, from Montrose, across Horsefly to Leonard, and
thence to Telluride. This was laid out in 1882, for the
purpose of freighting supplies to the then booming town
of Telluride. Montrose was the nearest rail point, and
this portion of the D. & R. G. R. R. was the main line
from Denver to Salt Lake City.

In 1882, immediately following the opening of the Indian reservation in the valley, the first farming was done
in the district surrounding the present town of Olathe. The
town was then called Colorow. Colorow was a Comanche
Indian by birth, and joined the Utes for the sake of easy
living. He had a small band of renegade Indians as his followers, and was a source of much trouble to all concerned.

It was near this site that he tried to run his bluff on General McKenzie, at the time the Utes were being moved to the reservation in Utah. However the general was posted, and he stationed his troops along the mesas overlooking the river bottoms, ready for any actions which Colorow might display. However, Colorow decided that the opposition presented was too strong, and as the story goes, the exodus of this outlaw chief and his followers was accomplished by the jeers and yells of the Indians, accompanied by the barking and yapping of the numerous dogs, wails of the squaws, all protesting against being transferred to the new grounds. General McKenzie, however, stood firm, and the thing was accompished without bloodshed.

Horsefly Mountain received its name during the days of the early freighting through this country on the Dave Wood road. It is a fanciful name, and applies to the shape of the mountain. It was called by some, "Mosca Hill," mosca meaning fly in Spanish.

On the road a saloon and roadhouse were established at the foot of what is now known as Dew Drop hill. The remains of the dwellings and old buildings are gone, but this portion of the road still retains the name of Dew Drop hill, originating from the name of this early road house.

CHAPTER XXXII

EARLY SAWMILLS AND OPERATORS IN THE UNCOMPAHGRE NATIONAL FOREST OF WESTERN COLORADO

(As compiled by Ranger Keep, of the Uncompahgre National Forest, and copied by Arthur W. Monroe, field survey worker for the Colorado Historical Society.)

The first sawmill of any record or consequence, was erected by the government, near what is now known as Government Springs, near the present boundary of the forest, west of the town of Colona. The mill was operated by the soldiers located at Fort Crawford, and it is said to have cost around $40.00 per M ft. B. M. to produce the lumber. Their operations extended to the yellow pine regions only.

The next mill was erected by Elisha Darling, of Montrose, in the year 1884, west of Montrose, in the yellow pine stands. This lumber was produced cheap, and brought a price of $14.00 at the mill. After the establishment of the sawmills, the lumber industry was a big factor for Montrose, in those days. Enormous quantities were necessary to supply the needs of the fast building community, as well as the construction of the railway, and the mines in the vicinity of Ouray. As high as 126 M ft. B. M. of R. R. bridge timber was being loaded out of Montrose in one day.

A large part of the present day roads through the forest were first constructed by the early sawmill men. As the yellow pine stands became exhausted, it was necessary for them to extend their operations to the spruce belt higher up on the mountain. Portions of the Divide road were constructed by Mr. Darling during the life of his operations.

In the early days the stumpage appraisal of the timber was handled by the Department of the Interior, until the Bureau of Forestry was established. Much timbered land was brought under the old Timber and Stone act, quite a lot homesteaded, and it was usually the best stands of timber thus secured for patent.

CHAPTER XXXIII

CREEDE

In the year 1890, Nathan C. Creede, discovered rich silver ore in what was then called King Solomon's Mines, and the camp of Creede was built up to a town of several thousand people in a few weeks.

Cy Warman has said "Life in Creede was of necessity rapid. The doings of a day comprised a cycle of time. Locations were made in the morning, sold at noon, jumped at night. The arrival of a freight train with the rising sun indicated a new place of business at sunset."

Creede was one of the great boom camps of the West, and I think it is ably described by the pen of Harry P. Taber as follows:

CREEDE CANDLE TO DISCONTINUE

Announcement is made in the December 13 issue of the Creede Candle by its publisher, L. G. Schwalenberger, that publication will be discontinued with the issue of December 27, says the Del Norte Prospector.

Mr. Schwalenberger gives as reason for discontinuing, ill health, and lack of business. The publication, though small, has been a credit to Creede and its publisher, and the people of Creede will regret its cessation.—Durango News.

The above item records the virtual passing out of another one time great mining camp. Thirty-seven years ago when we came to Gunnison, Creede was one of the truly great producers. It began to die with the final demonetization of silver that year. The Creede Candle was one of the best weeklies in the state then, and has been on our exchange list most ever since. We regret its passing.

And in the recording of its close we clip and print the following story of the camp's wild young days:

There recently have been two celebrations which marked the twenty-fifth anniversary of the passing of certain places in the history of civilization. One was Dearborn, Michigan; the other was at Kitty Hawk, down on the sand hills of the Carolinas. At Henry Ford's museum they paid homage to Mr. Edison for his successful effort in throwing the oil lamp in the discard; at Kitty Hawk they put laurel wreaths on Orville Wright because he and his brother had taught us that the days of the earthbound might be numbered.

It may be argued that these festivals were for the greater honor of Mr. Edison and Mr. Wright for their discoveries, but these discoveries marked the passing of interesting phases none the less, and it is a curious commentary on the fitness of things that when we welcome the coming guest with open arms we turn with deep regret to watch the one who had been with us a long time and who is just going around the corner to oblivion. It is a question what all the shouting's for: whether for the coming of one or the going of the other.

There wasn't much of a celebration out in Mineral county, Colorado, this year, but there might have been, for it was just 40 years ago that Nicholas Creede made his trip from Willow Creek down the valley of the Rio Grande carrying the news of his discovery of a tremendous silver bearing lode—a mine which he had named, with curious significance, the Last Chance. The rush to the location began. Thousands of miners and prospectors struggled through the snows to the upper reaches of the river and into the hills. An extension of the railroad was pushed up the valley from Wagon Wheel Gap, 12 miles, to the little settlement which was first known as Jimtown. Some sentimentalist, observing the coloration of the rock outcrop named it Amethyst, and the town worked under this name for a few months. Then it became officially Creede, and has thus remained for 40 years.

When I first saw the place there were perhaps 30 cabins in the gulch. Within a year it was a city of 17,000 adventurous souls. Now there are perhaps 700 people here, and they are mining lead and zinc, for silver passed with Mr. Bryan's Cross of Gold in 1896, and at that time, too, began the gradual fading of the last of the great mining camps. Creede became "one with Ninevah and Tyre," one with Virginia City—one with John Oakhurst and the outcasts of Poker Flats.

With Creede went glamorous days. With it went tradition, and with the tradition went something of the lure of adventure, for when we visit mining camps today we are guests of a syndicate, and over the syndicate's property there is a sign, "Hands Off." Forty years ago we went to mining camps on our own. There were no such signs posted. There was no need. We knew mighty well what would happen if we didn't keep our hands off the other fellow's property. Still, there were variations on the theme.

Afterward he was the Hon. Anthony Gavin, attorney general of the state of Colorado, in the cabinet of Governor Waite—he of the "Bloody Bridles"; but when we knew him down in Creede he was Tony Gavin. Even at that time he had the highly impressive dignity which so distinguished him when he came to his high office in the state house at Denver. He wore a silk hat and a Prince Albert coat, both of vintage years, and his whiskers were as picturesque as those of John Ruskin. They have been the model for those of which Mr. Chesterfield wrote: "one may not grow such whiskers in a moment of passion."

He was an authority on all subjects—on everything and anything that might come up for discussion. He pointed out the essential wrongness of President Harrison's attitude in international affairs, and argued convincingly on the sanity of the senator from Kansas. He discussed the probabilities, based on the study of Richard Proctor's "Theory of Chances," of a straight flush, playing with deuces wild, in a two-card draw, and in attempting to prove his theory one night he lost all he had charged David Gillespe for conducting a suit against the railroad company— and lost it to Dave, which intensified his grief. He didn't speak to us for three days.

He was justice of the peace and practiced law—such as

it was in what at that time was a virtual No Man's Land. There was some argument about the surveys of county lines, and the district immediately surrounding that part of the valley of the Rio Grande didn't seem to belong to anybody. Those who had staked claims up Willow Creek gulch in the rush after Nick Creede had located his Last Chance and had a good deal of a job to hold onto their claims. To leave a claim unwatched was simply to invite the jumper to get busy and a claim jumper who is firmly intrenched is a difficult thing to move—or was a difficult thing to move in the days of 1890. Sometimes he could be dislodged by process of law and sometimes one had to argue with him with a gun. The gun was the more effectual weapon, and the one who made warlike moves first usually won. But there really was little bloodshed. A reconnaissance in force was ordinarily all that was necessary. The case of Jimmy Pike and Bug Patterson was an exception.

It happened this way: Jimmy Pike had been prospecting the hills for some months and finally came upon a promising outcrop. There was little of it visible on the surface, and Jimmy decided to drift in from lower down the slope to see if by any chance he could cut the vein. Accordingly, he laid out the claim and staked it to cover the outcrop and his proposed mine opening. Then he went to work singlehanded and made such progress as was possible under the circumstances.

After he had worked on the claim for a month or so Jimmy had drifted in about 20 feet. He opened up the entrance sufficiently to make a fair sized room — big enough to contain a camp bed, a few cooking utensils, his grub and such supplies as were necessary. He boarded up the entrance and dug himself in properly. Everything was set for some intensive mining operations. Then one day he fell, broke his arm and had to go over to the hospital at Pueblo. He was gone six weeks.

When Jimmy's arm was in shape so that he could work again he came back to Creede and went up the Sunnyside trail to his claim. There at his cave home he met a disagreeable surprise. In the doorway was a tall, be-

whiskered person, a dangerous looking .45 in his holster,
a Winchester casually resting in the crook of his arm and
a not particularly welcoming smile on his face. It was
the sort of smile that Philip Hale's friend Old Chimes used
to call "canister." There was no use arguing, but Jimmy
wanted to know what the interloper was doing there, so
he stopped about 30 yards away and asked him.

"I'm reckonin' on doin' some work on this 'ere claim
o' mine," said the man with the gun.

Jimmy turned and walked back to camp and straight to
the office of Tony Gavin. He told the lawyer what had
happened. Tony, as has been said, was an impressive person. His law library in his cabin-office was no less so.
It consisted of a volume of Walker's "American Law," two
volumes of "The Count of Monte Christo," the Denver city
directory of 1887, and an old Bible on which those who
had to swear to things in his office took their oaths.

Tony listened to Jimmy's story and reached for one
of his reference books. That it happened to be the Denver
directory didn't matter, for Tony's knowledge of law was
sufficient for this case. Still, he had to make a showing,
and the psychological effect of looking up authorities in
the matter, right in the presence of the client, is well
enough known to every disciple of Coke. Tony worked
over the directory for some minutes, making notes and
tapping his pencil uncertainly on the table. Finally, "What
did you say this claim jumper's name was?" he asked.

"Didn't say," said Jimmy, "but he looked like this 'ere
Bug Patterson from over Silverton way."

"Aint he the feller that threatened to shoot Dave Day,
the editor of 'The Solid Muldoon' over in Ouray, for printing something about his being a horse thief?"

"Yes, same feller," said Jimmy.

"You think he meant what he said when he told you he
was all for holding onto that claim?"

"Seems like," replied Jimmy.

"Looked like he was going to do some shooting if you
argued with him?"

"Sure did."

Tony turned back to his reference books. He worked

over them for half an hour while Jimmy figited in his
chair. He took off his silk hat, chewed his cigar, looked
out into Creede's Main street, put the ends of his fingers
together judicially, forgot the vernacular, and said: "The
law in this case made and provided is to this effect and
substance. Time is of the essence. If a man has a claim
properly staked out and entered on the records, and works
out his assessments regular and on time, said claim is his
and he can hold it, according to law. If another man
comes along and jumps his claim he's acting against the
people of the state of Colorado, their peace and dignity.
He can't hold it, because the original claimant has title,
and said claim jumper can be evicted, put out, and made
to vacate peaceably by processes well known in legal practice."

"Sounds reas'nable," said Jimmy.

"But," continued Tony, "you say this Patterson person
is now in possession of your claim, and you say he's armed
with a couple of guns and will probably shoot anyone who
comes near the place with intent to put him out. You said
you had to be away for six weeks on account of your
broken arm, and consequently no work was done on your
claim at that time. Was your first assessment worked out
before you broke your arm?"

"All but one day," said Jimmy.

"Well, there you are. You just missed out. Now this
Patterson man has just a shade the best of it. He's got
possession and he will probably do some shooting if you
try to monkey around him. You ain't got a case. You're
dished. Buttoned up. The fee will be $15."

Jimmy Pike silently paid over three $5 bills and started
for the door.

"What you aiming to do?" asked Tony.

"Why, see Patterson," replied Jimmy.

The next afternoon Tony, Doc, Lon Hartigan and I were
playing stud in the back room of Doc's drug store. A
man came in asking for the doctor, who was also the
coroner.

"Say, Doc," he said, "there's a couple of dead men up
by Jimmy Pike's room. Better have 'em looked after. Both

of 'em shot through the heart, looks like. One's a chap from over Silverton way. Name's Bug Patterson. The other's Jimmy Pike."

"Hell!" said Tony. "I told him he didn't have any case. Your deal, Lon."

Creede, as an entity did not realize that it was without the visible means of salvation until the coming of Parson Reed. In other words, it had not thought much about being without a church or a minister of the gospel. Thomas Reed had established the People's church up in Denver and had done a great work among the unregenerate, who had not been touched by the ministrations of the regular organizations. His church had no particular creed other than one of right living, and he himself was the type of preacher whose religion is backed by physical strength that indicates the spiritual strength of his arguments—straight-forward, easily understood and convincing.

Somebody informed him that way down in the mountains some 400 miles from Denver there was a new mining camp of 5,000 or 10,000 people who had no church and no minister to lead them into paths of righteousness. He decided to come down and talk to us. William B. (Bat) Masterson, who became a warm friend of President Theodore Roosevelt's and companion on some of his hunting trips (he afterward was one of the editors of "The Morning Telegraph" in New York) together with Mart Watrous had opened a restaurant, saloon and gambling house in Creede shortly after the boom began. It was a big place and run on the square and thoroughly business like principles. Any one who ever knew Masterson will know that that's the only sort of thing he would have.

Along one side at the right, as one entered the place, was a long mahogany bar, one of the finest in all Colorado. Back of this were the usual mirrors, glasses, bottles and appliances such as may be remembered by those who grew up before 1900. In front of the bar filling the wide space at the left, were many small tables where two or more could be gathered together for the discussion of the fate of nations, timely arguments and the transaction of such other business as might properly come before the meeting.

The back part of the big room was a space possibly 40x60 feet, and this was devoted to the devices for the testing of one's skill at keno, roulette, faro, craps, chuck-a-luck, stud or straight draw as one chose. Here, too, were small and large tables, baize-covered with an eye-comforting green and surrounded with chairs of reasonable comfort—altogether an admirable place for public gathering. When it became known that Parson Reed had indicated a desire to come down and lead us to the mourner's bench, Masterson and Watrous promptly offered the use of this big room for his endeavors.

It was Cy Warman, the engineer poet, who wrote the lines which gave the camp much advertising:

"It's day all day in the daytime. And there is no night in Creede."

Also there were no Sundays—as such—so far as camp activities were concerned, and camp activities meant the carrying on of such things as were considered necessary. Gambling was one of them. Consequently, on the Sunday on which Parson Reed chose to perform his first operations on our unregeneracy was not particularly different from other Sundays. Things went on as usual. We met the parson at the railroad station, conducted him to the Brainard house, saw that he was properly cared for and arranged the time of his meeting for 7 o'clock that evening.

Word was passed around the camp and when time came for the services the place was more than filled. It was packed, and every gambling table had more than its quota of players. It was a gala night—something like the opening of the Follies, but considerably more picturesque, for it was the passing of an era. We can always have our Follies, or something like it but we can't have any more wide open mining camps. As Dick Bradshaw said, "They won't let us."

When the parson arrived, Bat Masterson escorted him to a place at the end of the bar and asked with all possible courtesy, if he'd have something. "Not now," said the minister. "I'll wait till afterward and then I'll have a glass of milk." His Bible lay open on the bar. Masterson rapped for order and asked Lon Hartigan to introduce

the speaker. Lon was a big and very handsome Irishman
who was born down in the old Chatham square district of
New York. He had drifted into newspaper work and all
over the country in the doing of it. He had achieved a sort
of oratory which, added to his natural gift, made him
pretty near being great. His speech that night should have
a place in the anthologies. Maybe it will be there some
day. He introduced Parson Reed.

Meanwhile play at the tables had stopped. The players
turned their chairs to face the minister, and settled back
comfortably. Their hands though, were busy. The chips
on the tables were handled absent mindedly and were allowed to slide through their fingers slowly, making a sort
of purring noise—not disturbing, rather comforting. The
faro dealer shoved the cards from his box with a rythmic
motion, halting regularly at the period of the card-turn,
as if waiting for the placing of bets—but he was not
watching the cards. His eyes were on the speaker. His
hands were only doing their second-nature stuff. Big Dan
Butler, the bartender, casually wiped a glass—the same
glass—all through the sermon.

Outside it was snowing with that continuing persistence
to be found only in the storms at high altitudes—silently
and uncompromisingly. And in this saloon, 11,000 feet
above the level of Broadway, away up in the top of the
Rocky Mountains, 200 men, gamblers with adventure, listened to the story of the Prodigal and his return, told to
us in the gorgeous voice of Parson Tom Reed, minister of
God and believer in the divinity of forgiveness.

Then we sang "Rock of Ages," and if it was a bit off
key in places nobody cared. There were no music critics
there. It was sincere singing, and it is doubted if a single
one of the 200 men who sang the old hymn failed to remember something far back—back when on summer Sundays he sat in church somewhere where home was—some
place where bees drifted in and joined their droning with
the pastor's and where the congregation sang the same old
hymn and little boys wriggled with expectancy of the final
Amen and an afternoon of freedom and possible adventure
—maybe with a dog . . . and a fishpole . . . maybe.

Anyway, when the benediction had been said I turned to Dick Bradshaw and asked him what he thought of it.

"I think the fatted calf got a damned bad break," said Dick.

Then Soapy Smith took up a collection. The proceeds were turned over to Parson Reed. He had his glass of milk with the rest of us, who had something else, and returned to Brainard house. This hotel, our Savoy-Ritz, was conducted by the father of Clint Brainard. Maybe you'll recall him as Clinton Bainard, publisher, and president of a couple of newspaper syndicates. In any case, he's the same Clint Brainard who, when he was showing us some quite mystifying slight-of-hand tricks in his off moments of night-and-day clerking at his father's hostelry, hardly thought how far his affability and genius for making friends would carry him. It was this same Clint who showed Parson Reed to his home and it was he, too, who pointed out to Joe Palmer where the room was. But that comes later in the story.

After the services were over and the play at the tables had been restored to its normal routine, somebody wondered audibly how much money had been taken up in the collection. Soapy Smith said he hadn't counted it before he passed it over, and Masterson said that whatever the amount was it wasn't enough. Somebody suggested that we ought to double it, anyway, and the practical Dan Butler chipped in with "How the hell you goin' to double things when you don't know what you're doublin'." Here was obviously a sticker. Then Soapy said he had put the canvas bag containing the collection in his trousers pocket. "He's probably got the money," argued Soapy, "right there where he put it. Probably he ain't thought to lock it up in Clint's safe. Careless folks, preachers. All we got to do is steal his pants and count the money."

This suggestion needed consideration, and when serious matters are to be discussed they can better be decided upon to the accompaniment of refreshing drinks. The accumulation of six rounds of Dan's soothing mixtures brought a rosy glow to everything in sight, and it was finally voted that Joe Palmer, one of Soapy's partners, act as chief burg-

lar. He went away with two or three other conspirators
to act as lookouts, and a half hour later came back with
Parson Tom's pants. Clint Brainard had shown a helpful
spirit.

We found the collection in his pocket, as had been pre-
dicted. It amounted to about $346. Mart Watrous allowed
that we could double that all right and another collection
was made which brought the lot up to $700 even. Then
there was a further discussion. Would it be best to return
the pants plus the added collection? It was evident, as
Mart Watrous pointed out, that the parson couldn't go
back to Denver without any pants. Some conventions
must be observed, even up on the Continental divide. It
was equally evident that if the pants were returned with
the added funds and nothing said about it the good minister would not know that anything had been done, and that
would spoil our whole evening. Probably he had not counted the money before he went to sleep.

"No," said Mastersen, "that wouldn't be the thing to
do. Let's send the pants back. Joe can get 'em into his
room maybe easier than he got 'em out. We'll keep all
the money here. Then he'll think he's been robbed, seeing
his pants there and the money gone. Then he'll set up a
holler. Let's hear him. He's got a fine voice."

So Joe Palmer, as he put it, unburglared the parson's
pants. He took them back to the Brainard house, put them
in Parson Tom's room and we called it a day. Monday
morning Bat Masterson's prophecy came true, and Dick
Bradshaw told about it afterward:

"You should have heard it," he said. "Parson Tom
comes down to the diningroom with fire in his eye, and
lets out a holler you could hear clear down to Alamosa—
maybe farther. When he emits said hollers, he also
makes a few short sayin's about honor among thieves or
somethin' like that. Then he turns to Clint and says, 'Clint,
you're a layman. I wish you'd make some fittin' remarks.'
Of course all of us was just there in the dinin' room
waiting for the explosion. Well, we heard it."

There seemed to be only one thing to do. Those of us,
who with Bradshaw, had come up to the hotel to hear the

outburst, told Parson Tom we'd better go down to Bat's place and talk it over with the boys there. Word had been sent in advance, and the place was crowded. Everything was moving along smoothly enough, but there was an abnormally large crowd at the tables for such an early hour on Monday morning. Bat stood behind the bar smiling a welcome. He didn't wait for anyone to make any remarks.

"They've been telling me," said he, "that somebody robbed you last night, Parson Reed."

"Well, at least they didn't lie to you," said the parson. "I don't believe my sermon last night did much good."

"Maybe not," said Bat, "and again maybe it did. You see it was this way. We got to tellin' each other how much good it really did us, and we decided that we hadn't made enough of a collection to show how much we appreciated it all. We didn't know how much the collection was and the only way we could find out was to count the money so's we could double it. You'd filled us so plumb full of religion and generosity that we wanted to dig up some more funds while the spell lasted.

"We didn't want to wake you up, so we did the only other thing possible—stole your pants. Joe Palmer here kindly assisted in that little affair"—Joe bowed graciously—"and we counted the money and sent your pants back sort of minus, but leavin' 'em so's you could come down here this mornin' and we could have the pleasure of tellin' you how much we liked your sermon—in a sort of general meetin'. Here's the $340 and $20 added as a sort of a rider to run 'er up to $700. Here it is."

Parson Reed took the money and wiped his forehead. "Mr. Masterson"—he began.

"Oh, call me Bat, same as all my friends do."

"All right, then I'm Tom to all you folks. And Bat, will you please ask Dan there to ask the boys—all of 'em—just ask Dan to ask all the boys what they'll have? This is on me."

Bein' as it was about the first drink time in the morning, we all said what we'd have, but Big Dan held up a warning hand when Parson Tom attempted to pay for the drinks. "Nothin' doin'," he said, and began wiping up the bar.

So Parson Tom Reed's pants wandered, Ulysses-like, and were beset by many and stark dangers and when they came again to their home place they brought with them $700 of men's money for the addition to the funds of the People's church of Denver, and for the help in the saving of bad men's souls.

Yes, there should have been a greater celebration of the anniversary of the founding of Creede. It marked as definitely the beginning of the end of a phase as did the lighting of Mr. Edison's lamp or the tentative flight of the first Wright plane over the dunes of Kitty Hawk. There's something definitely missed with the passing of the old mining camps. We have nothing to take their place. Too much color has gone out of the picture.—By Harry P. Taber.

CHAPTER XXXIV

PERTINENT FACTS ABOUT WESTERN COLORADO

E. J. Braund has been court reporter and stenographer of the Seventh Judicial District for more than fifty years.

W. G. Haney, justice of the peace at Montrose, came to Ouray County as a small boy, and lived on a farm below the town. He later engaged in blacksmithing in Montrose and has held the position of city commissioner, county commissioner and justice of the peace.

Frank Hovey, present sheriff of Montrose County, has been engaged in the cattle business in Western Colorado for the major portion of his life.

One of the hardest fought election battles Montrose County ever had was the fight between Ed Deguelle and Mac Callaway for sheriff, about 1909. Callaway was declared the winner after the matter had been taken to court.

It is a matter of record that the first name in the jail record of Montrose County, was the name of the first county sheriff, who was arrested on a charge of murdering one Cal Irvin.

During the World war, Sheriff J. H. Gill walked down into a dark cellar to arrest an army deserter. He heard the man's revolver click twice as he pulled back the hamme, and then kicked it out of the fellow's hand. He brought in his man.

The first high tension electrical transmission line in the world was constructed in the Telluride district.

L. L. Nunn, president of the Telluride Electric Company, gave $100,000 for the establishment of the Telluride Institute, which has graduated many electrical engineers in the succeeding years.

J. F. Krebs was one of the prominent old timers who

accumulated considerable property during his lifetime, most of which was spent in Western Colorado.

Montrose County was organized March 12th, 1883, when the board of commissioners which had been appointed from Gunnison County, met at 10 A. M. The board consisted of O. D. Loutenhizer, S. H. Nye and Chairman A. E. Duddecke. Joseph Selig was appointed county clerk, George Simmonds, county judge, and Frank Mason, county sheriff.

The first bill presented to the Montrose county commissioners was a bill for care of an insane person. The claim was made by Wm. Bruce and a man named Miller, and was disallowed by the board.

Man's habitation in the Uncompahgre Valley probably dates back as much as 30,000 years. Arrow points made by the Folsom man, who is thought to have existed that long ago, have been found in this valley.

Before the time of good automobile roads, Silverton has been isolated from the world for as long as two months at a time, on account of snow slides.

The town of Olathe has had three names. It was first called Colorow, then Brown and later was named Olathe.

When Gunnison was established it was slated to be the iron and steel center of the state.

The building now occupied by the Goodwin Hardware store in the 200 block on Main street, Montrose, was used by Montrose County as a court house for many years.

Montrose County has had some famous murder cases. Mrs. Nancy Jane Bush was convicted of the murder of her son and grandson. She was supposed to have made soap out of the bodies, boiling them in a large kettle with several cans of lye. The Hecox murder case occurred in western Montrose County about 1920. Dean Meyers and John Miller shot Lemuel Hecox through the head, cut his head off and carried it two miles on horseback, then buried it. They were given penitentiary sentences after the case was solved. J. J. Baker killed Jim Kelley, and shot his brother, Daniel S. Kelley, and his father, Daniel M. Kelley, in the elder Kelley's real estate office on Main stret, Montros. Cash Sampson and Ben Lowe, long time enemies, met and killed each other in an isolated section in Escalante Canyon. (There have been scores of killings in the San Juan country, and scores of Mexican killings in the Uncompahgre Valley since the coming of so-called civilized man.)

Many men have escaped from the old county jail in Montrose, some having dug out with case knives, others, with outside help, have bashed in the windows with railroad rails.

Rear Admiral Emory S. Land of the United States Navy, was in school in Montrose in 1885. His name is on the census list of District No. 1 for that year.

John J. Tobin was one of the first superintendents of schools. He later served many years as state senator.

W. L. Knous, justice of the state Supreme Court, was born in Ouray and went through elementary and high school in that town, where his father and uncle were prominent men.

Considerable difficulty was encountered in establishing the county lines between Montrose and Ouray counties and between Montrose and Delta counties.

All of the original road and ditch maps and plats are now in the Montrose County court house.

William B. Upton, father of Walter Upton, of Spring Creek Mesa, served Montrose County for several years as county clerk. His son still lives on the original Upton ranch, one of the first places settled on Spring Creek Mesa.

Solomon Edwards, C. E. McConnell, J. W. Owens, H. S. Hammond, John Adams, S. H. Baker, D. L. Markley, J. W. Dalrymple, C. Musser, E. B. Sawyer were some of the now almost-forgotten men, who were prominent in affairs of early Montrose County.

Judge William Rathmell, of Ouray, found a scrap book full of clippings from Revolutionary War papers in an old barn in that town. He prizes it highly, as he should, and will turn it over to the State Historical Society when he dies.

The first school district in Montrose had its eastern boundary on the top of the Poverty Ridge and its west boundary on the top of the Uncompahgre Plateau.

James B. Johnson was one of the early day sheriffs
of Montrose County.

The Woodgate road, south of Montrose, was named
after J. B. Woodgate, who was chairman of the board of
county commissioners in 1884.

Thomas J. Black came to Montrose as a young man.
He served as county attorney, and later was district judge,
of the Seventh Judicial District.

Nat Young, first superintendent of schools of Montrose
County, was dismissed after he was charged with embez-
zlement.

T. B. Townsend was a member of the board of county
commissioners in the early eighties and was a very prominent citizen of Montrose at that time.

The CCC colony was organized by a group of Socialists
who first settled at Pinion, on the San Miguel River, west
of Montrose. It was a co-operative venture, and many
of the citizens of western Montrose County are descendants
of the original settlers.

Evans Willerup settled the land across the railroad
tracks in Montrose when it was a brush-filled river bottom.

David Wood built the Montrose-San Miguel County
cutoff road, known today as the Dave Wood road. He
and Otto Mears operated it as a toll road. The county
commissioners voted to offer Wood $4500.00 for his part
of the road and Mears $2500.00 for his share, then later
withdrew the offer.

Jaky Fist, early day saloon-keeper in Montrose, was
always in trouble. He was up before the court with every
change of the moon, it seems, and the vicissitudes of life
were many for him.

The opening of the Gunnison Tunnel was the biggest
event that ever occurred in Montrose. National attention
was focussed on this town at that time by the visit of President William Howard Taft to the city.

Some of the most exciting trips ever taken by Western
Colorado citizens have been the attempts to traverse the
Black Canyon of the Gunnison River. In 1901 Messrs. Torrence, Curtis, Anderson, Hovey and Pelton made the first
recorded attempt, and failed. Later Torrence and Fellows

tried again and failed to get clear through. Many attempts have been made since that time and few have succeeded.

Probably the most sensational trial ever held in San Miguel County was the case of Vincent St. John in 1906. It was a murder trial and claimed national attention. The Steve Adams case also attracted much attention to that county.

The last shot in the construction of the Gunnison Tunnel was fired in July, 1909.

For several consecutive years Al Neale, prominent cattleman, won the grand championship on Hereford steers at the Chicago International Livestock Show.

The Rico News was one of the best early day newspapers in the State of Colorado.

Dave Wood hauled most of the equipment for building the Rio Grande Southern Railroad from Vance Junction to Rico.

Tom Walsh made millions of dollars out of the Camp Bird Mine. He gave the Walsh Library to the town of Ouray. His daughter, Evalyn Walsh McLean, is the owner of the famous Hope diamond.

Capt. N. G. Clark operated one of the first flour mills in Montrose, and also served as county attorney in 1884.

In the early days, when there was just one 50-pound sack of flour in Ouray, it was sold for $50, or a rate of $1.00 a pound.

O. C. Skinner, early day publisher of the Montrose Enterprise, was speaker of the House of Representatives of the State of Colorado.

The first electric light company in Montrose was operated at a sawmill, across the tracks on North Fourth street by Pete Hiebler.

R. B. Rives was an early day road overseer in the Cimarron district.

E. L. Osborn was the second county treasurer of Montrose County.

A son of Evans Willerup died while the family was enroute between Ouray and Montrose and lies buried in an unmarked grave somewhere along the Uncompahgre river.

The Kittleson family have long been identified with affairs in the Uncompahgre Valley, Randolph Kittleson being the mayor of Montrose at the present time.

Andrew J. Thompson was county judge of Montrose County for eight years, from 1890 to 1898.

Travelers were ferried across the Gunnison River, above Delta, before the old State Bridge was built.

Morgan H. Payne, sheriff; John B. Killian, county clerk; James D. Gage, county commissioner; P. T. Stevens and W. H. Crecelius were prominent in early day affairs in Montrose County.

George S. Craig, father of W. S. Craig, of Montrose, delivered beef to the old Indian Agency, under contract with Otto Mears in 1876. He was at the home of Chief Ouray, south of Montrose, when the Packer party arrived there from Salt Lake City. His brother, Alec Craig, was a soldier on the Hayden survey party and also served at Fort Crawford.

Mr. W. N. Doolittle states that he arrived in Montrose the night McClease was hung.

Captain M. W. Cline, of Cimarron, was the grandfather of Ernest Benson, who is a resident of Montrose.

One of the fine pioneer mothers of the Uncompahgre Valley was Mrs. Louisa J. Bryant, mother of Bob Bryant, of the Montrose fire department, E. Earle Bryant, deputy district attorney at Montrose, Mrs. Kerr, wife of J. C. Kerr, state representative, and Mrs. Myrtle Ross.

The late Fred Donley was for many years one of the foremost sheep men of the valley.

Frank Turner was for twenty years a rural mail carrier out of the Montrose post office.

A. E. Walther, the pioneer banker of Ouray County, had many experiences in the placer mining game throughout Western Colorado, before he finally became a fixture in Ridgway, where he now resides.

The family of Cora Culver McClure are among the early pioneers, who have lived on their home place for many years.

CHAPTER XXXV

ADIEU! PIONEERS!

In the old days silver was king in Western Colorado. Today, we might say, the potato is king. Agriculture has replaced mining as the most important industry, followed closely by the cattle and sheep business and there are some lumbering operations in the national forests. The tourist business is coming to the front rapidly.

The old days of the silvery San Juan are gone forever. The Indian has departed and his ancient trails are silent. A new order has replaced the old. A new and energetic generation has come to "carry on," where their fathers and grandfathers left off. Many of the farms of the Uncompahgre Valley still show the transition from the old to the new. The original log cabin built by the first settler still stands, although it is today used as a bunk house or a milk house. In front of the old shack is a newer and more modern house built as the squatter became more prosperous. Then there is sometimes a nice, comfortable farm house, modern with its electric refrigerator and lights and radio aerial.

So goes the march of time. Ever the new to replace the old. The valley of the Uncompahgre has kept abreast of this relentless march. Modern highways cross the time-worn trails of the Utes, his war-cries have long been stilled and the ashes of his little camp fires have long returned to the earth, to be erased forever by the overwhelming force of the grass, which covers all.

The barren flats have blossomed into productive fields and orchards, and clean modern towns have sprung up.

Western Colorado takes a back seat to no section on earth. We have the climate, the people, the fertile soil, and the most gorgeous scenery on earth. Truly it is a little bit of paradise for us. We are satisfied for we love it.

Never has anyone attempted a complete history of the Western Colorado country. Sidney Jocknick wrote "Early Days on The Western Slope," but it is out of print and unobtainable now. Martha and Henry Ripley wrote the history of the Ripley family. Rev. Darley wrote of the San Juan region in the early days, and Judge Bell wrote of his life. Little else has been written on this particular locality.

It is the sincere hope of the author that this book is received by the public—as it is written. I have made no effort to fictionize, but only to tell the stories contained here as they were told to me. I hope this is received as a fairly complete history of the San Juan region and the Uncompahgre Valley. Many of the pioneers, who would have had interesting stories, I have failed to contact, and for this I am sorry.

Some of the stories may conflict with each other, but, of course, no two people see an incident or experience the same.

So, now we say to our old friends, the pioneers: "Adieu, dear friends, may the future treat you well."

TO THE OLD TIMER

You came when the country was wild and untamed
    You came with no fear in your heart,
Yours was a task that took courage and nerve,
    But you valiantly held up your part;
You came when the land was a desert waste,
    And oh, it was dry and hot,
You tilled the soil and labored to make,
    This beautiful garden spot.

Old Timer, we owe you an unpaid debt,
    A debt that can never be paid.
Yours was the work of a true pioneer,
    And we thank our God that you stayed;
We'll help you today and pay homage to you,
    As you call back the day that you came,
May we live as well as you have, our friends,
    And play as you played the game.

THE END

Printed in the United States
142607LV00005B/1/P